A Brief Course On TECHNOLOGY MANAGEMENT

A Brief Course On TECHNOLOGY MANAGEMENT

K NAGARAJAN

Professor, School of Management
Sri Krishna College of Engineering and Technology
Coimbatore, Tamil Nadu

NEW AGE
MANAGEMENT

An Imprint of

NEW AGE INTERNATIONAL (P) LIMITED, PUBLISHERS

New Delhi • Bangalore • Chennai • Cochin • Guwahati
Hyderabad • Kolkata • Lucknow • Mumbai
Visit us at **www.newagepublishers.com**

Published by New Age International (P) Ltd., Publishers
First Edition: 2015

BRANCHES

- **Bangalore** 37/10, 8th Cross (Near Hanuman Temple), Azad Nagar, Chamarajpet, Bangalore-560 018, Tel.: (080) 26756823, Telefax: 26756820
  E-mail: bangalore@newagepublishers.com
- **Chennai** 26, Damodaran Street, T. Nagar, Chennai-600 017
  Tel.: (044) 24353401, Telefax: 24351463,
  E-mail: chennai@newagepublishers.com
- **Cochin** CC-39/1016, Carrier Station Road, Ernakulam South, Cochin-682 016
  Tel.: (0484) 2377004, Telefax: 4051303,
  E-mail: cochin@newagepublishers.com
- **Guwahati** Hemsen Complex, Mohd. Shah Road, Paltan Bazar, Near Starline Hotel, Guwahati-781 008 Tel.: (0361) 2513881, Telefax: 2543669,
  E-mail: guwahati@newagepublishers.com
- **Hyderabad** 105, 1st Floor, Madhiray Kaveri Tower, 3-2-19, Azam Jahi Road, Near Kumar Theater Nimboliadda, Kachiguda, Hyderabad-500 027, Tel.: (040) 24652456, Telefax: 24652457 **E-mail: hyderabad@newagepublishers.com**
- **Kolkata** RDB Chambers (Formerly Lotus Cinema) 106A, 1st Floor, S N Banerjee Road, Kolkata-700 014 Tel.: (033) 22273773, Telefax: 22275247
  E-mail: kolkata@newagepublishers.com
- **Lucknow** 16-A, Jopling Road, Lucknow-226 001, Tel.: (0522) 2209578, 4045297 Telefax: 2204098, **E-mail:lucknow@newagepublishers.com**
- **Mumbai** 142C, Victor House, Ground Floor, N.M. Joshi Marg, Lower Parel Mumbai-400 013, Tel.: (022) 24927869, Telefax: 24915415
  E-mail: mumbai@newagepublishers.com
- **New Delhi** 22, Golden House, Daryaganj, New Delhi-110 002
  Tel.: (011) 23262368, 23262370, Telefax: 43551305
  E-mail: sales@newagepublishers.com

ISBN: 978-81-224-3688-4

₹ 250.00

C-14-04-7574

Printed in India at Ajit Printing Press, New Delhi.
Typeset at Aakriti Graphics.

PUBLISHING GLOBALLY
NEW AGE INTERNATIONAL (P) LIMITED, PUBLISHERS
7/30 A, Daryaganj, New Delhi - 110002
Visit us at **www.newagepublishers.com**

Dedicated to the loving memory
of my pets

Whitey, Browna, Subbi, Araika, Manda, Baskar,
Bayangar, Gimmy, Nimmy, Ish and a lot more

who made my life meaningful
during their short tenure in this world

Preface

Technology changed the way of life subsequent the industrial revolution which lasted for a period of about 80 years from 1760 B.C. During this period, there was transition to new manufacturing processes and practices. Machines that could produce more efficiently were developed that replaced human labour. Mass production of goods was made possible by machines. New energy sources were identified and developed. Communication and transportation systems improved a lot. Industrial revolution had its beginning in England and spread to Europe and USA. It gave economic strength to Europe and USA which enabled them expand their power worldwide. The second phase of industrial revolution took place in Germany, Japan and Russia between 1870 and 1960 B.C. The development of technology brought about changes in the economic, social and political systems. Mass production of goods, industrial capitalism, increased standard of living, expansion of international trade etc., are some of the economic changes brought about by technology. The political changes took the form of increased power of industrialized nations, growth and expansion of democracy, increased Government involvement in society etc. Increased leisure time, increase in population, growth of urban slums, unequal distribution of wealth, economic insecurity to a section of people etc., are some of the social changes brought about by technological development. Thus, technology has a greater impact on the socioeconomic conditions of any country.

When India achieved independence, the initial thrust was to set up industries in the basic and strategic sectors by the Government, which led to the establishment of many public sector units, thus giving the country a strong infrastructure. During the Seventh Plan Period (1985–1990), the public sector was freed from a number of constraints and the needs for improved productivity and technological modernization were felt and a number of measures were initiated towards achieving this. The new industrial policy, 1991 had very lofty objectives, including dismantling of the regulatory system, attaining international competitiveness, encouraging technology collaboration and foreign investment. The impetus given to these areas had stressed the need for assigning greater importance to technology. The importance of technology is only expected to grow further in the days to come.

The importance of technology for any business having become one of paramount importance, managers are expected to be exposed to different facets of technology. Students pursuing their business administration courses, who are the future managers of the business world, come from different educational and technical backgrounds. Though all managers cannot be expected to be technically qualified or technology savvy, they must know how to handle technology for the betterment of their organization.

This brief course on Technology Management, aimed at providing the basic and essential inputs in the realm of technology, innovation and intellectual property rights will prove to be of use as an introductory textbook to undergraduate and postgraduate students who pursue courses on Technology Management, Innovation Management and Intellectual Property Rights.

Suggestions and views of readers on improvement of the course content are most welcome.

Dr. K. Nagarajan

Acknowledgements

I am grateful to my students who were the motivating factor for me to come out with a book that explains the concepts in a nutshell. It is the difficulty expressed by them in not getting a simple book that introduces the subject to them that made me take up this work.

In writing the book, I was inspired and guided by the writings of many authors of books and research articles on the subject and I feel greatly indebted to them all.

I thank Mrs. S. Malarvizhi, the Chairperson and Managing Trustee of Sri Krishna Institutions, Coimbatore for her support and encouragement.

I extend my sincere thanks to Dr. S. Annadurai, Principal and Dr. L. Sivakumar, Vice-Principal of Sri Krishna College of Engineering and Technology, Coimbatore for their encouragement.

I wish to place on record my sincere thanks to Dr. C. Ramakrishnan, Director, Sri Krishna Institute of Management, Coimbatore, who has painstakingly gone through the manuscript and offered valuable suggestions.

Last, but not the least, I thank the publishers M/s New Age International (P) Limited, Publishers, New Delhi for their continued support in publishing my works.

Dr. K. Nagarajan

Contents

CHAPTER 1

Technology and Its Importance to Business

1.1. TECHNOLOGY

Technology can be defined as the knowledge and systems employed for the production of goods and services, using processes, methods, tools and techniques. In simple terms, technology is the way by which things are getting done. Knowledge, per se, cannot produce goods or offer services. Application of knowledge becomes technology which can produce goods/services. It is only when knowledge is practically implemented to create new things or offer some new services, we enter the realm of technology.

Technology refers to the totality of means employed to provide objects necessary for human sustenance and comfort. Objects include not only goods but also services and know-how.

The word 'Technology' is derived from the Greek word *techno-logia*. *Techno* means skill and *logia* means science. Thus, Technology refers to the application of scientific knowledge for practical purposes. This definition expands the scope of technology beyond products and processes.

1.2. SCIENCE VERSUS TECHNOLOGY

For a business enterprise, wherever scientific knowledge is made use of for achieving competitive advantages, all such issues will fall under the domain of technology.

Science	Technology
Science deals with the natural world.	Technology deals with man-made world.
Science studies the natural laws of the universe.	Technology focuses on the application of scientific laws. Technology is the application of scientific knowledge for

(Contd...)

	practical purposes. Man makes use of scientific knowledge for his benefit and devises products, methods, techniques etc., which all fall under the domain of technology.
Findings of scientific research become public property. They can not be patented and no one claim rights over the findings. For example, no one can claim right for the Law of Gravity. Issac Newton only discovered the Law. It was existing already.	Technology can be both public and private knowledge. For example, a new technology that is developed by a firm and patented by the firm will be a private property. Once the period of patent expires, the technology will become a public property.
Scientific development is an on-going process. New laws are discovered and added to the existing pool of knowledge. It may also so happen that some of the scientific laws might get altered/modified due to subsequent findings. But, science keeps growing and does not have a declining or death phase.	Technology once introduced, can not remain relevant for ever. When new technologies emerge, the existing technologies that have already become obsolete will have to leave the field. Thus, technology has a life cycle. It is born, it grows, matures and finally dies when a new technology takes over.
Cost-benefit analysis can not be applied for scientific research. Most of the times, the costs will appear to exceed the benefit. This is because, the benefits of scientific discoveries will bear fruits only after some time, i.e., after the scientific discovery is transformed into some form of value added product/process that benefits mankind. Till such time, the benefits can not be known and can not also be measured. Hence, scientific researches are continued without applying cost-benefit analysis.	Technology is a business proposition. Hence, it is subject to cost-benefit analysis. A firm will be induced to spend resources towards technology development, only when the benefits are in excess of the costs.

1.3. ESSENTIAL FEATURES OF TECHNOLOGY

We can understand the role and meaning of technology if its features are understood. Some of the essential features of technology are listed below:

(*a*) Technology is the application of scientific knowledge to produce various products/provide services that are used by human beings.

(*b*) Technology is not restricted to the physical object (or the hardware part of the object). It also includes software meant to be used with the concerned product and the know-how that is needed to use/operate the product.

(*c*) Technology adds value to a product/process. The magnitude of value addition decides the level of the technology.

(*d*) Technology is a dominant factor in modern life and it touches upon many spheres of activities of human life.

(*e*) Technologies are interdependent. For example, a product with one technology requires another product (with a different technology) for putting it into use/ operation. For example, Diesel engine and Alternator are two different products with two different types of technologies. They are combined to form the product 'electricity generator'. Here, the output from one product acts as the input for the other product. Another example relates to all those products that make use of an electromotive force (by way of an electric motor or some other product) that drives a machine/part of a machine.

(*f*) Technology, in general is complex in nature. Some of technological aspects of a product may be difficult to understand/comprehend except by those who have relevant technical knowledge.

(*g*) Technology adds value to the assets of a firm. The value of a firm is not the value of its physical assets alone. The technology possessed by the firm has got greater value. While the physical assets are visible and tangible, technology as an asset is intangible and it exists in an organization in the form of software, brain ware and know-how. Technology is present in an organization in its people and in the technical systems.

(*h*) Every technology has a life cycle. It is born, it grows, matures and finally dies. When it reaches the stage of maturity, it is exposed to the risk of getting substituted by an emerging technology or it becomes obsolete and dies down, giving way for a new technology.

(*i*) It is technology that drives business performance and gives an organization competitive edge.

(*j*) Technology encompasses the whole organization. Considering technology as something separate that is related only to production (of a product) or to some manufacturing process is a narrow and incorrect view of technology.

1.4. IMPORTANCE OF TECHNOLOGY TO BUSINESS

An organization is a vehicle that introduces one or more technologies to the society. Technology is vital for all business enterprises, especially for enterprises engaged in production of goods. When the importance of technology was not correctly perceived, the value of a company was assessed only on the basis of physical assets owned by the company. The real value of a company is much more than its physical assets. It is technology that adds value to assets. Hence, it is obvious that technology is the backbone of an enterprise that is engaged in production. Technology helps a production unit in the following ways:

- To get competitive advantage in terms of technology.
- To improve productivity.
- To reduce cost of production.
- To bring innovations in products.
- To gain greater market share by virtue of superior technology and lower cost, thereby improving the profitability.
- To help sustain in business, overcoming the threat of obsolescence.

The growth and survival of a business organization depends upon how effectively it satisfies customer expectations and how efficiently it makes use of its resources. Only efficient utilization of resources will bring down the cost. In a competitive environment only those firms that have a cost advantage over its competitors have a better chance to survive. Cost reduction can be made possible only through technology. Meeting the customer expectations by offering them with the types of products/services they look for is a great challenge for an organization. Here again, technology comes to the rescue. While customer expectations can be studied by conducting opinion surveys/field studies etc., giving shape to their expectations by offering new products/ services, adding additional expected features in the existing products etc., can be made possible only through technological innovations. Technology plays a major role in improving productivity. Though an organization (be it a manufacturing organization or a service organization) is run by human beings, they make use of technology in some form or the other to carry out their operations. Since the productivity depends to a larger extent on technology, the survival of an organization depends on technology. Thus, it is only technology that gives an organization competitive advantage. Hence, no organization can ignore technology. Technology is important for the survival and growth of an organization.

1.5. BENEFITS OF TECHNOLOGY FOR A BUSINESS FIRM

Technology aids all business firms. Both production oriented firms and service oriented firms derive benefits by the use of technology. Of the two, production oriented firms stand to gain a lot from technology since technology leaves a greater scope for the improvement/modification of products and for the creation of new products. Some of the benefits that technology offers are as below:

(*a*) Technology helps a firm to make optimum use of available resources and thus to bring down the cost of production.

(*b*) Technology helps a firm to bring out new products/new services to satisfy customer expectations. This in turn, will help the firm to retain its market share and improve it further.

(*c*) Technology helps a firm to find new business avenues by identifying new market segments, by identifying the needs of the customers in these segments and offering them the products/services that are expected by them.

(*d*) Extending the life cycle of a product is one of the requirements for any business to gain advantage. Technology comes to help for extending the product life cycle.

(*e*) Technology helps a firm to exploit the benefits of economies of scale. With mass production, the production cost per unit gets reduced substantially due to economies of scale.

(*f*) Technology helps in developing low cost substitutes (in products as well as processes) which are helpful both to the customers and to the business firm.

(*g*) For achieving business turnarounds wherein a loss making firm is made into a profit making one, technology has a greater role to play. Though a firm needs the support of many business processes for making a turnaround, the role of technology is vital.

(*h*) Technology helps a firm in its long term survival.

(*i*) In short, technology helps a firm to gain competitive business advantage, to sustain for long, to improve profits and to become a market leader in the domain in which the firm operates.

(*j*) If the products manufactured have export potential, the firm can earn foreign exchange through exports.

(*k*) In a globalised environment, a firm that produces quality products can compete in the world market where there is good scope for getting premium price and high volume sales.

(*l*) Building up customer base worldwide will help the firm to handle domestic fluctuations with confidence and ease.

(*m*) A firm that has developed and perfected a technology that is sound, robust and cost-effective can also explore the scope for earning through technology transfer arrangements.

1.6. IMPORTANCE OF TECHNOLOGY FOR THE ECONOMIC GROWTH OF A NATION

History has proved time and again that technology has played a major role in the development of nations. All the economically developed nations, at any point of time have had technology advantage as well. A country may be rich in natural resources. But, for the exploitation of the natural resources, what is required is technology.

Prior to the Second World War, Germany and Italy were two great economic powers in the world. Their economic power also gave them the ability to become military super- powers. However, after the end of the Second World War, USA and Soviet Union emerged as the top two super powers in the world. This was because of the reason that they were able to win the war against Germany, through better technological management of the military resources. The economy of Japan was totally destroyed during the Second World War. It is a relatively small country in terms of territory and population. The country also lacks natural resources. There is no oil/coal/iron which are important natural resources for a country. Only about 12% of the country's land is suitable for cultivation. The country is also known for natural disasters. Japan has up to about 5000 earth quakes every year. Volcanoes are another common natural hazard found in Japan. Japan has nearly one tenth of world's most active volcanoes. Apart from this, there are a large number of inactive volcanoes, whose danger can not be ruled out. Typhoons are another major natural hazard in Japan. A typhoon is a tropical cyclone that has the wind speed of more than 17.2 meters per second. Japan has a rough estimate of about 29 typhoons per year. This type of natural disaster is one of the most deadly of them all. The typhoons bring heavy rain over wide areas which cause flooding and gale winds that damage homes and forest resources. In addition to this, the country also gets worst affected by Tsunami.

In spite of all the above shortcomings and limitations, Japan emerged as the world's third largest economy, next only to USA and China. In 1951, Japan's total GNP was only one-third of Britain's and one-twentieth of the United States. Thirty years later it had reached half of the US's and double that of the Britain's. This has been made possible only through technology development supported by the firm determination of the people of Japan. Since the country has to rely only on value addition to improve its economy, it resorted to improving its manufacturing sector through technology. Japan imports all major raw materials required for industrial production. It is one of the world's major importer's of oil, coal and iron ore. By improving technology base of industries, Japan produced manufactured goods of high quality at cheaper cost and captured the world market, defeating the major players. This proves the point that technological development has an important role in the economic growth of a nation.

1.7. TECHNOLOGY AND HUMANITY

Gone are the days when man looked at technology with an eye of suspicion. The voices that rose against the adverse effects produced by technology on human life have got mellowed down and man has now understood that technology is his best friend. But, he should know how to make use of it and how to overcome some of the adverse effects that technology may bring on human life. It is like a sharp knife. Just because a knife can accidently harm a man (if used carelessly), it can not be said that the tool as such is not desired. The benefits that technology has brought to humanity and that it will bring to humanity when correctly used are immense. Let us see some of the benefits that technology has offered to humanity.

(*a*) Technology helps to improve productivity, which helps in better utilization of resources.

(*b*) Increase in productivity will lead to reduction in the cost of production and hence consumers will be getting the products/services at a comparatively cheaper price.

(*c*) Technology creates new jobs (due to the introduction of new products/new avenues of production) and also increases the standard of living of employees, which leads to economic prosperity of the society.

(*d*) Technology has made the entire world accessible within a few seconds, through internet.

(*e*) Faster exchanges of information have been made possible by technology.

(*f*) Technology has made a total change in the teaching-learning process. Knowledge sharing across the globe takes place instantaneously.

(*g*) Advancements in technology helps to identify diseases in human beings and also helps in the treatment of diseases.

(*h*) Technological advancements create a more informed society. By this, the nation as a whole becomes well informed and hence the nation can take important decisions quickly.

1.7.1. Technology — A Boon or a Bane

In spite of the fact that technology has made human life more comfortable, there is another side of technology which brings some harmful effects. But, man can always devise ways and means to overcome these hurdles. Some of the negative effects of technology that cause concern are discussed below:

(*a*) Latest/improved technology mostly comes with lower manpower. Hence, there is always the threat of machine replacing man on jobs, leading to unemployment.

(*b*) While technology is an aid to mankind, there is a chance of man becoming totally dependent on technology for everything. Replacing man with machine at all places will have the negative consequence of making man a slave t technology.

(*c*) Technology creates disparity between technologically developed nations and underdeveloped/undeveloped nations. There is possibility of developed nations exploiting undeveloped nations. This will create regional imbalance and social injustice.

(*d*) Environmental hazards created by technological developments are many. Polluting the land, water, air, atmosphere etc., are some of the after-effects of technology.

(*e*) Technology, no doubt, brings latest gadgets, tools, equipments etc., for the benefit of mankind. Technology is like a double-edged sword. When it lands in the hands of anti-social elements who can use it for their ulterior motives, technology will only prove disastrous.

(*f*) High-tech crimes, which are the outcomes of perverted minds is another misfortune of technological development.

(*g*) The younger generation gets addicted to technology and spends their leisure time (and at times their valuable time also) with technical gadgets like video games, internet, ipod etc., which robs them of the joy of natural play and enjoyment. This culture of the younger generation getting addicted to technology based entertainments and misusing technology will only develop a generation that will be sick, both physically and mentally and this will be a great threat to the country's future.

Thus, while the benefits of technology are a boon to humanity, the misuse of technology and the after-effects of technology can bring negative consequences. This makes some people consider technology as a bane and not a boon to humanity. However, logical reasoning will make it clear that it is man who devices technology and man can very well modify it to suit his convenience and comfort. When done so, technology will always remain a boon to humanity.

1.8. ACHIEVING COMPETITIVE ADVANTAGE THROUGH TECHNOLOGY

Technology has become the most essential component for achieving competitive business advantage. In a firm, technology resides in the intangible assets like technical knowledge, expertise, skill, know-how etc., which are possessed by the employees of the firm. Any business has to follow certain strategies to be successful amidst competition. Technology has an important role to play in the strategy of a business entity. It will help gain competitive advantage over other players in the field, in the form of reducing costs of products/services, improving functionality of products, in creation of product differentiation etc. Technology can be used both as an offensive and as a defensive tool. Technology can be used offensively by developing new products, by developing new modes of offering service, by improving existing lines of products etc., and it can be used defensively by sustaining the competitive advantage already gained in the form of cost reduction, by product differentiation etc.

Technology helps a firm in the following ways in achieving competitive advantage:

- The firm can innovate new products/processes; the firm can improve upon existing products/processes and thereby gain a sizable market share and overcome competitions.
- The firm, with its innovative products, can identify new market segments.
- Technology will drive efficiency and will help reduce cost of production and improve productivity.
- Lower cost of production and increased market share will lead to increased profits.
- Technology will help reduce product development cycle time.
- Technology will also aid in extending the life cycle of existing products through suitable incremental innovations.
- Technology always comes with improved production techniques and enables large scale production. Mass production will help achieve economies of scale, which in turn will lead to increased business profits.
- Technology will safeguard a firm from becoming outdated and will improve its survival period.
- Technology will give a firm the flexibility to respond to the changing market needs at a faster rate.
- Use of technology in operations area in a firm makes it possible to improve the delivery process, to standardize and improve quality and focus on customization, apart from reducing cost, which will add value.

1.9. TYPES OF TECHNOLOGIES

Technology can be classified into the following types:

- New Technology
- Emerging Technology
- High Technology
- Low Technology
- Medium Technology
- Appropriate Technology
- Codified Technology
- Tacit Technology
- Hybrid Technology
- Generic Technology
- State-of-the-art Technology
- Cutting edge, Leading edge, Bleeding edge Technologies

New Technology

It is any newly introduced technology that changes the way a company produces its products/offer services. A new technology will have a profound effect on improving productivity and competitiveness of a business enterprise. A technology need not be totally new to the world to be termed as 'New Technology'. It depends on the situation. A technology that is in use in some part of the world for quite some time can be introduced into a particular country for the first time. For this country and for the enterprise that is going to make use of the technology, it is a new technology.

Example: Marketing products using internet web site; Using computer software for developing engineering drawings, replacing the manual drafting techniques.

Emerging Technology

It is the technology on the anvil. It is a newly introduced technology that has not yet been fully commercialized, but has good scope for commercialization. Since it is not yet perfected, the technology may be currently in limited use. It may have the potential to spread significantly after being perfected and fine-tuned. They can bring about substantial changes in the way companies operate and can even bring about changes in the society as a whole.

Example: Nano Technology, Genetic Engineering, Super conductivity, Stem Cell therapy.

High Technology

An advanced and sophisticated technology can be termed as 'High Technology'. Organisations using high technology employ people with high levels of education and skills (like scientists & engineers). These organizations will have high levels of R&D activity. Hence, the proportion of expenditure on R & D will be substantial. There will be competition among peer companies in Technological innovation. The risk is that the technology may be changing at a faster rate and hence organizations should be able to cope up with the change in phase of technology.

Example: Nuclear Power Plant

Low Technology

These are technology that are diffused into larger section of the society and will make use of manual/semi-automatic methods of production. They employ people with relatively low levels of education and skill. Since the technology is stabilized, it will remain stable with little or no changes and there will be practically no expenditure on R&D activities.

Example: Technology used for food manufacture, clothing, shelter etc., – that satisfy basic human needs.

Medium Technology

The set of technology that falls between High and Low technologies can be termed as 'Medium technology'. The technology will be a matured one. Since the technology is not likely to undergo many changes, these technologies are more suitable for technology transfer.

Example: Automobile technology, consumer products manufacturing technology.

Appropriate Technology

It is the Technology that is suitable for the social and economic conditions of the geographic area in which it is to be applied, is environmentally sound and promotes self-sufficiency on the part of those using it. It is a technology that is considered suitable and reasonable for a particular purpose that conforms to the existing cultural, social, economic and environmental conditions.

The Technology could be of any level – Low, Medium or High. Utilising the appropriate level of technology results in better use of available resources and achieving better production efficiency.

Under given circumstances, an organization should give due consideration to the type of technology that is suited for its status. It is not always likely that the latest technology will be the appropriate technology for a firm. It depends on so many factors like the cost of acquiring the latest technology, the cost advantage offered by the latest technology, the readiness of the firm to acquire the latest technology, the capacity of the firm (in terms of financial and human resources) to acquire the latest technology, the scope for marketing products/services produced using the latest technology, the strength/advantages of the existing technology, customer acceptance of the latest technology, etc. When there is lack of infrastructure to make use of the latest technology, it will not be advisable for a firm/country to opt for the latest technology. The technology that is appropriate for one country may be inappropriate to another country. Similarly, within a country, a technology that is appropriate for one region may not be appropriate for another region. The same differentiation is applicable even at firms' level. What is an appropriate technology for one firm may not be an appropriate technology for another firm within the country.

The identification of appropriate technology for a country is of vital importance since only the appropriate technology makes better use of the available resources and results in better production efficiency.

Example: Solar powered bulbs (for regions where solar power is available in plenty and other sources of power generation are scarce/costly.)

Pot-in-pot Refrigerator (where usage of electric power for the operation of refrigerator is to be restricted in order to conserve energy or where the negative environmental impacts due to the release of chloro-fluoro carbon into the atmosphere is not desired.)

Codified Technology

This classification is based on the way in which a technology is preserved. A technology can be effectively and conveniently transferred if it is well documented and preserved in a codified form. Such technology is known as Codified technology. Transfer of technology becomes easier when the technology is in a codified form. Engineering Drawing, computer software etc., are some of the codified forms of technology. A Codified Technology may be in a high or a medium level of the technology development.

Tacit Technology

The word 'tacit' means 'implied', 'implicit' or 'unexpressed'. A technology that is not explicitly articulated and can be leant by one, only by being with the person/firm possessing the knowledge and observing demonstrations and assimilating the knowledge, is called Tacit technology. As the name implies, the technology is not documented or codified and it remains known only to the person/firm who/that developed the technology. The technology remains only in the minds of the developers. A technology becomes inexpressible when it involves nuances specific to the filed, requiring special knowledge and skills on the part of the transferors and transferees. Hence, one has to necessarily learn the technology through observation and assimilation. Training/apprenticeship programmes are some of the ways through which such technology can be transferred.

Hybrid Technology

Hybrid Technology is a technology that combines together the salient features of two or more technologies in such a way that the resulting product will have a combination of the superior features of the individual technologies that are combined.

Examples:

- **Diesel-electric hybrid locomotives:** This hybrid locomotive uses diesel power and electric power. It can run by drawing electric power from overhead electric power lines. It will also have a diesel engine and can run on diesel when the locomotive moves to places where overhead electric power lines are not available.

- **Hybrid power system:** This system combines two or more modes of electricity generation together. Combination of wind energy technology and solar power technology results into a hybrid power system. The rotation of the blades of the wind mill will run a turbine, which is connected to a power generator, where the mechanical energy is converted into electrical energy. The solar power that is harnessed generates electrical energy through photovoltaic cells. The electrical energy generated through both the sources is combined into one battery inverter (or Storage Unit). The storage unit saves the energy generated from both the sources, from where the energy can be drawn for the required use.
- **Hybrid car:** It has a fuel tank that supplies gas to the engine like any regular car. It also has a set of batteries that run an electric motor. The gas engine does not directly power the car. The engine turns a generator. The generator can either charge the set of batteries or power the electric motor that drives transmission. Advanced electronics allow the electric motor to act either as a motor or as a generator (Refer figure 1.1). When required, the motor takes power from the batteries to accelerate the car. When the car slows down, the motor acts as a generator and returns energy to the batteries. This technology is called Regenerative Braking by which the motor (acting as generator) gains energy when the car slows down. Normally the energy will be lost due to braking when the car slows down. In the hybrid model, the energy that would otherwise have been lost when the car is slowed down by applying brakes is gained and the energy gained is returned to the set of batteries.

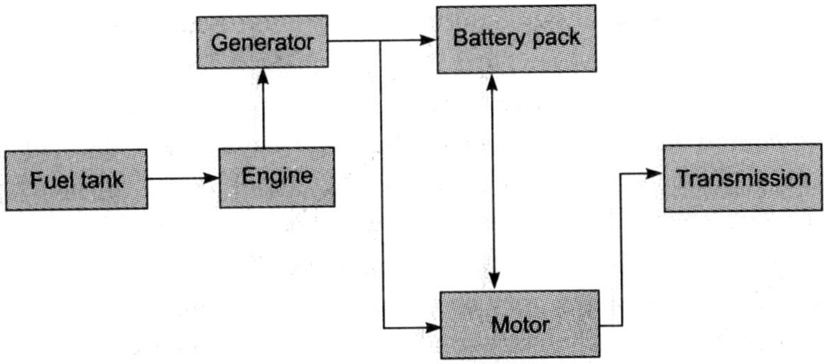

Fig. 1.1 Hybrid car

- **Hybrid cooking stove:** Cooking stove that combines burners that make use of cooking gas and induction plates that converts electric energy into heat energy is another example of a hybrid product wherein two altogether different technologies are combined in one product which offers a greater value to the consumers who can use either of the heating methods depending upon their convenience and availability of the two energy sources, viz., LP Gas and Electricity.

- **Digital camera:** This hybrid product combines the features of photography and digital technology.

Generic Technology

The technology that has its use spread across many industries is called Generic Technology. The word 'Generic' refers to something that is common to the entire group. Dry cell batteries, belt/chain conveyors, power transmission Gear boxes are some of the examples of Generic Technology, which are widely used across many industries.

State-of-the-art Technology

It is the technology that reflects the highest stage of development achieved in a specified technology at a particular point of time. A technology that is considered 'state-of-the-art' today may become an ordinary technology in the future, with the passage of time.

Cutting Edge, Leading Edge, Bleeding Edge Technologies

These are evolving terms to denote the different types of technologies. These are advanced technologies with subtle differences between them. The technology that is at the forefront of any field is called the Cutting Edge Technology. Bleeding Edge Technology refers to a new technology that has a greater degree of risk associated with it for the firm that adopts it. The risk associated may be due to uncaught problems, lack of compatibility with other systems, fear/hesitation of the consumers to accept etc. Thus, while 'Cutting Edge' refers to a new technology that is risk-free, a 'Bleeding Edge' refers to a new technology with associated risks. The adjective 'bleeding; depicts the inherent danger of risk that may be harmful to the firm that adopts the technology. 'Leading Edge' is also a technology similar to the Cutting Edge technology; but while the Cutting Edge technology is at the fore-front, Leading Edge Technology is one among the advanced technologies, but not necessarily the most advanced and does not stand at the fore front of technologies. These are newer definitions of evolving technologies and more such new definitions may evolve in the course of time, depending on necessity.

1.10. TECHNOLOGY PORTFOLIO

Technology portfolio refers to the combination of the different technologies owned and used by a firm. Production of any product may require the use of a few technologies. A firm that is engaged in the production of a product may be owning and using all or a few of the technologies required for the production of the product. All the technologies owned and used by the firm is called its technology portfolio. For example, a firm that is engaged in the manufacture of refrigerators may be requiring the following technologies.

- Refrigeration compressor technology
- Metal body forming technology
- Heat exchanger technology
- Plastic technology
- Painting technology
- Welding technology
- Electrical technology etc.

A firm that manufactures refrigerators may own all the above technologies. Alternatively, the firm can own only a few of the required technologies and can outsource the remaining technologies. The different technologies that are owned and used by the firm for its production activities form the technology portfolio of the firm. The technologies that can be owned and those that need not be owned, but can be outsourced are to be decided taking into account many aspects like the initial investment required, the cost-benefit propositions of the different options, the expertise available with the organization with regard to owning and using a particular technology, the position of the technology in the technology life cycle etc. The portfolio of technologies should be decided after careful planning. If an organization owns a technology that is the state-of-the-art technology, then the organization can gain technological leadership. However, whether to have such technology in the portfolio is to be carefully decided. Simply opting for the latest technology will not always be a prudent decision. Another aspect to be considered is the balancing of the technologies contained in a portfolio. Suppose a firm has say, five technologies in its portfolio. These five technologies should be properly balanced. Suppose out of the five technologies in the portfolio, one technology is the latest and an emerging technology while the remaining four are proven and established technologies. The combination may not be a balanced one and synchronization of the technologies will not prevail. It will be like putting a pair of bullocks before a car for pulling it.

Designing the technology portfolio of a firm can be done following different approaches. The most popular approach for deciding upon the technology strategy of a firm is to study the importance of technology for the firm and the status of the technology in the firm. The process is explained with a Technology Portfolio Matrix. (Refer Fig.1.2)

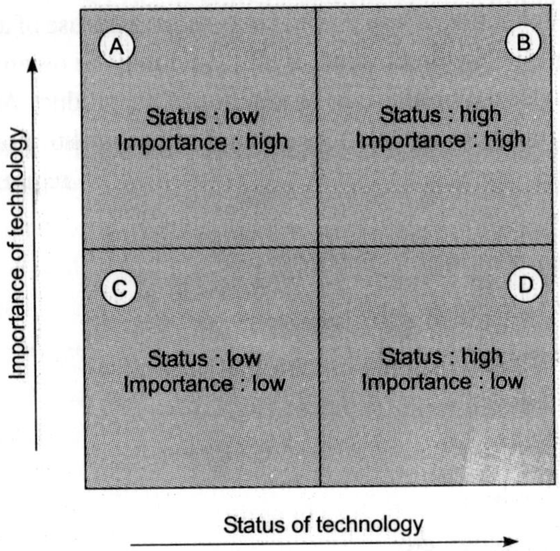

Fig. 1.2 Status of technology in a firm (Technology Portfolio Matrix)

Status of technology refers to the firm's technological competence, technological resources, manpower resources to handle the technology etc. A 'High' status indicates high level of technical competence and a 'Low' status indicates a low level of technical competence. Importance of technology refers to the degree of necessity of that technology for the sustenance of the firm. It depends upon the activities of the firm. A technology that is considered very important for one firm may be considered trivial for another firm.

Allocating all the technologies being used by a firm into the four cells of the technology matrix will reveal the technology strategy to be followed.

Cell-A

The technology is highly important for the firm, but the firm enjoys only a low status (or low level of technical competency) in this technology. (For example, for a company that manufactures refrigeration and air-conditioning equipments, the refrigeration-compressor technology will fall under the category of 'Very Important' Technology. This is because of the fact that compressor is the heart of any refrigeration/ air-conditioning system and a company should possess core technical competency in this area to emerge as a market leader. If the status of this technology in a firm is low, it reveals that the company will not be enjoying competitive advantage as far this technology is concerned. This shows the immediate need to strengthen the technology status. R&D activities should be strengthened in respect of this technology. Employees should be adequately trained in this technology and additional technical resources relating to this technology should be acquired in order to gain competitive advantage.

Cell-B

The technology that falls in this cell is highly important for the firm and the firm also enjoys high technological status as far as this technology is concerned. Hence, there is no need to panic. However, the firm should not rest on its laurels and should be ever prepared to face probable attacks from competitors.

Cell-C

The technologies that fall in Cell-C are relatively less important for the firm. The firm's technology status (or competency) is also low. There will be some other firms that will have a higher level of technical competency in respect of these technologies. Hence, the firm can study the possibility of removing this technology from its portfolio and outsource the process or the product/component that are produced using these technologies from other firms that enjoy a higher level of competency. This will free the men and material resources attending to these technologies and the resources can be profitably employed in other areas.

Cell-D

The technologies that fall in this cell are also having a lower degree of importance for the firm; but the technology status of the firm in respect of these technologies is high. How to take advantage of the situation? First, the firm can explore the possibility of exploiting its technological competency by executing work orders for other firms that are in need of these technologies. Further, the firm can also explore the scope for increasing the degree of importance of these technologies, i.e., moving these technologies to Cell-B so that the firm can make better use of its technological competency. For achieving this, the product/process may be required to be altered in order to improve the importance of the technologies in Cell-D so that the technologies can be upgraded to Cell-B. When there is no scope for making better use of the technologies, the firm can take a conscious decision to remove these technologies from its portfolio and divert the resources to other strategic areas. This decision is a crucial one and needs to be taken only after exhausting all other options to retain the technologies in the portfolio.

1.11. TECHNOLOGY LIFE CYCLE

Managing technology properly requires an understanding of the life cycle of technology. Just as any living being has a life cycle, viz., birth, growth, maturity and death, technology also has its life cycle. A technology is developed, it is introduced, it grows, it matures and finally it loses its relevance and vanishes. Fig. 1.3 shows the S-Curve for Technology progress. The life cycle stages of technology are discussed below.

Embryonic Stage

This is the stage when the new technology is developed in the laboratory and in the R&D centers. During this stage, a technology is conceived from a scientific law. The technology is given shape, experimentations are carried out, initial imperfections/hurdles are studied, teething troubles are identified and removed and the technology is made ready for launch.

Growth Stage

The technology that is developed is launched into the market and it is made available to consumers in the form of various products/services. Since the fundamental operating principles of the technology are perfected, many applications using this technology are explored and new applications are found out. The technology is fine-tuned based on the market requirements and customer feedback. During this phase, the technology exhibits a faster rate of growth.

Technology Maturity Stage

Over a period of time, the rate of growth of the technology starts to slow down. Further improvements in technology becomes difficult and do not prove cost effective. In other words, further developments in technology gives only limited returns. This indicates that a stage of limitation has been reached. Any technology has its limitations for growth in terms of physical parameters, technological saturations etc. This is a natural limit for any technology and any technology, sooner or later enters this phase when the cost of further development of a product or process by improvising the technology becomes very prohibitive. This stage is also referred to as the 'Technological frontier'. When the technology reaches its maturity stage, it becomes prone to substitution or obsolescence.

Decline Stage

This is the last phase of the technological life cycle. During this phase, there is decline in the utility of the technology. Once a technology reaches this stage, two things can take place. The technology may be rejuvenated and the technology may be made to enter a new phase of life cycle. Otherwise, the technology will become obsolete, lose its relevance and will get substituted by some latest technology that has superior performance features. Replacement of vacuum tubes by transistors is an example of one technology becoming obsolete and another emerging technology taking over its place and offering products with improved features and performance characteristics.

The S-Curve of technology progress (or Technology Life Cycle) is very much useful in forecasting of technology. Most of the technologies undergo the Technology Life Cycle.

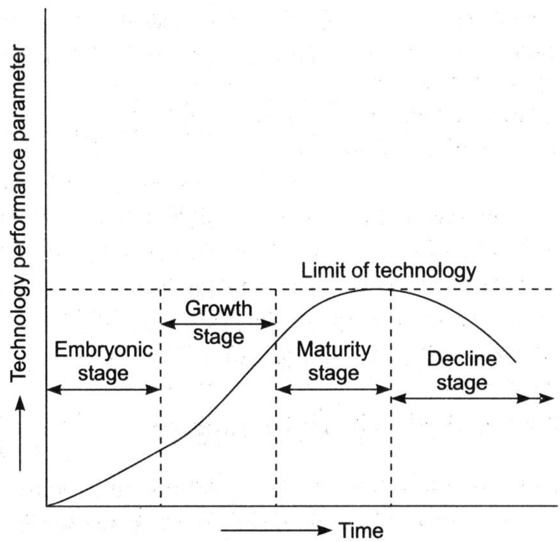

Fig. 1.3 S-Curve for technology progress

1.11.1. Competition Strategies During the Different Phases of Technology Life Cycle

During the embryonic stage, the technology does not normally remain perfected. The technology would still remain in a developing stage. This leaves scope for value addition through technology improvement. Hence, during this phase, companies rely more on improving the technology and the competition is on the basis of innovation. The company that surges ahead of its competitors gains the early-mover advantage.

Once the embryonic stage is over, the product enters the growth stage. During this stage, the companies become busy expanding their market share and every company wants to grab a larger slice of the market. Though companies compete by devising suitable marketing strategy for gaining greater share of the market, the importance of technology can not be ignored. Though the technology would have come out of the embryonic stage, there will be still scope for its further improvement/refinement. Hence, during this stage, a company has to keep on exploring the avenues for technology improvement and strive to improve upon the product through continued innovation. During the later part of the growth stage, the technology becomes refined and industry standards emerge. Competition among the players will be in terms of value addition, quality and cost.

After the growth stage is over, the technology reaches a stage of maturity and there remains little scope for further innovations. The rate of innovation gradually declines and the technology would be available to all the players. No one player will enjoy technological supremacy. Price and quality would remain the major factors based on which companies would compete with one another. Since the scope for product innovation would come to a stand-still, companies would concentrate more on process innovations as the way of reducing cost and improving quality.

Once the scope for process innovation and the scope for further cost reduction become extinct, new technologies start emerging. The new technologies that emerge substitute the existing technologies that have no further scope for either cost reduction or quality improvement. Hence, the existing technology would be gradually replaced by an emerging technology. Thus, during this phase (decline stage), companies gradually migrate to new/emerging technologies.

1.12. TECHNOLOGY AS AN INVESTMENT

Money spent on Technology is an investment and not an expense. It is inadvertently considered as an expense because of the reasons that the benefits derived from of technology are intangible in nature and the benefits spread over a longer period of time, which can also be not defined exactly. The activities of R&D department do not relate to the R&D department alone. They belong to the entire organization. The act of carrying out research and development work extends beyond the boundaries of the R&D department and extends to all the other functional departments. All other functional departments stand benefitted by the R&D department. When a R&D department comes out with a new product, and if the new product brings increased revenue to the organization, people will reckon that whatever money spent on R&D is an investment. On the other hand, when R&D efforts have come out with quality improvement of a product/process, it will not be recognized properly and the investment may not be considered as an investment, since 'Quality' becomes an intangible benefit. However, considering the facts, savings achieved due to improved quality or additional profit earned due to improved quality is a tangible benefit. Similarly, satisfied customers are an intangible benefit while increased customer patronage will be a tangible benefit of R&D efforts. Since some of the benefits of technology, which appear to be intangible in the short-run, become tangible in the long-run, money spent on technology is an investment and not an expense.

1.13. NATIONAL TECHNOLOGY POLICY — ITS IMPORTANCE FOR THE TECHNOLOGICAL GROWTH OF A NATION

The Government of a country has the responsibility to create an environment that allows industry to perform successfully in the domestic market and to compete successfully in the international market. For achieving this, the Government should frame a policy that supports the technological growth of industry, which in turn will support the country's economy as a whole. The national technology policy should be such that it creates healthy competition among industries. It should not breed inefficiency and bail out inefficient business units. It should not provide for unhealthy subsidies that will harm healthy competition. Subsidies should be judiciously decided, keeping in view the state of the different sectors of economy, the inherent strength of the economy, the stakeholders attached to the different sectors and their economic/social status, the uneven development of different geographical locations within a country etc.

Innovations in industry can be stimulated by a conducive technology policy at the national level. The Government of a country can create a climate conducive for innovation by forming suitable policies in this direction. Supporting R&D activities, subsidizing investment expenditure on research works, formulating easy, user-friendly and hassle-free procedures for technology transfer, framing appropriate policies with clear-cut and easily understandable procedures for transfer of technology into the country from abroad, creating a net-work of research institutions especially in the areas of fundamental research where private investment will not be forthcoming etc., are some of the activities for which a Government can give thrust in its technology policy for strengthening the climate for innovations in the country. Such arrangements will create a culture of innovation in the industry.

Any country requires continuous supply of manpower with technical knowledge and skill in order to progress technologically. Government has a greater role to play in ensuring that the requirements of the industry in terms of technical manpower are made available without interruption. A technology policy that supports creation of academic/research institutions and gives guidelines for effective industry-institute interaction will go a long way in supporting the industry of the country with the required manpower.

Every country has its own strengths and weaknesses. The technology policy of the country should identify the strengths of the country and initiate measures that will exploit the strengths. If a country has a strong reserve of a particular natural resource and if there is scope for the country to achieve strategic advantage by exploiting that particular resource, the Government's technology policy, for example, may give incentives to industries that make use of such resource. This will make the sector competitive globally and the country can capture global markets. Such initiatives will orient the technological growth of the country in the right direction.

Since all the industrial firms in a country work under the broad guidelines laid down in the country's technology policy, a correct policy that is framed taking into account the factors like the country's natural resources, the country's technological skills, the thrust sectors to be developed, the environmental damages to be avoided etc., will make all the industrial firms in the country to work on the lines of the technology policy, which will be beneficial for the individual firms as well as for the country as a whole.

Review Questions

1. Define Technology. Distinguish between Science and Technology.
2. What are the essential features of Technology?
3. 'Technology is important for the survival and growth of an organization'. Explain.
4. Explain the benefits of technology to a firm that is engaged in the manufacture of some products.
5. Discuss the role of technology development in the economic growth of a nation.
6. 'Technological developments bring greater boons to human life'. Explain.
7. Is Technology a boon or bane to mankind? Justify your answer with supporting arguments.
8. How does technology help a firm in gaining competitive advantage?
9. Explain the different types of Technologies.
10. What is meant by Technology Portfolio? Explain the factors to be considered in managing a technology portfolio.
11. Explain Technology Life Cycle (or the S-Curve of Technological Progress).
12. Explain the competition strategies to be followed by firms during the different stages of Technology Life Cycle.
13. 'National Technology policies are very essential for giving proper direction to the nation for the technological growth of enterprises'. Explain.

CHAPTER 2

Management of Technology

2.1. MANAGEMENT OF TECHNOLOGY (MOT) — AN OVERVIEW

Rapid developments in technology make a profound impact on business firms. New product technologies change the products and product features; new process technologies change the way in which products are produced. Use of new technology in supply-chain mechanism changes the way a business firm operates. A business firm must be prepared to adopt and adapt new technologies in order to sustain in business for long. In a competitive environment, where technology has become a key factor that decides the success of a business, every firm should know how to handle technology to its advantage. In other words, every firm should know as to how to effectively manage technology.

Management of Technology (MOT) can be defined as the process of keeping abreast of the technological developments taking place, planning for implementing the right kind/kinds of technology/technologies, modifying/altering the prevailing technologies in the firm, forecasting the possible technological developments that might take place in future and constantly updating the technological capabilities of the firm in order to gain sustainable technological competitiveness.

Since technology embraces all aspects of a business (and not just the products and manufacturing processes alone), MOT is concerned with the management of technology in all spheres of the business activity, starting from identification of the raw material to delivering the product in the hands of the consumer.

Management of technology is done not only at the enterprise level, but also at the national level. While the MOT at the enterprise level aims at ensuring that the enterprise attains strong competitive position in technology, MOT at the national level ensures that a nation achieves sustainable technological competitiveness so that the nation can perform well in the global scenario.

2.2. OBJECTIVES OF MOT (AT ENTERPRISE LEVEL)

At the enterprise level, MOT is important to ensure that the enterprise attains a strong competitive position in technology. The objective of MOT at enterprise level can be summed up as under:

(*a*) To ensure that the firm attains competitive technical advantage.

(*b*) To ensure that the firm sustains its competitive technical advantage and continues to remain as a technology leader.

(*c*) To help the firm improve its productivity.

(*d*) To help the firm improve its effectiveness and reap financial benefits due to technology and to ensure long term survival amidst competition.

Role of MOT at enterprise level

At the enterprise level, MOT has its role in many of the functional areas. The areas where MOT has its role to play are as below:

(*a*) Research and Development activities of the firm.

(*b*) Integrating the activities of R&D wing with the manufacturing departments for carrying out meaningful R&D activity.

(*c*) Integrating the manufacturing department with the sales/marketing department for achieving successful product development and for effective commercialization of new products introduced by the firm.

(*d*) Product design/Product modification, Process design/Process modification.

(*e*) Forecasting the technology that the firm may have to acquire/adopt/adapt in future.

(*f*) Managing the technology portfolio of the firm.

(*g*) Development of the technology strategy of the firm.

(*h*) Improving the technological capacity of the firm in terms of physical resources (by acquiring the required equipments, plant & machinery, tools etc.,) and human resources (by recruiting technically qualified and skilled employees and by imparting the required technical skills to the existing employees through effective training methods.)

(*i*) Coordinating with the stakeholders in the supply chain and customers for smooth diffusion of technology, for cost-effective production and for timely delivery of products to customers.

(*j*) Guiding the organization towards achieving the strategic objectives that are, in general, long-term in nature. MOT has a crucial role to play in this aspect. The organizational members should not be allowed to take decisions considering only the short-term benefits that might accrue to the organization, ignoring the long-term perspective. Management of technology has a greater role to play here. It should uncover the weaker areas in the system that are the results of short-term view point of the business and should strength them in the long run, in tune with the long-term strategies. In the absence of effective management of technology, the firm will be misled by short-sightedness of the organizational members and the firm might pursue only certain short-term goals, losing in the process, the implementation of any long term technology strategy.

(*k*) Conducting Technology Audit, where by the firm will understand its technology status and the need to upgrade technology to a required level.

(*l*) Shortening the product development times.

(*m*) Introducing more flexibility in the organization, so that the organization can embrace technology development with ease.

2.3. OBJECTIVES OF MOT (AT THE NATIONAL LEVEL)

Just as MOT has certain objectives to be fulfilled at the enterprise level, it has certain objectives to be fulfilled at the national level. At the national level MOT has the objective of making the nation gain technological competitiveness and become a technological power to reckon with in the international arena and to have long term sustenance of technological supremacy among other nations of the world.

Role of MOT at national level

A nation can attain technological competitiveness only through the many enterprises operating in the nation. However, at the national level, there are certain areas which need to be attended for creating a climate conducive for the growth of technology in the nation. Some of the areas are listed below:

(*a*) Developing a technology strategy for the nation that is relevant and appropriate keeping in view the resources and capabilities of the nation.

(*b*) Development of sustainable technologies.

(*c*) Planning a technology portfolio for the nation.

(*d*) Framing guidelines for technology collaborations with other nations.

(*e*) Framing a technology policy for the nation which provides a broader frame work for the individual business enterprises in the nation to operate.

(*f*) Knowledge management and management of Intellectual Property of the nation.

(*g*) Management of environment in the context of technological developments that adds to the pollution level, by way of increased emission of harmful gases, increased discharge of industrial effluents etc.

(*h*) Management of physical and mental health of the citizens of the nation in the context of increased work load,, higher level of mental pressure, increased level of damage caused to the environment etc.

(*i*) Management of imbalances in the economic status, life style etc., in the society due to disproportionate growth of technology in the nation.

(*j*) Management of technology transfer across the nation and within the nation.

(*k*) Management of technology absorption and technology diffusion in the nation.

(*l*) Creating linkages between research institutes, academic institutions and production/business enterprises for ensuring healthy interaction between them to aid technology development in the nation.

2.4. STRATEGIC MANAGEMENT OF TECHNOLOGY (SMOT)

Strategic Management of Technology (SMOT) refers to the management of technology considering the long-term future prospects of the organization.

Technology has become the greatest asset of all business firms. In order to meet with both domestic and global competitions, a firm has to have a well thought-out strategy for managing its technology. Strategic management of technology has thus become a core business strategy for all firms. This is especially so for production oriented firms where technology has a greater role to play.

Developing a technology/acquiring a technology, developing a product or process using the technology developed/acquired, launching the product in the market, getting customer feedback on the product launched, modifying the product/process based on customer feedback, keeping track of the advances in technology and adopting/adapting to the developments that have taken place in technology, carrying out technology audit of the firm for identifying the technology status and for knowing technology to be acquired, fostering technological innovations, keeping abreast with the technological developments among the peer group/competitors etc., are all essential for proper management of technology and these call for a strategy at every stage. All the different activities mentioned above form a chain of activities covering all stages of business. Strategic management of technology refers to having a strategy for every stage in the technology development chain. Every stage needs to be managed with a strategy since technology has the inherent risk of meeting with failures when it is commercialized. When a new technology is developed/acquired and a new product is brought into the market, it may so happen that the product is not well received by the market. At times, the product may be altogether rejected by the market. It all depends on many factors.

The span of time involved from conceptualization of a product idea to commercialization of the product may be very large and the investment required in terms of men, material and financial resources may be huge. In spite of these, a new technology may fail to impress upon customers. This emphasizes strategic management of technology at all stages of the technology development chain so that the technology/product will be accepted by the customers and the firm will reap the benefits of technology.

Strategic management when applied at each and every stage in the technology development chain will help in reducing the cost of production considerably and will add value to the product at every stage, thereby making the product a success. Value addition gives the product an edge over the competitors' products and thus helps the firm gain competitive advantage in the long run. Thus, strategic management of technology will help a firm achieve competitive advantage in the long run.

2.4.1. Strategic Technology Management System (STMS)

Strategic technology management system refers to a 'systems approach' to the management of technology in an organization, considering the future prospects of the organization in the long run. The term 'system' in respect of management refers to a set of different independent parts working together in an interrelated and coordinated manner to accomplish a set of objectives. If we consider the whole organization as one system, it consists of several sub-systems which are the different independent departments. Each sub-system influences all other sub-systems and also the main system as a whole. Each sub-system derives its strength by association and interaction with other sub-systems. As a result, the collective output of the organization is greater than the sum of the individual outputs of various sub-systems. Thus, when there is close coordination between the different sub-systems in a system, there is synergy.

During a longer time span, the technology in an organization moves through its life cycle from birth to decline stage and at every stage it needs to be managed with a strategy in view. The strategy is to make the organization attain a sustainable competitive advantage in the long run. The purpose of STMS is to integrate the various aspects of technology management and to make the technology managers manage the change process effectively.

According to Michael Porter, 'Technological change is one of the principal drivers of competition. It plays a major role in industry structural change, as well as in creating new industries. It is also a great equalizer, eroding the competitive advantage of even well-entrenched firms and propelling others to the forefront.' Accordingly, the top management of a firm has a greater responsibility in designing and executing organizational strategies that make the firm face the challenges and sustain in the long run.

The different processes involved in the technology development chain and the strategies that are to be followed in each stage in order to integrate the different stages are discussed below:

The STMS (Strategic Technology Management System) life cycle can be visualized to have eight distinct phases (refer Fig. 2.1).

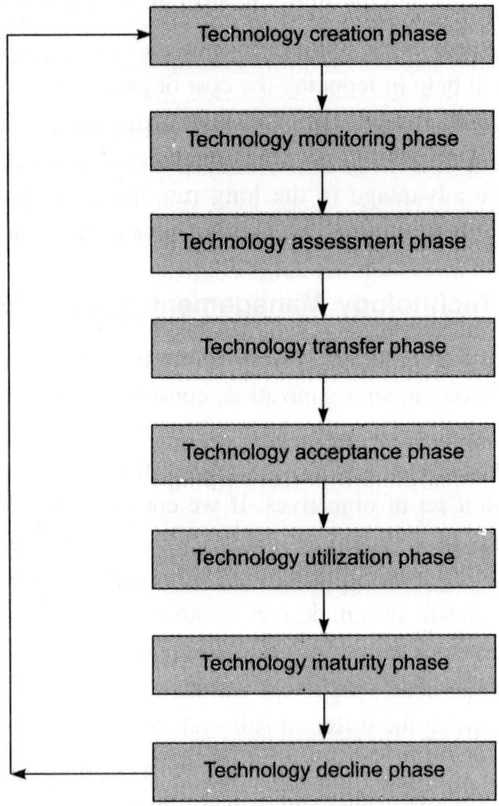

Fig. 2.1 STMS life cycle

A technology that enters the cycle completes its course with the final phase of 'Technology decline' after which a new technology takes over. Sometimes, the same technology may be rejuvenated and may appear as an improved version of an existing technology which will also undergo the different phases before reaching its 'decline' phase.

Technology Creation Phase

While invention refers to the creation of a new product, process or service, innovation refers to the introduction of a new product, process or service in the market. In other words, innovation is commercialization of invention.

Technology creation is the stage where new technologies are invented and innovated. Invention needs creativity. Innovation can happen only if there is a supporting and encouraging top management and a corporate culture that stimulates innovation.

Creativity $\rightarrow$ Invention

Invention + (Supportive top management + Supportive organizational culture) $\rightarrow$ innovation

Technology manager has a greater role to play in infusing creative thinking and in converting it into innovative products of value. He/she should be a visionary in identifying the new product/ new business areas and motivating the team towards achievement. Successive innovations can be made possible by spelling out the market needs identified and the long-term business objectives in clear terms so that the product team can orient its efforts to satisfy the business objectives, to create innovative products/ processes that fulfills the objectives and at the same time meet the needs of the market.

In the technology creation phase, an organization need not solely depend on its internal R&D efforts for creating innovative products. Once the market needs are identified, the organization can also look at the prospects of acquiring technology from any outside source and can choose either the technology developed internally or acquired from outside, whichever is best suited for the requirement.

Technology Monitoring Phase

Before implementing a new technology, a firm should attempt to ensure that the technology will be accepted by the market. Technology monitoring refers to monitoring the trends and changes that have taken place/are taking place in the market before implementing a new technology in the firm. Technology is growing and is getting updated at a faster rate and this technological growth/updating takes place throughout the world. Hence, it is a must that as a part of technology management strategy, a firm should continuously monitor the changes/developments taking place globally in order to identify the emerging technologies, the phases of different technologies in their life cycle etc. Once a firm implements a new technology without proper monitoring, the firm may end up with implementing a technology that is already old enough and likely to be substituted shortly by an emerging technology. A firm can engage 'Technology gate-keepers' who keep a watch of the latest developments taking place in technology and update the firm on the changes taking place. Competitive analysis programs will also help in monitoring of technology status of a firm and arriving at strategies to be followed to overcome competition.

Technology Assessment Phase

Technology assessment mainly aims at assessing the commercial feasibility of the prospective technologies. It also formulates plan for the integration of business strategy and technology strategy. For effective integration of business and technology strategies, both the business and the technology sides of the corporate management should agree on common set of priorities.

Technology Transfer Phase

Technology transfer refers to the movement of technology from some external source into the organization or from the organization's own R&D division to the production division. Since the scope of technology is very wide and cover all the departments in an organization, technology transfer may also takeplace from the R&D department to say, marketing department, wherein the research might have been done on the avenues of marketing. Technology management strategy during this phase will take the form of entering into strategic alliances for acquiring new technologies, choosing the right mode of acquisition of technology (viz., joint venture, research consortia, licensing, mergers and acquisitions etc.) , reducing the organizational barrier for the transfer of technology, sensitizing the product design team for accepting the technology and converting it into successful business opportunities.

Technology Acceptance Phase

A technology that is introduced will bring its impact at all levels. The management should identify the likely impact on various areas and prepare the organization to handle the impact comfortably. Technology acceptance will involve activities like building a supportive organizational structure, nurturing a supportive organizational culture, removing/smoothening barriers for technology acceptance etc.

Technology Utilization Phase

It is the phase of actual utilization of technology in products, processes or services. In a fast changing world of technology, it is not the firm that first succeeds in innovation that succeeds in business, but it is the firm that brings the innovative product to the customer first that succeeds in business. Time has become a very crucial element in deciding success. For ensuring timely delivery of products and services to customers, the technology manager shall resort to project management approach in producing and delivering the product so that products can be delivered to customers at the shortest possible time. During this phase, technology growth also occurs which will add to the increase in sales/turnover and improve quality.

Technology Maturity Phase

When a product moves into maturity stage, it shows that technology has already stabilized and further improvements/advancements are going to be only meager. This is a vulnerable stage and once this stage is reached, the end for the life of the technology is not far away. Hence, the technology manager should act without further loss of time to identify the technological alternatives before the profitability gets affected. Some of the features that indicate that the technology has reached its maturity stage are as under:

(*a*) Competitors have increased their market share considerably over a period of time.

(*b*) Productivity is increased only through efficiency of production rather than due to effectiveness in production. (In other words, productivity improves only by doing things right than by doing the right things.)

(*c*) R&D efforts do not yield product/service improvements to any appreciable extent.

(*d*) R&D efforts in the given technology have become highly expensive.

(*e*) Evidence of customers drifting away from the firm's products/services and delayed purchases.

(*f*) Restructuring/reorganization of the enterprise has not taken place for a long period.

(*g*) No or very few research papers appear in the given technology.

(*h*) Small players enter the field and perform well with radical technologies; radical technologies that were once beyond the reach of small players have now become affordable and implementable by small players.

(*i*) Creativity level in the organization has fallen down.

(*j*) The skill levels of technical personnel have not improved for quite some time.

Technology Decline Phase

After a product remains in its maturity phase for some time, the product and its technology enters the 'decline phase'. The product would have lost its charm and it would become an ordinary product. The technology would also lose its significance and would become obsolete. The technology would gradually get withdrawn and would give way for new technologies to take its place. Once a new technology replaces an existing technology in its decline phase, the new technology will go through the cycle, starting from the Technology Creation Phase and ending up with the Technology Decline Phase.

The Technology Manager shall be watchful of the life cycle phases of the existing technologies that are being used by the firm and when a technology that is currently being used by a firm enters the decline phase, the technology manager should prepare the firm ready to switchover to the new/emerging technologies when required. This being the last phase of the Technology Life Cycle, after this phase, the technology that is currently being used becomes obsolete and a new technology takes its place. By the time the currently used technology being phased out, the firm should have already planned for and acquired a new technology; the organization structure should have been refined/fine-tuned to accept the new technology.

2.5. EXPLOITATION OF TECHNOLOGY

Technology exploitation refers to identifying the best possible ways of utilizing the technology, so that the technology improves the competitive strength of the firm (that has invented and innovated the technology and owns the technology) in the long run and improves its long-term sustenance.

Technology is an asset for a firm. It is in fact technology that adds value to other physical assets. A machine, for example, derives its value due to the processes that it can carry out and for the different uses for which the machine can be put into. In other words, a machine derives its value due to the technology it has. A firm makes use of technology to improve its competitive position. Technology is at the background of the various products and services offered by a firm. Since technology itself is an asset (an intangible asset that has the capacity to give tangible benefits), a firm should explore the possibility of making the best use of a technology that it possesses. In other words, a firm should know as to how to exploit the technologies that it possesses. To explain the meaning of exploitation of technology further, let us assume that a firm has developed and perfected a new technology. The firm can use this technology for the manufacture of some products/offering certain services. By this way, the firm can use its technology to its advantage and can become a pioneer in its field of activity. If the firm retains the technology within itself and uses it for its own manufacturing/service activities, the firm may have to invest heavily towards production/service activities in order to gain a greater market share. The firm can, instead, explore the scope for licensing out the technology.

Licensing out the technology is a technology strategy and should be done with proper planning. Licensing of technology will ensure faster rate of diffusion. Licensing is an ideal strategy if the technology has got a wide range of applications. The firm that has invented and innovated a technology may not be able to explore all possible avenues of utilizing the technology because of resource constraints as well as due to lack of technical knowledge/skills in making use of the technology in diversified applications. Under such circumstances, the best option would be to license the technology. The advantages of licensing option is that the technology will bring remuneration to the firm by way of licensing fee and at the same time the technology will get diffused fast. Faster diffusion of technology is another greater advantage to the firm since it will act as a barrier for the introduction of substitute technology by competitors.

When a firm owns a technology that is very unique and distinct and if the firm is confident of earning good returns in the short-run, the firm can defer the licensing option to start with and exercise the option at the appropriate time. If the firm wants to retain the technology within itself due to its uniqueness, but it finds itself short of resources to make use of the technology in production activities, the firm can explore the options of contract-out manufacture or can also study the scope for entering into joint-ventures.

Thus, it is not only important for a firm to innovate technology, but it is equally important to exploit the benefits of technology by exercising the right action at the right time in retaining/sharing/diffusing the technology. Technology exploitation as a strategy helps the firm in enhancing their competitive advantage and in ensuring sustenance.

2.6. PRINCIPLES OF MOT

A sound management of technology is based on certain fundamental principles. Once these principles are followed in designing and implementing a technology management initiative, things will fall in line and the organization will achieve its technological objectives. Some of the widely accepted principles of MOT are detailed below.

2.6.1. Management of Technology Involves Holistic Management of All the Functional Areas

The definition of Technology from the point of view of a business organization is to be understood first. From an organization's point of view, technology not only means anything related to science and engineering but includes all those that are required to transform the organizational resources into useful products and services. All tools and techniques that are used for this purpose come under the purview of technology. It often so happens that organizations manage Production, R&D, Training, Marketing, Finance etc., as independent functions. When they are viewed and managed as independent functions, they will lack orientation and each department will function in a way that is considered best for it. This will not help in the optimum use of resources. Technology management is not something related to technology alone. It is holistic in nature. Technology can bear fruit only if all the functional departments work in an integrated manner. It has been found that lack of scientific and engineering knowledge is not always the reason for the failure of projects/products. Most of the times, the reasons are beyond the knowledge/expertise in science and technology. If the marketing department is not able to identify the market gap to design a new product or to modify an existing product, if the production department is not competent enough to produce a product as per the specifications/requirements of the R&D department and if the HR department fails to understand the importance of recruiting adequate number of scientists, engineers and technically skilled personnel to carry out the technology mission of the organization, the organization will fail in its technology management.

2.6.2. Designing a Conducive Organizational Structure

Every organization has its goals. The organizational structure should be one that aids the organization in achieving its goals. This is the only objective based on which the structure should be designed. Designing an organizational structure should not be considered as a formality to be complied with. Wrong structure will lead to wastage of resources. There can be no hard and fast rule as to the number of levels on the structure. Fixing up levels in the structure mechanically, without giving a thought to the need for such hierarchical levels will only create barriers to communication which will eventually lead to inefficiency. It has been found that in manufacturing organizations, technology related functions contribute to about 65% or more of the sales value of production. Hence, technology related issues deserve to be given top priority in designing the structure of organizations, especially manufacturing organizations. Span of control is another aspect that is to be correctly decided. The span depends upon the capability of personnel. A qualified technical manager can easily manage the activities of over 20 or 25 technically qualified personnel, if they really have professionalism in their approach to their work. This shows that the structure should be designed keeping the people who occupy positions in the hierarchy, rather than forming a hierarchy and then fitting people in the structure. The structure should be so designed that efficiency, effectiveness and economy are achieved.

2.6.3. Reviewing Current Managerial Practices for their Relevance and Suitability

Policies and guidelines are no doubt required for streamlining the operations. But, they should not act as barriers for development. The only way to make them not to act as barriers is to make them flexible. There should not be rigid policy framework. Rigidity will kill enthusiasm and will spoil creativity. Hence, for efficiently managing technology, a lot of flexibility is to be built into the policies and guidelines. It should not be misinterpreted that a flexible policy will be a weaker one and will be exploited by the employees. The damage that will be caused by rigidity will be much more than that may be caused by flexibility. Identifying the Chief Technical Officer, placing the technical personnel suitably in the hierarchy, communicating the need for technology to all the members of the organization, encouraging all the organizational members to become technology literate etc., will go a long way in improving the technology standard of the organization, Coupled with this, a guiding policy that is appropriate and flexible to accommodate the changing circumstances will be more suitable for a technology driven organization. Thus, frequent review of the managerial practices being followed needs to be carried out to identify their relevance and to modify them whenever and wherever required.

2.6.4. Integrating Technology Related Issues into Business Strategy

The business strategy should be formed taking into account technology related issues like Research & Development, innovation, technology transfer, technology scouting, manufacturing techniques/options etc. A business strategy that is formed taking into account only financial and marketing strategies, as is normally being done, will not be a correct one. Marketing and financial strategies do have their place. But, they can not stand alone; they should be linked with technology. Since it is the business strategy that gives direction to the business activities, a business strategy that is formulated without considering the technology aspects will not take the organization in the right direction. Further, since technology keeps changing fast, the business strategy should be capable of accommodating all such technological changes.

2.6.5. Managing the Internal and External Interfaces Effectively

Interfaces between the different functional departments (internal interfaces) and the interfaces between the organization and the external world (external interfaces) are important areas to be strengthened. Interdepartmental barriers should be broken down which is a prerequisite for improving organizational efficiency. Good business strategies will fail in the presence of such barriers. One of the ways of removing interdepartmental barriers is not to have a rigid organizational structure. The employees must be made to understand the importance of not having any internal organizational barriers within the organization. They must be educated to realize that such barriers will pull down the organization, despite the organization having strong resources. Breaking down the internal, interdepartmental barriers can be done if the CEO has it at the top of his agenda.

However, barriers in external interfaces are not fully under the control of the organization. For example, interfaces with customers (where the marketing, sales and R&D departments will be involved) and interfaces with the suppliers (where the marketing, sales, finance and administrative departments will normally be involved) are to be made barrier-free for effective management of technology. Both internal and external interfaces will add value to the business if they integrate the organization as one unit without offering any resistance/barriers. Hence, for technology driven organizations, ensuring conducive interfaces assumes greater importance. Since this is one of the areas that is overlooked, the top management should realize its importance and take steps for managing the interfaces correctly.

2.6.6. Investment in Technology must be a Carefully Studied Business Decision

Any investment for that matter is a business decision. Investment in technology is to be studied in detail as a business decision, keeping in view the short and long term impacts of the technology on the business fortunes. Not every new technology acquired/ developed by an organization succeeds. There can be failures. Failures can not be avoided totally. But, the process of investing in technology should go through certain time-tested, well-proven stages like evaluation of alternative technologies available, evaluating the availability of technical, financial and man-power resources for implementing the chosen technology, improvement in business performance consequent to technology acquisition/updating of technology, anticipating problem areas and arriving at possible solutions to tackle problem situations, updating the market and economic assumptions continuously etc.

2.6.7. Reacting to Technological Changes

Changes are taking place in all spheres of business. Changes in technology are happening faster. The business should be prepared to adapt to the rapid changes taking place in the field of technology. When it is said that technology is changing fast, it does not necessarily mean that new/breakthrough technologies occur frequently. In fact, breakthrough technologies happen only occasionally. Modification/improvements in existing technologies, however, happen quite frequently and technology driven organizations must keep themselves abreast of the latest developments taking place. Technology forecast is another area to be concentrated which gives an organization the road map for switching over from the current technology to the latest technology. Despite all the changes taking place, an organization should study the changing technologies and should opt for that technology that is appropriate for the organization. Choosing the appropriate technology (and not the latest technology) is a crucial decision that will decide the sustainability of the business. A company can identify the appropriate technology only if it has thorough knowledge of the existing and emerging technologies, the pros and cons associated with them, the resources available at the disposal of the company, the technology that will best suit the expectations of the customers etc.

2.6.8. Managing Technology Requires Managerial Competence

Many technological failures are not failures in technology as such, but are failures in the management of technology. Hence, for managing technology correctly, the manager should possess overall managerial competence. He should have technical as well as general managerial knowledge and skills. It is not expected that the top level executives who are in decision-making position in the hierarchy and all those managers who are entrusted with the job of managing technology related issues should be experts in the field of the concerned technology. What is required is good understanding of the fundamentals and the ability to manage issues rationally and intelligently and the ability to put the available resources into optimum use. Technological decisions have substantial impact on the business. Technological decision should support the organization in achieving competitive business advantage. This requires greater acumen and clear foresight for the manager to integrate technology for enhancing business competitiveness.

2.6.9. Shortening the Concept-to-Commercialization Cycle Time

In a fast changing world, any new product/process/business model should be given shape in the shortest possible time. Delayed implementation will rob the opportunity to tap the benefits from the market and will make the new product/process/business model meaningless if during the time some new technology/concept has already started emerging or a few competitors have already made use of the emerging technology/ concept. Further, customer preference about products might have changed over a period of time and hence any delayed introduction of a new product is more likely to meet with failures.

The life cycle of new products have been gradually getting shortened. About five decades ago, new products had a life cycle of about 15 to 20 years. The present day scenario is that the average life cycle of new products have got shrunk to the range of 5 to 7 years. The shorter life cycle of products have made it all the more important that new products are to be launched at the shortest possible time. Hence, cycle time is of paramount importance. It is not just the product development cycle time that is important. It is the concept – to – commercialization cycle time that is important. This is because, aiming to shorten the product development cycle time alone leaves much to be desired. On either side of the product development there exist a number of activities which are all to be completed in the shortest possible time in order to bring the product to the market at the earliest. It requires a holistic approach to optimize the concept – to – commercialization cycle time.

2.6.10. Extending the Scope of Project Approach

Project management approach is not restricted to getting done tasks that are time-bound and that have resource constraints. Though project management as a branch has been devoted to efficient management of projects which are one-time affairs, the core values of the approach can be made use of wherever possible. In fact, every business activity needs to be completed within the shortest possible time, within the given resource constraints. Hence, project management approach to managing the business activities can be introduced wherever possible. This may require a change of the existing organizational structure. But, it is worth pursuing as it will eliminate most of the unwanted work. In an organization that has an organizational structure that is ill designed, most of the employees will be busy doing works that are unproductive; higher priority will be assigned to tasks that are not in tune with the organizational objectives. The project approach will remove such inefficiencies in the system and will release a lot of man-hours from unproductive/trivial jobs, which can be channelized for better performance.

2.7. THE ROLE OF R&D IN AN ORGANIZATION

In-house R&D unit is a vital department for any progress oriented manufacturing organization. Research is a systematic activity using both basic and applied sciences aimed at discovering solutions to problems, while development refers to creating new products/processes based on the findings of the research. Though the primary responsibility of R&D unit is to work on new products/processes, in general the R&D unit of an organization carries out the following activities:

(*a*) Offers total technical support and backup facilities to the organization's manufacturing activities.

(*b*) Works on product and process standardization and updates the standards in tune with the developments in technology.

(*c*) Sets quality standards for products.

(*d*) Keeps a watch on the products/processes developed/being developed by competitors and develops new products/processes.

(*e*) Develops new products that suit the company's resources and strengths; the new products can be in line with the company's existing products or diversified products.

(*f*) Identifies new applications for existing products and carries out the required modifications to make the products suitable for new applications.

(*g*) Identifies new/emerging technologies and acquires them through a suitable process.

(*h*) Trains the employees in various production, testing, quality control operations.

(*i*) Prepares periodical technical reports on the activities of the department and submits to the top management for perusal and directions.

R&D is an important activity for all business firms, especially to the firms engaged in production of goods. The R&D department should work in close coordination with all other departments in order to undertake meaningful research and development activities. The steps that should be taken for strengthening the R&D department can be summarized as under:

(*a*) There should be very close integration between the overall business strategy and the strategy of the R&D department.

(*b*) Technology audit shall be conducted at adequate intervals to assess the current status of technology in the organization, to study as to how effectively the firm's technology is competing in the market and to identify the technology shift required, if any.

(*c*) R&D department shall be provided with adequate resources. It should not be given a step-motherly treatment in allocation of resources. R&D departments require greater resource allocation at times of business slowdown in order to revive the firm's position.

(*d*) Employees at all levels should be encouraged to come out with new ideas; all new ideas should be rewarded, however small their contribution may be.

(*e*) Failures are quite common in research and developmental works. The top management should encourage people in spite of their failures, errors and mistakes. The top management should have high degree of tolerance in dealing with the R&D activities and should allow people to learn from their mistakes so that the mistakes will not get repeated again. Looking down upon people for their failures, finding fault with their approach etc., will kill motivation and initiative towards research and developmental activities.

(*f*) An organizational culture that encourages creativity and that promotes sharing of innovative ideas among the peer group without any hesitation and inhibition shall be nurtured and developed.

(*g*) The technological life cycle shall be studied and the management shall be watchful of the stage of the life cycle up to which the different technologies in the firm have moved. When there are signs of reduced growth rate, it signals that the product is about to move into 'saturation' stage and hence the management has to intensify its efforts to either introducing incremental improvements so that the saturation phase will get postponed, or introduce new technology/product so that the life cycle will restart with a new 'S-Curve.

(*h*) The core technical competency area of the firm shall be identified and R&D efforts shall be focused more towards this area so that tangible results could be easily achieved.

(*i*) Above all, the R&D project portfolios should be aligned in accordance with the organization's business strategy.

(*j*) There must be close coordination between the R&D and the Finance departments. Investment in R&D efforts is a key factor for innovations and for the survival of organizations. This investment, however, competes with many other investments that a company needs to make. The finance department is a critical participant in deciding resource allocations. The finance department is a partner in the development and execution of R&D plans and is instrumental in providing the required resources for the R&D activities. Hence, the finance and the R&D departments should work in close coordination and each department should understand the priorities and limitations of the other department in order to have realistic plans.

(*k*) The R&D department should consult the marketing department in the process of idea generation for the development of new products as well as for product modifications. It normally so happens that the marketing department makes many of its plans for product developments/improvements on its own, based on customer feedback, without consulting the R&D department. When it comes to implementation, such plans usually suffer either because of the reason that the R&D department is not equipped with the required resources and competency to carryout the plans or because of the reason that the people in the R&D department show a detached attitude since the R&D plan is not something conceived by them on their own. At times, it may also so happen that only the R&D departments think about the future of the company and develop new products/product modifications, without the active participation of other departments in the company. This will also lead to ineffective commercialization of the developments since the R&D department might not have felt the pulse of the market.

2.8. NEW PRODUCT DEVELOPMENT PROCESS

The important ingredients for successfully managing the new product development process are:

(*a*) Accumulated technological knowledge from previous experiences, technological capabilities, complete technical knowledge about the proposed product and its features.

(*b*) Market knowledge.

Before venturing upon introducing a new product into the market, a company should get itself satisfied about the following:

(*a*) There must be adequate demand for the proposed new product.

(*b*) The product should fit into the present production structure and facilities of the company.

(*c*) The company should have the required financial resources to successfully develop and introduce the new product into the market.

(*d*) The product should fit into the present market structure of the company.

If the above aspects are prima-facie in agreement, the company can proceed further. It does not mean that a company can not venture upon a totally new product that does not fit into its present status. In that case, the company may have to put forth extra efforts and resources in aligning the organization in line with the new product.

Further, the following points are to be kept in view while developing new products and during product innovations:

(*a*) The new product must be less expensive for the consumer than the existing products.

(*b*) The new product should have better features, both functional and non-functional than the existing products so that the new product can offer greater benefits to the consumers.

(*c*) The new product should not have any switching or adoption costs. If at all there are any such costs, they should be very minimum and affordable to customers. If the switching or adoption costs are more, it will act as an impediment for attracting customers who are using existing products, in favour of the new product.

(*d*) The new product must be made readily available in the market, so that it will be within the easy reach of consumers.

The steps involved in a new product development process are given in the flow diagram below (Refer Fig. 2.2):

(*a*) Idea generation

Any new product development starts with searching for ideas. Ideas that are generated keeping the customers aside will not prove to be successful. Problems expressed by customers, expectations and preferences revealed by customers are the most fertile grounds for the generation of new product ideas. Formally, Brain-storming and Synectics are the two techniques employed in the idea generation process.

In Brain-storming session, a small group of people are posed with a specific problem and are encouraged to deliberate upon the problem and come out with their suggestions and ideas. The difference between Brain-storming and Synectics is that while the problem is posed to the group in the Brain-storming session, the real problem is kept away from the group in Synectics. In Synectics, only a broader framework of the problem is given to the group without disclosing the specific problem at hand. The group is encouraged to think broadly in all possible dimensions. As the idea generation process progresses, slowly the actual problem is exposed to the group and their ideas are fine-tuned and refined in line with the problem at hand. Synectics is a creative problem solving technique that stimulates the thought process of which the subjects may not be aware of. The method depends on creative thinking, use of analogy and informal discussion among a group of individuals. The individuals in the group are with diverse qualifications, experiences and background. The word 'Synectics' comes from the Greek word *synectokos* which means bringing different things together. Synectics relies on the idea generation process with the use of analogies. Analogies allow the group members to move away from the original problem, discuss the analogy in order to develop solutions and to arrive at a solution to the problem on the basis of the solution to the analogy. Synectics require a skilled facilitator to use analogy/ metaphor for creative generation of new ideas.

(*b*) Idea screening

The objective of idea screening is to give up poor ideas at the initial stage itself. The task of segregating the ideas generated and screening them can be entrusted to a committee of experts. The ideas generated can be grouped into three categories to start with, viz., (*a*) Promising ideas (*b*) Marginally promising ideas and (*c*) Ideas to be rejected.

After grouping the ideas as above, a second stage of screening can be done to identify the ideas to be retained. From the group of 'Marginally promising ideas', those that can be categorized as 'Promising ideas' and 'Rejects' are first identified and regrouped. Now, we are left with only two categories, viz., 'Promising ideas' and 'Rejects'.

Every promising idea and every idea under the rejected category are again examined critically to avoid the following two types of errors which are common:

(*a*) The error of rejecting a good idea that has a great potential.

(*b*) The error of accepting a poor idea that may either be not possible to be implemented or will turn out to be a failure even if implemented.

After the above exercise, the set of promising ideas are arrived at. From out of the above ideas, the one that is most promising is taken up for proceeding further.

(*c*) Concept development

Concept is a detailed description of a product idea, expressed from the customers' perspective. The concept should be expressed effectively. It should be brief, presenting a true picture of the product in the minds of the customers, without much of technical details; it should use simple, understandable language; it should not understate or exaggerate the product features/qualities; it should describe the uses and values of the product. In short, the concept should answer the customer's question of 'What is in it for me?'

The product concept should give the benefits that the product offers to customers in terms of the basic benefits (like nutritional value, sensory appeal etc.,), package benefits (like size of the packing, ease of storage, ease of disposal etc.), usage benefits (like convenience in buying and handling) and psychological benefits (like aesthetics, prestige value, user friendliness etc.).

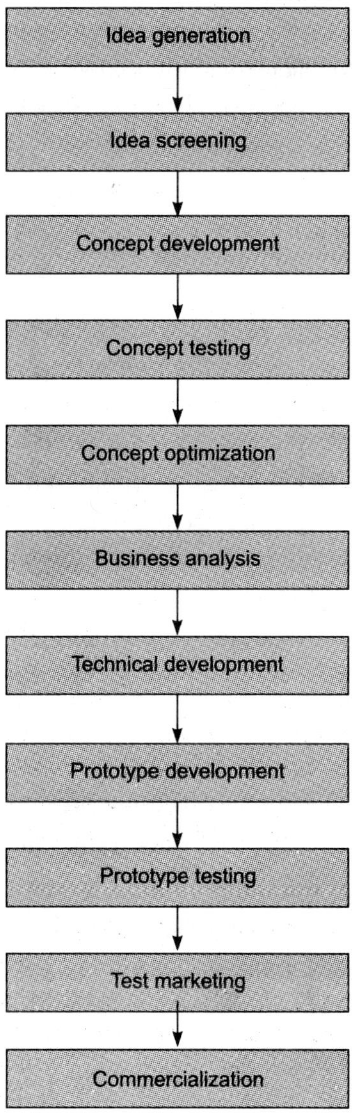

Fig. 2.2 New product development process

(*d*) Concept testing

It is a product development process wherein a product concept is presented to prospective customers and their opinions, buying intentions, preferences and objections/ reservations if any, are obtained. Concept testing is done using field surveys, personal interviews and focus groups. It is an attempt to predict the success or otherwise of a new product idea, before actually putting the product in the market. It is usually done by getting the responses of targeted customers to a product concept through a statement that describes the basic idea of the product and getting their Yes/No, Pass/Fail, Go/ Stop responses. Apart from the dichotomous questions indicated above, a concept will seek answers for the following questions from the customers.

- Is this product idea acceptable to you?
- In your opinion, what are the improvements that should be done before going for production/re-launch?
- Which is the product attribute/benefit that is most important to you?

For concept testing to be successful, both qualitative and quantitative data inputs should be obtained from the customers and analyzed.

(*e*) Concept optimization

It is the process where in the views, opinions and preferences of prospective customers/users are obtained regarding the best features of the new product with the objective of carrying out the required modifications in the product in order to offer the customer the best value for their money. Concept optimization aims at the following:

- Incorporating unique features in the product that are not available in competitive products.
- Improving the value to the customer, by enhancing its worth to the users and reducing the cost.
- Meeting the customer expectations better than the competitors' products.
- Offering a product of relatively better quality than competitors' products.
- Removing problems/ shortcomings that customers come across in competitors products and thus offering customers a defect-free product.
- Introducing innovative features, thereby making the product the first of its kind.

(*f*) Business analysis

Once the product concept is finalized, the next step is to carryout a business analysis from financial and marketing point of view. Market study shall be carried out to assess the likely demand for the product and to decide upon the proposed volume of production. The volume of production depends upon, apart from the market potential, the financial capacity of the company. Expected sales, revenue, cost and profit are projected and the financial profitability of the project is to be studied to ensure that the project will be an acceptable business proposition.

(*g*) Technical development

The new product development may relate to a totally new product or modifications of an existing product. In both the cases, the company may have to invest in new technology/modify the existing technology to suit its production requirements. It is the stage in which a tangible new product emerges or modifications to an existing product are finalized or the specifications of a new service are determined. For a new product, the first stage in technical development is the development of a product protocol.

A product protocol is a document giving the product details, specifications and other deliverables that the multidisciplinary product development team arrives at by mutual agreement between them, after discussions, consultations and deliberations. The product protocol is signed by all the concerned parties in order to authenticate the consensus arrived at. The product protocol communicates details about the product to all the concerned departments and specifies the contribution to be made by each department/team in order to deliver the final product to the customer. It focuses on developing the product or service that is most desirable to the customer. The product protocol is prepared in order to give a direction to the different team members who are involved in the product development and who would have come from different departments, so that all the team members could work effectively and efficiently towards product development. The product protocol gives clarity to the product development team, avoids wastages and reworks/redesigns. Since the product protocol is communicated to all the concerned departments/teams, all the teams that are involved in the product development process can contribute their best towards developing the product with features/attributes desirable to the customers.

Apart from giving the details/specifications and designs about the product, the product protocol also gives in clear terms, the time frame for the completion of different works during the product development cycle so that each team will come to know about the time-bound tasks to be completed by them.

The product protocol also gives clear-cut definitions as to what the requirements of a successful product are. By this, the product protocol gives the appropriate measures/metrics to be used in measuring the product features/attributes/performances. Some of the aspects that are included in the product protocol are as under:

- Details of product attributes

- Details of product designs/specifications
- Product positioning
- Time schedule for product development
- Product differentiation and its competitive advantage
- Foreseeable problems, if any in product development
- Comparison of competitors' products
- Financial requirements like BEP, NPV etc.
- Production requirements
- Regulatory requirements connected with the product
- Special marketing issues, if any

Design for Excellence (DFX)

Under technical development, the product design plays an important role. Product design is an important stage wherein the desirable features and characteristics are finalized. In a competitive environment of new product development, organizations can not wait for problems to surface and then attempt to solve them. Instead, organizations should anticipate likely problems and address them in the product design stage itself so that the products will not exhibit problems at a later date. The following are some of the technical design aspects that should be given consideration:

- The design should be such that the product is user friendly.
- The products should be fail-safe. (a fail-safe device is one that will not cause any harm in the event of its failure.)
- The products should be free from posing hazards to users during usage. For example, sharp edges, slippery handles, unsafe exposure of electrical wire/ contacts etc., should be avoided.
- Proper earthing should be ensured for electrical gadgets.
- The product should be capable of being repaired easily.
- Moving parts/components should be so designed that they are separated and that they don't pose any danger of coming into contact with the users' hands/ other parts of the body. Fixing of screens/guards and allowing adequate clearances can solve this problem.
- The controls used to operate the product should be so designed that the user need not have to take up an unnatural position to operate/use the product.
- The raw materials of parts/components should be so chosen that critical, load-bearing parts are made of high strength, impact-resistant materials.

DFX is a proactive approach which has the following advantages:

- Reduces the time taken to take the final product to the market.
- Reduces manufacturing costs.
- Reduces changes/reworks in product design at a later design.
- Reduces product defects.

(*h*) Prototype development

Prototype is the first unit of a manufactured product that is tested for its use and whose design can be changed/modified if necessary before the product is manufactured commercially.

Uses of Prototypes

- Prototypes aid in discovering and avoiding costly mistakes in the product designs before the product is taken for large scale production.
- Prototypes developed are used, tested, improved and tested again. It is an iterative process through which the product design is refined and finalized. Prototypes help to design the product to perfection by conducting field trial tests, observing the functioning of the product in the field and perfecting the design based on the feedbacks.
- Prototypes help to reach the market faster. Since design adjustments / corrections / modifications are done at the prototype stage itself, it avoids further time in taking the product to the market.

In developing the prototype, the following aspects are to be critically examined:

Technology

The technology to be used for building the prototype should as far as be the latest one, except under situations where cost considerations may impose a restriction in the use of the latest technology. When the company has opted for an emerging technology and has developed a new product, in order to safeguard against any infringement of intellectual property rights by others, the company shall register the patent rights. This will help the company gain temporary monopoly when the product is introduced in the market.

Ease of use

The product/equipment shall be user friendly. The design of the product should be done in such a way that human-machine interaction is smooth so that the product will gain customer acceptance. A product/tool/equipment that is easy to use will improve productivity, safety and satisfaction level of the users.

Cost – Function relationship

Cost being a major influencing factor for any product, the prototype design should aim at cost reduction without sacrificing the functional requirements. If a product is designed ignoring the cost aspects, even a technically sound and superior product may become a failure when commercialized. Before designing the prototype, the price that is affordable to the target customers is to be arrived at based on which the likely cost can be zeroed in. The cost-function tradeoff should be such that the functions/features/ specifications are so designed that the cost arrived at is not exceeded.

(*i*) Prototype testing

Prototype testing is very critical to new product development. Prototypes are tested for design flaws, if any and for ease of use by the end-users. The effect of prototype testing is ultimately to increase the bottom line since a product that fails in the market due to improper testing of the prototype is going to eat away the profits. Time is another crucial element in prototype testing. If the testing of the prototype takes longer time duration, then company is likely to lose the first-mover advantage since a competitor who works on a similar product might enter the market earlier. Hence, prototype testing should be done giving due importance to both the extent of testing and the time taken for testing.

The two modes of testing a prototype are Alpha testing and Beta testing. Alpha testing refers to testing the prototype for its functioning within the firm while Beta testing refers to testing the prototype for its functioning at the customers end wherein the customers are given the prototype and are asked to use it and give their feedback. The Beta testing is in effect market testing of the prototype.

(*j*) Test marketing

This is the stage when the product and the marketing program are introduced on a small scale into one or more selected cities or regions. Test marketing provides the company with an opportunity to know the customer behavior towards the product in real market situations. The marketer can identify the potential problem areas and rectify the defects noted if any, before going in for full-fledged production and marketing.

(*k*) Commercialization

It is the final stage of new product development. It is the process of launching the new product into the market. It normally involves heavy promotion expenditure. The timing of the product launch should be so chosen that it coincides with the good economic condition that is conducive for improved sales.

2.8.1. Failure of New Products

Some of the factors that are responsible for the failure of new products are as under:

1. Inadequate/inaccurate market analysis is the major factor responsible for the failure of new products. It is customer acceptance that is responsible for the success of any product. A market analysis that is biased and that does not correctly capture the customer opinions is more likely to give misleading findings and any new product that is launched based on such incorrect market studies is bound to face problems in its market acceptance. There is a tendency on the part of the entrepreneurs, engineers and scientists to assume customer behavior pattern and to go ahead with the development of products on such assumptions. They take it for granted that the customers would behave in the way that they expect them to behave. But, this is not the case often. Thus, new products often fail to take off due to inadequate, inaccurate market analysis
2. Products develop defects when manufactured on commercial scale. Newly developed products are perfected at laboratory before taken for commercial production. If the working conditions at the field level where the products are actually put into use differ from the working conditions in which products are tested in the laboratory, the products may not give the same result/output as given in the laboratory. The product may also develop defects due to changed working conditions. Thus, the difference between the laboratory conditions and the actual field conditions is another factor responsible for the failure of new products.
3. A new product that has been successfully developed and that has a potential to be accepted by the market may fail if the product is not correctly marketed. Poor/weak marketing strategies may make the product do not gain ground and capture the market share that it is capable of gaining.
4. In spite of launching a new product with relevant and appropriate marketing strategy, the product may face hurdles if a strong competitor comes with an effective counter move introducing a modified/improved product.
5. A new product should be launched at the appropriate time. Poor timing of the launch may spoil even a good product. The time of launch of a new product may be made to coincide with a trade/industry fair to be more effective. For products that show seasonal variations in the consumption pattern, the product launch should immediately proceed the peak season. Introducing the product in off-season time will be a very bad choice. Once the product launch date is identified and finalized, the product should be made available in its complete form. Absence of certain features/attributes from the product at the time of launch (due to paucity of time) with a promise that the product will soon be

available in complete form will produce a disastrous effect. Customers who use the incomplete product may spread unfavourable comments about the product which will become very difficult to set right later.

Review Questions

1. What do you understand by the term 'Management of Technology (MOT)'?
2. What are the objectives of MOT at enterprise level? Indicate the areas where MOT has its role at an enterprise level.
3. What are the objectives of MOT at the national level? Indicate the areas where MOT has its role at the national level.
4. Explain Strategic Management of Technology (SMOT).
5. Explain Strategic Technology Management System in detail.
6. Give a brief note on Exploitation of Technology.
7. Explain the fundamental principles of Technology Management.
8. How can R&D activities in an organization be strengthened?
9. Explain the stages involved in New Product Development.
10. Explain some of the factors responsible for the failure of new products.

3

CHAPTER

Technology Forecasting

3.1. TECHNOLOGY FORECAST

The word 'Forecast' refers to prediction of a future event. Technology forecast is the prediction of the characteristics of future technology. Traditional forecasting techniques depend on the past data, which are projected into the future for arriving at a forecast of the future. For example, if population is to be forecasted for a future period, the growth of population in the past can be plotted and the curve can be extended into the future period. Technology forecast, however, can not be done by simply projecting the past data, especially when the technology being predicted undergoes rapid changes. Hence, special techniques need to be used for forecasting the technology. Technology forecast can not be simply reduced to a relationship between two variables in numeric terms since assessment of the magnitude of technological growth has more subjective elements in it.

Technology forecast predicts the new developments in technology. The main objective is to identify the emerging technologies on the anvil that may change the operations of an organization. For example, 'vacuum tube' went out of business once 'transistor' emerged and this made a total change by which electronic products were made and the industry as a whole went through major changes in its mode of operations. An aggressive organization will keep itself updated with the latest developments taking place in the industry and will become prepared to adopt new technologies. Technology forecast is of great use in this regard. It may be noted that technology forecast does not define any technology strategy, but only predicts the likely technology status in the future. It is left to the judgment of the management to accept the findings of the technology forecast and to go ahead with switching over to the technology predicted to prevail in the future. This is because, customers are the ultimate decision makers and they accept only those products that offer substantial benefit to them over the existing products. Customers are not averse to new technologies. But, they will accept a new technology only if the technology offers substantial benefit to them. A technology that does not offer any additional benefit from the customers point of view will not be received well by the market, however advanced the technology may be.

Advantages of Forecasting Technology

(*a*) Technology forecast indicates the rate of progress of technology so that the technology planning can be made correctly.

(*b*) Technology forecast exposes the likely technologies that are available for adoption and hence a firm can make a deliberate choice of the required technology.

(*c*) Technology forecast gives warning signals to firms that have a slower phase of technology updation/acquisition, since a firm that is not in tune with the phase of development of technology in its field will find its survival difficult unless it takes appropriate steps to speed up its phase of technological growth.

(*d*) Technology forecast will help a firm to overcome its competitors through appropriate strategic technology planning.

(*e*) Technology forecast will help in the long term sustenance of a firm provided the firm updates its technology in tune with the phase of the technological growth.

(*f*) Through technology forecast, a firm can make appropriate capacity planning and facilities planning and this in turn will help in investment planning.

(*g*) With the knowledge of the findings of technology forecast, a firm can plan its technology in such a way that it gains competitive business advantage.

(*h*) Technology planning will be of help in planning for new product development.

(*i*) Strategic decisions of technology licensing, joint venture etc., can be taken with the aid of the findings of technology forecast.

(*j*) Technology forecast will be of use in prioritizing the R&D activities of the firm.

3.2. METHODS OF FORECASTING TECHNOLOGY

Trend Analysis

This method uses past data to predict the future. It is extension of time series data into the future. It is based on the assumption that the past trend will continue in the future also. It requires substantial volume of reliable, good data to predict the future status of technology. It is useful only when quantitative data is available. Since the technology trend may not remain the same in the long run, this method is useful only for short range technology forecast.

The trend analysis is to be judiciously used and extension of the past trend requires a careful prediction. Physical limitations of technology, influence of social and environmental factors etc., may alter the trend. Physical limitations of technology will reduce the phase of growth. Influence of social and environmental factors may either reduce the phase of future growth of technology or accelerate the phase depending upon the type of the factor and the prevailing conditions that influence the growth of technology. (For example, people's apprehension about the safety of nuclear power plants will reduce the rate of growth of nuclear power plant technology.)

Refer Fig. 3.1 which shows the likely trends that technological growth may assume in the future.

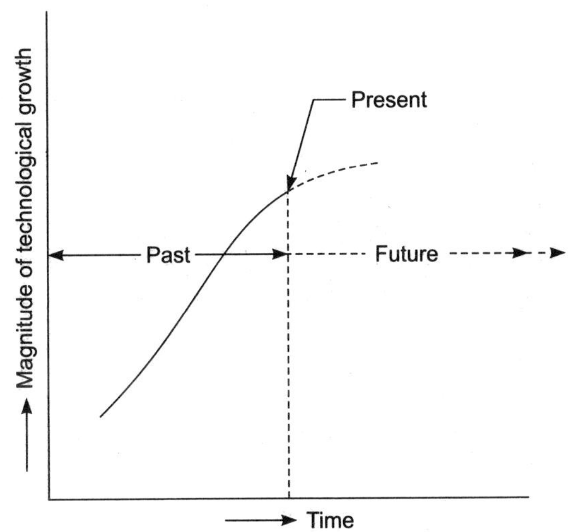

Fig. 3.1 Technology trend

Technology Discontinuity

Technological discontinuity happens when new technologies emerge. Refer to Fig. 3.2.

S_1 is the technology progress curve of Technology -1, which is the current technology. Portion "BC" of the curve 'ABC' refers to the extension of the past trend (or projection of the past trend) of the existing technology (Technology-1) into the future. By now, another technology (Technology -2) would have already started to emerge. Thus, as of the present (the present time 't_1' is indicated by the dotted line drawn parallel to the Y-axis in Fig. 3.2), Technology -1 might be with a higher status of development while Technology -2 (which is the emerging technology) might have a slower level of growth; but, Technology-2 will have a greater potential for a steeper growth in the near future. A firm that presently owns Technology –1 can survive till time period 't_2'. By this time, Technology-2 would become equal in status to Technology-1. Beyond time 't_2', Technology-2 will overtake Technology-1.

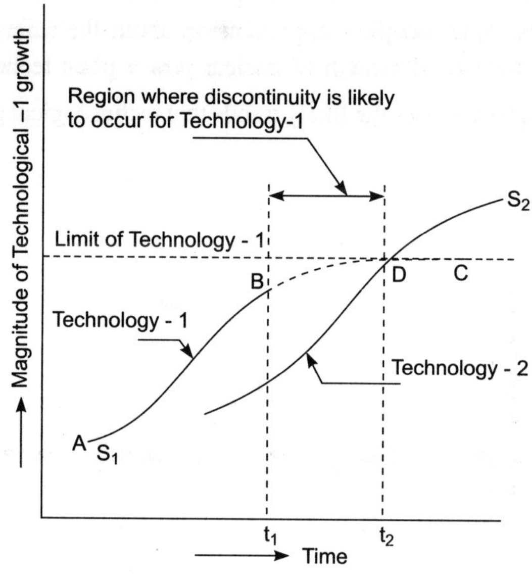

Fig. 3.2 Technology discontinuity

The growth rate of Technology – 1 will be limited by physical and technological factors and hence the growth rate will fall down drastically and will virtually become a straight line, indicating no further growth. After time period 't_2', Technology-2 would surpass Technology -1 and firms that are struck up with Technology-1 will find the going tough. For these firms, it would be futile to continue to use Technology-1 and these firms need to switch over to Technology-2, well ahead of time period 't_2' and the managements of the firms need to plan for the migration from Technology-1 to Technology-2, at the appropriate time. Melting of metal/alloys using 'Arc furnace' was a widely used technology during the 1970's and 1980's. By this time, 'Induction furnace' technology that is an advanced and an altogether different technology had already started evolving. The Induction technology very soon replaced the Arc-melting technology for the process of melting metals and alloys. Thus, while forecasting technologies, apart from projecting the growth rate of technologies currently being used, the emerging technologies are also to be studied, so that the forecast will throw some useful light on the steps to be taken to remain technologically updated.

A new innovation is called discontinuous innovation when it creates some product using an entirely new knowledge base than what is presently being used to produce the same product. For example, digital photography is a discontinuous innovation, because, when it was innovated it was on a totally different knowledge base when compared with the chemical photography (Silver-halide printing process) that was the technology prevalent then. A firm that does not give importance to technological forecasting might be caught unawares when a new technology replaces the technology currently being used by the firm all of a sudden. (Refer para 3.4 for more details on Technology Discontinuity.)

Expert Opinion

Expert opinion method of technology forecast can have the following two forms:

(*a*) Expert committee opinion

(*b*) Delphi technique.

Expert Committee Opinion

It is a qualitative forecasting method. A group of experts in the chosen area are identified and a committee of experts is formed. The committee is entrusted with the task of forecasting the technology for the future. This method is based on the belief that some individuals know more about a particular area and that a group of such experts are better able to forecast the technology of the future by their collective wisdom. The experts may be drawn from internal as well as external sources. The experts meet, interact, exchange their views and arrive at a consensus about their forecast. They may require a few meetings before arriving at the consensus.

Though this method has the advantage of collective wisdom and consensus opinion (which by their nature are capable of correctly predicting the technological trend), suffers from the following setbacks:

(*a*) It may turnout to a time-consuming process if arriving at a consensus is delayed. Sometimes, arriving at a consensus may be elusive.

(*b*) Since arriving at the consensus is an important milestone in this method of forecast, there is the danger that the opinion of the majority will prevail, rather than the more valid opinion; a member who is more powerful, may influence the views of others and may force a consensus.

(*c*) The committee members, may, at times, involve in emotional conflicts and this may harm the process of arriving at the forecast.

Delphi Technique

It is also a qualitative forecasting method similar to obtaining the opinion of an expert committee. In this method also, a panel of experts are assigned with the task of forecasting the technology. The experts in the panel work separately and they do not meet in person for discussions/deliberations. They are coordinated by a skilled coordinator (or moderator). Only the coordinator knows who the members of the panel are. The panel members do not know who are all in the panel. The coordinator gets the predictions of the panel members in writing (about technology forecast). Usually a well thought-out and pre-designed questionnaire is given to the panel members for answering and giving their forecast. The coordinator consolidates the predictions of the panel members, summarizes them, frames another questionnaire and poses the second questionnaire to the panel members for getting their answer. The second questionnaire is formed in such a way that ambiguity/misinterpretations, if any in the first questionnaire are removed, additional questions required to clarify some of the answers given for the first questionnaire are included etc. Along with the second questionnaire, the coordinator also provides to each of the panel member with the views/predictions given by the other panel members, the degree of consensus, the agreeing/conflicting view points of the panel members etc., and the panel members are asked to reassess their predictions on the basis of the views of the other panel members. The responses of the panel members for the second set of questions along with their revised/modified views/opinions are obtained. The coordinator summarizes the responses obtained from the panel members in the second time and he/she repeats the process of passing on the feedbacks to the panel members and refining their responses obtained until consensus of opinion is obtained. Thus, Delphi method overcomes the disadvantages associated with the face-to-face group interactions of Expert Committee Opinion method. However, the success of Delphi method depends to a greater extent on the knowledge and skill level of the coordinator.

Mathematical Modeling

A model is a simplified form of representing the structure and dynamics of some part of the real world. Models are developed by segregating the essential system aspects from the unessential details and identifying the variables (or determinants) that act as drivers for the system. The behavior of the system is developed by studying the relationships between the variables (determinants). The relationships may be in the form of flow diagrams, simple/complex equations or computerized simulations. Modeling of the technological change will help forecast the technology for the future period. Since models are developed using quantifiable parameters, some important factors that are not amenable for quantification may be left out and to that extent the prediction capacity of the model will suffer. Modeling is used as a tool for technological forecasting whenever the system is too complex which requires to be reduced to manageable proportion for the purpose of analysis and future prediction.

Scenario Building

Scenarios refer to snap-shots (one-time picture) of some aspect. It is a narrative form of forecast that describes a course of events that are likely to happen sometime in the future. Usually, three scenarios are developed, viz., the worst-case scenario, the best-case scenario and the most-likely scenario. Experts are entrusted with the task of building the three types of scenarios. A study of the three types of scenarios developed about the likely future course of events at some specified point of time in the future will provoke thought as to how the firm could handle the problems/issues associated with each of the scenarios. It is the practice for firms involved in scenario building, to plan for achieving the results predicted by the most-likely scenario. At the same time, firms should have identified plans to fall back upon in the event of the worst situation (as predicted by the worst-case scenario) happening.

Decision Trees

Decision trees originally evolved as a graphical representation of indicating the alternative choices available at each stage. It is a diagrammatic representation of the logical relationship between the different parts of a complex situation and the possible outcomes of the different decisions.

Decision tree approach can be used for analyzing the pros and cons of alternative decisions and choosing the best possible course of action.

Decision trees present a number of 'Yes/No' choices. The subsequent questions depend on the answer to the immediate previous question. Following the branches of the decision tree, starting from the top leads to a final destination that gives the anticipated solution. In respect of technological forecast, the final destination will indicate the forecasted technology. With the development in computer technology, designing of much more complex decision trees have become possible with feed-back loops and multiple alternatives. Decisions are no longer limited to dichotomies (requiring only 'Yes' or 'No' responses), but permit multiple alternatives by assigning different probabilities to the likelihood of any particular path. The application of Bayes' theorem (which gives a formula for determining conditional probability values) has enabled the modification of probabilities initially assigned so that decision trees get more and more refined as new evidences are introduced.

Hybrid Methods

Every method of technological forecasting has its own strengths and weaknesses. Some methods rely only on quantifiable data and some methods purely go by qualitative data. The reliability and accuracy of technological forecast depends on the nature of the technology and the method used for the forecast. Obviously, a method that relies on qualitative data will give a better result for a technology whose attributes are qualitative in nature and are difficult to be quantified. Similarly, for a technology with quantifiable data, a forecasting method that relies more on quantified data will give better results. Hence, all the different methods of technological forecast have their own relevance and none can be ignored. A hybrid method combines the different methods (or approaches) of forecasting in order to gain different and divergent views about the technologies that will rule the future.

3.3. TECHNOLOGY OBSOLESCENCE

A Technology is considered obsolete when the technology and its related products, services or processes have become irrelevant since a better technology has already evolved, which is superior in terms of cost-effectiveness, technical efficiency, operational convenience and effectiveness, consumer preference etc. Technology obsolescence is said to occur when a product/service is no longer wanted by the customer, though it would still be in working/useful condition. This is because a new product/service has already been created to replace the older version and the new product/service is superior to the old product/service in terms of cost, efficiency and effectiveness. A firm should remain ever watchful to see that if any of its technologies are likely to become obsolete in the near future and should guard against such technological obsolescence by switching over to the latest technology at the appropriate time. Ignoring technological obsolescence will land a firm in trouble. Technological obsolescence is inevitable and is bound to occur due to one or more of the following reasons.

- Technology is always being improved upon and perfected and hence better technologies emerge with the passage of time.
- A technology that is still relevant may be planned to be phased out due to reasons like the high level of pollution that it causes, the occupational hazards that the technology might possess, the higher manpower that the technology may demand etc., and the Government of a country may come up with a plan for phased removal of such technologies and replacing the same with a technology that does not suffer from such shortcomings. Under such circumstances, the prevalent technology (that will be replaced by a new technology in the near future) will become obsolete in the short run.

- When a country that has so far been conservative in not opening up its economy to the international economy decides to open up and become global, the current technologies that are being used by the firms in the country will become obsolete due to the acquisition of new/latest technologies from abroad.
- A technology that involves higher manufacturing cost, higher maintenance cost, lower productivity etc., will make it become obsolete since such a technology can not stand for long and R&D efforts will be diverted to bring out a technology that is superior, free from such shortcomings.
- Technology policy of the Government may give thrust for certain technology/ technologies and the Government may support such technologies with financial and non-financial incentives. This may be on the basis of national priorities to develop a particular technology. Such a move by the Government may make an existing technology lose its importance in the course of time and the existing technology (if it is not under the category of 'thrust technology' of the Government) will become obsolete.
- Tastes and preferences of consumers change fast. Firms may have to go for a technology that suits the tastes and preferences of the consumers, thus making the existing technologies become obsolete.

3.3.1. Managing Technology Obsolescence

While technology discontinuity (discussed later) overtakes an existing technology all of a sudden, technology obsolescence is to some extent predictable. When we say that technology discontinuity emerges all of a sudden, it does not literally mean that the new technology is developed instantaneously; it only means that the new technology that is being developed lies unnoticed or a new application of an emerging technology has just been identified.

When a product reaches its maturity phase of life cycle, the chances of it becoming obsolete are to be assessed. Sharp decline in sales volume is an indication that the product/technology is entering the phase of obsolescence. Since technology obsolescence occurs due to the arrival of improved/better technologies and innovations in the market place, the old technology has to necessarily give way. A firm can not cling to the old technology and try to survive for long.

To overcome the effect of technology obsolescence, firms should start switching over to the latest/emerging technology when the product is in its maturity stage itself, by surveying the market, scouting for the emerging technologies in the concerned domain and entering into strategic technology alliances. If such a proposition is beyond the financial and technical capabilities of a firm, the best option is to gradually withdraw from the market, allowing those with better technology and capacity to compete.

Technology obsolescence is not a thing to be analyzed at the fag end of a product in its life cycle. Even at the time of planning to build a product, opting to buy a technology, deciding to buy an equipment etc., a firm should assess (of course, within all the limitations) the likely time period until which there can be no possible threat of technology obsolescence. If due attention is not given at this stage, the product/ technology may become obsolete within a shorter time. For example, the Indian textile weaving sector was dominated by handlooms and semi-automatic power looms. High-speed projectile looms entered India during 1990s. These looms were mostly imported second-hand from Europe. Used, TW-11 Model 'Sulzer' brand projectile looms were imported into the country in large numbers as these looms were costing around Rs. 3.00 lakhs which was considered very cheap considering the output that these looms could give. But, the crux of the issue was that the production of these looms were already stopped by the manufacturer Sulzer Ltd., Switzerland, way back in 1978. A company opting for buying such looms should weigh the consequences of not getting adequate spare parts and take a conscious decision. This is because, the production being stopped, finding spares for maintaining the looms would become difficult and the looms would face obsolescence at any point of time.

Electric Arc furnaces were widely used during the 1980s in India by small foundries for the melting of iron/steel. During the late 1980s and early 1990s, Electric Induction furnaces entered the market. The Electric Induction furnace was designed on a different technology that was superior to the Arc furnace technology. Electric Induction furnaces were energy efficient as compared to electric Arc furnaces. Further, they offered a better way of controlling the melting process and provided dust/pollution free operating environment and came with a wide range of capacity in the range of 1 kilogramme to 100 tonnes. These advantages of the Electric Induction furnace tilted the market in their favour. Thus, the entry of Electric Induction furnaces signaled the threat of technical obsolescence for the Electric Arc furnaces. Seeing no way out, the manufacturers of Electric Arc furnaces, either stopped their production or diverted their production efforts to special category areas that are free from the competition of Electric Induction furnaces.

3.4. TECHNOLOGY DISCONTINUITY

Technology discontinuity is said to occur when a technology is replaced by another improved technology rapidly, within a very short period. Technology discontinuity occurs in every industrial sector. Biotechnology, Genetic engineering, Polymer technology, Computer data storage system, mobile phone etc., are some of the areas that have experienced technology discontinuity in the recent past. It is sometimes regarded as a special case of technological obsolescence. However, the term

Technological obsolescence is used for the decline of technology over a period of time. One can predict that a technology will become obsolete, based on the time duration of its existence, the developments in technology taking place elsewhere that have the potential to replace the existing technology etc. On the other hand, technological discontinuity will be very fast and the technological changes will be very substantial. When a new technology with substantial improvements in key parameters emerges, it will replace an existing technology very quickly. New firms will be set up using the latest technology which will give them an edge over the existing firms (that are using old technology). In a world of fast changing technologies, technology discontinuity creates opportunities for some companies while sends some other companies out of business. Since technology discontinuity has become unavoidable, it has become obligatory on the part of all organizations, especially manufacturing organizations, to anticipate technology discontinuity and to take steps to overcome it. Hence, as compared to Technological obsolescence, it is Technological discontinuity that demands a greater and faster response from firms to remain competitive.

Technological discontinuity occurs due to one or more of the following reasons:

- Arrival of disruptive technologies may change the way products are manufactured and business is done and this will lead to a discontinuity in technology. The disruptive technology will have far reaching influence and will breakaway from the existing technology.
- Research findings that point towards harmful effects of some technology may force the Government to impose a ban on such technologies and direct manufacturing firms to switch over to an acceptable technology.
- Government/statutory authorities/regulatory bodies/Courts may direct manufacturing firms to abandon an existing technology and switch over to a new technology. The direction of the Government and other agencies towards this effect may be due to social/environmental considerations, in the overall benefit of the society/country. Under such circumstances, there will be sudden discontinuity in the technology status.

A company has to identify potential discontinuities, assess the discontinuities, analyze the impact of discontinuities, take strategic decisions and implement the strategic decisions.

Technology discontinuity often becomes unpredictable due to the faster phase of technological developments taking place, which brings up a new technology all of a sudden. Scenario development and market pressure forecasting are the two techniques that can be used to foresee technical discontinuity (Refer Fig. 3.3). These techniques involve talking to customers, listening to their needs and requirements and arriving at a scenario that will depict the market requirement in the near and distant future.

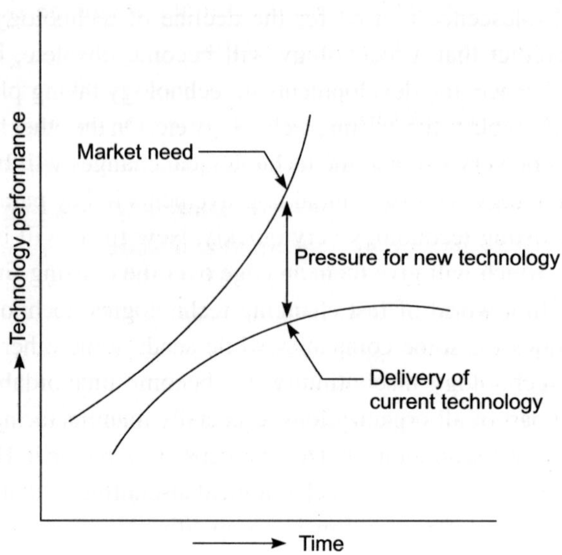

Fig. 3.3 Pressure for new technology

If the existing technology promises scope only for incremental improvements, leaving much to be desired when compared to the market pressure, it indicates that there is a greater threat in the form of technology discontinuity. To predict the likely onset of technology discontinuity in the near future, a firm has to seek answers to the following questions:

1. What is the expectation of the market in the long-run?
2. Are the technologies presently used/owned by the firm promise greater scope for improved performance or is there scope only for incremental improvement?

When answers to these questions are obtained and studied, it will expose the vulnerability of the firm for technology discontinuity.

3.4.1. Handling Technology Discontinuity

Technology discontinuity can not be predicted with accuracy. Hence, most organizations may face a situation of technology discontinuity one time or the other. When a new technology emerges all of a sudden, threatening the continuance of an existing technology, a technology discontinuity is imminent and a firm faced with such a situation can react in any one of the following ways:

(*a*) Defending the new technology

(*b*) Building the new technology

(*c*) Buying the new technology

(*d*) Exiting.

Since technology discontinuity can threaten any sector, an organization has to find the best possible way to handle the situation.

Defending the New Technology

The substitute technology (i.e. the new technology that threatens to substitute an existing technology) is often found to be more expensive. Further, the new technology is and remains poorly understood for some period of time. These are the two factors that will come to the rescue of a firm facing the threat of technology discontinuity. For example, the circular knitting machinery sector in India faced such a situation during the early 1990s. Earlier to that, the market was dominated by indigenous circular knitting machine manufacturers, most of them located in Ludhiana. When computerized, high-speed, high-precision circular knitting machines from Japan and European countries started flooding the Indian market, the indigenous machines faced a technology discontinuity. The indigenous machines can not compete with the imported machines on the quality front. The imported, high-tech machines also came with a high production rate, almost in the order of about 10 times the production rate of indigenous machine. But, the high-tech machines were also priced more than 10 times the price of indigenous machines. Taking advantage of the price difference the Indian circular knitting machine manufacturers defended the substitute technology. Since knitted fabric finds its use in the production of garments meant both for indigenous use and for exports, the indigenous manufacturers of knitting machines concentrated more on manufacturers of cloth meant for indigenous use, since the quality of fabric produced from indigenous machines was considered enough for local consumption. Thus, the indigenous machinery manufacturers defended the substitute technology for some time. But, it should be noted that a defensive strategy can not succeed in the long run. It can only be a short term strategy. In the long run, the price of the high-tech knitting machines also came down substantially and by this time, the indigenous manufacturers of conventional knitting machines had to withdraw from the scene.

Building the New Technology

A firm facing the threat of technology discontinuity can build the technology on its own provided the technical entry barriers are not high and there are no IPR restrictions. The advantage of a firm in building the new technology is that, the firm already knows the customers well and hence design the product keeping the customer requirements in mind. A new player who comes to the market afresh may not have this advantage. Hence, if otherwise possible, a firm can capitalize on its customer contacts by building the new technology on its own.

Buying the New Technology

If the substitute technology relates to a product/component that is strategically important and if building the new technology on its own will be faced with problems, a firm can plan to buy the technology. This is a strategic decision and should be taken after due analysis. If the firm is hopeful of building the technology on its own in the course of time, as a short-term strategy, the firm can buy the new technology through a licensing agreement.

Exiting

If the new technology satisfies the customer need much better than the existing technology of a firm and if the firm is not well placed to switch over to the new technology, the firm can opt to withdraw from the field and allow the new comer to take up the market. Though this option might appear to be a meek one, it can turn out to be the only possible and only judicious option when a firm is not having the expertise and financial strength to opt for the new technology. There is no point in defending, building or buying the new technology, if a firm is not comfortably placed to do so. Quitting can as well be a strategic decision, when other options do not offer promising solutions.

3.5. TECHNOLOGY AUDIT

Technology audit is an analysis carried out to assess the technology status of an organization. It will attempt to identify the strengths and weaknesses of the organization with regard to technology.

3.5.1. Objectives of Technology Audit

Technology Audit is carried out with the following objectives:

(*i*) To assess the technology status of a firm in relation to its competitors.

(*ii*) To compare the technology status of the firm with the State of the Art Technology.

(*iii*) To know where the technology of the firm is located in the technology life cycle.

(*iv*) To identify the 'Technology Gaps'. (Technology gap will show the latest technologies that the company must acquire in order to remain technologically competitive).

(*v*) To identify the strengths and weaknesses of the firm in terms of technology.

(*vi*) To identify the core technical competencies of the firm.

(*vii*) To develop a framework for the formulation of Technology strategy of the firm.

Since developments in technology take place continuously, Technology Audit will be a continuous process. It will be conducted at frequent intervals, say, at a frequency of once in a year. It is a self-examination process to understand the efficiency and effectiveness of technology utilization by the company. It helps a company to identify its technological strengths and weaknesses and to plan accordingly so that the company won't lag behind in terms of technology. It is a tool for continuous technology improvement.

3.5.2. Phases of Technology Audit

In order to comply with the objectives, Technology Audit for a company is conducted in three phases. They are:

- Technology Audit of the company concerned
- Technology Audit of the competitors of the company
- Audit of the State-of-the-Art Technology

(i) Technology Audit of the company concerned

This audit covers the following aspects:

1. The products and services offered by the company, the production processes used by the company and the technology used by the company for its production/service.
2. The R&D projects being undertaken by the company.
3. Technology strategy followed by the company and the shifts in technology strategy needed, if any.
4. Incremental product/process/service improvements being done/aimed at by the company.
5. Analysis of technical partnerships/joint ventures to ascertain whether they are in line with the overall strategy of the company.
6. Study of the Technology Transfer processes being followed by the company with regard to their effectiveness.
7. Study of the organizational structure of the company from the view point of its conduciveness for technological development.

(ii) Technology Audit of the competitors of the company

This audit covers the following aspects:

1. The products and services offered by the competitors, the production processes

used by them and the technology used by them for their production/service activities.

2. The R&D projects being undertaken by the competitors.
3. Technology strategy that is being followed by the competitors.
4. Incremental product/process/service improvements that are being done/aimed at by the competitors.
5. Study of the Technology Transfer processes being followed by the competitors.
6. Overall strengths and weaknesses of the competitors in the domain of technology.

(iii) Audit of the state-of-the-art technology

'State-of-the-art Technology' refers to the highest level of development in a particular domain at a particular time.

This audit covers the following aspects:

1. Understanding the latest technological developments that have taken place in various fields, through studies, market analysis reports, magazines, product launches, Government policies/reports, published patent specifications, industry research reports, technical papers/seminars/workshops etc.
2. Carrying out forecast of various technologies, assessing the technological breakthroughs that are likely to occur and identifying the emerging technologies in the domain in which the company is operating.
3. Reviewing the technologies that are currently being used by the company, the technologies that the company is interested to acquire, comparing these with the State-of-the-art Technology and identifying the company's position vis-à-vis the State-of-the-art Technology.

3.5.3. Technology Audit Process

Though the objectives of Technology Audit are known and evident, it is an intricate process and the methodology should be carefully designed so that the audit will bring out the facts genuinely. The technology audit team is formed by including technical experts, both from within the company and from outside. The team should be provided with the technology policy of the company, the technology goals being pursued by the company, the technology portfolio of the company, the R&D activities of the company, the technology strategy followed by the company, the technology that the company aspires to acquire in future etc. The audit team will review the technology status of the company on the basis of the information provided. The team will also interview key technical personnel in the company, apart from visiting the R&D labs and understanding the R&D activities. The technology audit report will throw light on the present technology status of the company, the company's technology position vis-à-vis its competitors, comparison of the company's technology with the State-of-the-art Technology. The report will help the company to know where it stands in terms of technology, the improvements in technology required, the technology strategies to be followed by the company etc.

The technology audit report will contain both qualitative assessments and quantitative evaluations. Both are complementary to each other. Out of these two, quantitative evaluation is more demanding and requires to be done carefully, covering all aspects of technology. Every aspect of technology is assessed on a five-point scale (with rating '1' indicating 'poor', rating '2' indicating 'below average', rating '3' indicating 'average', rating '4' indicating 'good' and rating '5' indicating 'very good'). For example, if 'Technology Transfer' is one of the aspects of technology that is assessed under this head, the following can be some of the elements that are assessed on a five-point scale.

Technology aspect: Technology Transfer

Elements	Poor (1)	Below Average (2)	Average (3)	Good (4)	Very Good (5)
Transfer procedures					
Transfer teams					
Strategic alliances					
Handling of barriers for transfer					

The sum of the scores assigned to the individual elements gives the overall assessment. When the audit is carried out next time, the overall score indicates whether there is improvement in the technology strategy of the company or not. The audit report will have to spell out the ideal situation that should be reached so as to get a score of '5' for each technology element. This will offer a 'standard' towards which the company can progress in order to improve its technology status.

3.6. TECHNOLOGY SCOUTING

Technology Scouting is an organized approach followed by organizations, with the objective of identifying the needs, opportunities and gaps in technology and then finding solutions to the issues, preferably from outside the boundaries of the enterprise. Technology Scouting has the following three phases:

(*a*) Identification of the emerging technologies in the concerned product/process domain.

(*b*) Channelizing into the organization the technology related information gathered.

(*c*) Supporting the organization in technology acquisition process.

In a fast moving world, where knowledge and technology have got very widely distributed, companies are under compulsion to look beyond their internal R&D department for identifying sources of new technology and innovation. Looking beyond the boundaries of one's company for innovative ideas and practices is very much required to remain updated with regard to technology. Technology Intelligence has become an important field of study which aims at identifying opportunities and threats arising from advances in technology. In this respect, Technology Scouting is a process that can lower the time lag between the advances that have taken place in technology and their detection. In an environment of increasing technological complexity, faster phase of changes in technology and the globalization of R&D, the successful identification and usage of external sources of knowledge will give a company an edge over competitors on the technology front. In the sourcing of technology, the scouts can also play an important role in identifying valuable technology sources and in facilitating the sourcing of technology.

Looking for technology and product knowledge beyond the boundaries of one's company is also known as 'Open Innovation'. Technology scouting is an essential tool for any organization that strives for open innovation. Technology scouting helps to identify new and emerging technologies and the gap between such new/emerging technologies and the technology presently being practiced in the company. Technology scout, the person who is entrusted with the task of scouting for technology, can be an employee of the company or an external consultant. He must be a person with knowledge in science and technology. He must have the capacity to think laterally and should preferably have orientation towards cross-disciplines. Technology scouting helps to identify the different prevailing technologies and the technological trends. It will also help avoid technological shocks that a company might face. 'Search and see' is a form of scouting, wherein the scout (the person who undertakes scouting) goes for technology scouting without any specific direction and objectives. Though it may be tempting for anyone to prefer 'Search and see' approach to scouting, it is very unlikely to give the desired results. Hence, a systematic approach to Technology Scouting will be always beneficial. The technological findings of scouting are made use of in strategic innovation management. Technology Scouting will become a fruitless exercise if there is no clear strategic intention that is based on a compelling business requirement. Technology scouting can be either directed towards a specific technological area or it may be undirected. Technology scouting relies on formal and informal information sources, including the personal networks of the scouts.

Technology Scouting complements internal R&D efforts. Since it aims at arriving at a strong fit between need and idea, it can reduce the risk of launching products that don't have market. When a formal scouting process has the approval and support of the organizational members, it can help overcome internal resistance to externally-generated ideas.

The steps involved in Technology Scouting are as given below:

- Defining the technology search areas.
- Selection of information sources.
- Looking for opportunities in technology/technology-related areas.
- Evaluating and assessing opportunities and capabilities.
- Determining and negotiating win-win deals.
- Implementing the deal and monitoring its success.

Companies assign few of their employees with the required skills to act as technology scouts, or they employ external consultants for the purpose. The scouting of technology can be either directed towards a specified technological area that the company is in immediate need of or it can be undirected.

3.6.1. Qualities Expected of a Technology Scout

A technology scout is expected to have the following qualities/traits:

- Strong aptitude to learn a wide range of scientific disciplines and ability to arrive at technology options from the scientific knowledge gained.
- Up-to-date knowledge about the emerging technologies.
- In-depth knowledge of market trends.
- Ability to negotiate and arrange partnership agreements with a win-win status.
- Good communication skills, both oral and written.
- Capacity to handle multiple tasks at the same time.
- Effective project management skills.
- Extensive network of contacts.
- Competence to carry out technical due diligence study.
- Good knowledge of Intellectual property rights.
- Creative thinking ability.
- Readiness and willingness to work towards the strategic goals of the company.
- Entrepreneurial skill-sets.
- Risk taking ability.

- Good listening capacity.
- Ability to give proper direction to technology related projects.

Review Questions

1. Define the term 'Technology Forecast'. What are the advantages of forecasting technology?
2. Explain in detail the different methods of forecasting technology.
3. What do you understand by the term 'Technology Discontinuity'? What are the reasons for Technology Discontinuity to occur?
4. Explain how to handle Technology Disconitinuity?
5. What is meant by 'Technology Obsolescence'? Enumerate the reasons due to which a technology becomes obsolete.
6. Define 'Technology audit'. What are its objectives?
7. Explain the different phases and the process of conducting Technology Audit.
8. What is meant by 'Technology Scouting'? What are the qualities expected of a Technology Scout?

4 CHAPTER

Technology Generation and Innovation

4.1. ROLE OF R&D IN TECHNOLOGY GENERATION

Research and Development activities play a key role in technology generation in an organization. Research and development activities are oriented towards new as well as existing products and processes.

(*a*) Technical support to the production department

Though the R&D department is mainly concerned with research into new areas and development of the research findings by designing new products/formulating new processes, it has a great supportive role to play. It should act in close coordination with the manufacturing department and offer solutions to the day-to-day problems/ issues that crop up in the course of production. It can work on the ways of improving productivity, reduction in the consumption of power and fuel, improving the user-friendliness of the different operations involved in the production department etc.

(*b*) R&D for product improvement

R&D wing of an organization has a greater role to play for improving the product features of existing products or for expansion of an existing product line. The modalities of product improvement/expansion of product line are to be decided jointly by the R&D department and the manufacturing department. At times, interaction of manufacturing/sales department with the R&D department may also become necessary. The R&D department must receive inputs from the sales/marketing department and proceed with the research and development activities. Consultations with the manufacturing department will throw light on the scope for carrying out manufacture of products with additional /modified product features. In the absence of proper interaction between the R&D department and the manufacturing department, both the departments will stand to lose. The customer feedback on the requirements of product improvements is a vital input for the R&D department. Hence, the marketing and sales departments should also maintain cordial and continuous interaction and coordination with the R&D department.

(*c*) R&D and new product development

Research work for new product development is not the exclusive work of the R&D department alone. A new product can be successfully brought out by a company only with close coordination of all the functional departments. A new manufacturing process, a new product design, a new type of raw material etc., will call for substantial changes in the resource requirements of the manufacturing department. The manufacturing department should be ready to take up production once the new product developed by the R&D department is passed on to it by the R&D department. This level of preparedness will come only when there is close coordination between the R&D and manufacturing departments.

(*d*) R&D for process improvement/new process development

The same product, when manufactured by a different process or improvements/ modifications in the existing process will require consequent changes in the resource requirements of the manufacturing department. Moreover, the personnel of the production department need to be trained on the new processes. Thus, R&D and manufacturing interface is vital for the success of process improvements, process modifications and new process developments.

4.2. CREATIVITY

Creativity is the ability to produce some novel, unique and useful work, using one's own thought or imagination. Creativity is the mental characteristic that allows a person to think out-of-the box which results in innovative approaches to a particular task.

According to Webster's dictionary,'Creativity is artistic or intellectual inventiveness'. Some of the well-known definitions given by experts in the field are as under:

Creativity is any act, idea or product that changes an existing domain or that transforms an existing domain into a new one.

– Mihaly Csikszentmihalyl

Creativity is generating new ideas and concepts or making connections between ideas, where none previously existed.

– Michell Rigic and Keith Harmeyer

I define creativity as the act of turning new and imaginative ideas into reality. Creativity involves two processes: Thinking and Producing. Innovation is the production or implementation of an idea. If you have ideas, but don't act on them, you are imaginative but not creative.

– ***Linda Naiman***

Creativity is seeing what everyone else has seen and thinking what no one else has thought.

– ***Albert Einstein***

Creativity is the process of having original ideas that have value.

– ***Prof. Sir Kenneth Robinson***

Creativity is seeing something that does not exist already.....you need to find out how you can bring it into being.

– ***Michele Shea***

4.2.1. Characteristics of Creativity

- Creativity is a process and not a product. Creative ideas originate in the minds of individuals. When given shape, these can be transformed into innovative products.
- Creativity involves both conscious and subconscious mind. Conscious mind is that part of one's mind that deals with reason and logic. The subconscious mind does not need to reason to make things happen. When an impression is made on the subconscious mind (by the conscious mind), the subconscious mind will proceed to work on it automatically. If the conscious mind that functions on the basis of reason and logic finds the behavior of the subconscious mind unacceptable, the conscious mind interferes and makes a conflicting impression on the subconscious mind which will undo the impression made earlier. Thus, for creativity to happen, both conscious and sub-conscious minds should work together.
- Creativity is a pattern-breaking process. It involves breaking out of established patterns in order to look at things in a different way.
- Creativity will flourish with a higher degree of awareness of the happenings around. Hence, in an organization, there is a need to develop cross-functional expertise among the employees. When employees are not exposed to all functional domains, their mind can accept and react only to those ideas that

pertain to their area of specialization and they may miss good creative ideas pertaining to other functional domains.

- Creativity being a mental process involving the generation of new ideas/ concepts and/or new associations between existing ideas/concepts, it can be stimulated at the individual level as well as at group level. The advantage of group-thinking is sharing of cross-functional knowledge.
- Creative thinking can be both systematic and unsystematic. Even if it is taken for granted that new ideas strike to the mind only by chance, only a mind that has strived systematically for catching up with new ideas has a greater chance to succeed in coming out with creative ideas. (*Chance only favours the prepared mind* – Louis Pasteur.)
- Creativity is not a one-time activity. It is an on-going process.
- Creative thinking is made possible by posing open-ended questions and allowing the mind to look for all possible answers. Open-ended questions open up curiosity and a curious mind has a greater probability of striking at creative ideas.

4.2.2. Creativity Gap

People are not living up to their creative potential. Hence, there always exists a creativity gap. It is the difference between what an individual can contribute in terms of creativity and what he/she actually contributes. A 2012 Adobe study on creativity shows that eight out of ten people feel that unlocking creativity is critical to economic growth and nearly two-thirds of the respondents feel that creativity is valuable to society, yet only one in four people believe that they are living up to their own creative potential.

If an individual employee in an organization perceives that the work environment in his organization imposes restrictions or does not encourage creative ideas, a gap develops between the individual's creative potential and his delivery. This gap indicates an important untapped potential which the organization had failed to capitalize on. This untapped potential is very vital in a competitive business environment. To capitalize on this potential, the organization should provide a climate conducive for creativity.

Employees need support for their creative talents from three levels, viz.,

(*a*) At the supervisor level

(*b*) At the work-group level and

(*c*) At the organizational level.

Supervisors must be supportive of creativity. They should value employee contributions, stand as role models, encourage and motivate their subordinates in bringing out new ideas and guide them by giving clear directions instead of simply controlling them. When we say support from the supervisor, it is applicable at different levels in the organizational hierarchy since in an organizational structure there are many levels wherein an employee may supervise the work some of his subordinates, while he himself may be under the supervision of his immediate boss in the hierarchy. Thus, the employee-immediate boss relationship should be supportive for bringing out the creative talents at all levels.

In an organization wherever group activities are planned/involved, the group should be so formed that the group members have diverse backgrounds. The group should be encouraged to be open to new ideas. The group leader should be an effective communicator and should allow/arrange for meaningful interactions/discussions, constructive criticisms and effective feedbacks between the group members so that the group can come out with some tangible outcomes.

The organizational support for creativity may take the form of providing autonomy, making adequate resources available, encouragement for contributors, readiness to accept failures that occur despite genuine efforts put forth by the members etc.

4.2.3. Role of Creativity in Organizational Growth

Creativity has very many roles to play in the overall growth of an organization, some of which are discussed below:

(a) Generation of new ideas for product development/improvement

Creativity will bring forth new ideas that can be made use of in creating new products, new manufacturing processes, new types of services etc.(Motorized tooth brush meant for children is an example of a new product developed from creative thinking. Children are playful, but they do not like to be directed. Hence, asking them to brush their teeth everyday is a hectic task. One way to accomplish this is by producing tooth pastes that taste good, smell good and appear attractive to children. The other way is to make the process of brushing playful and attractive. A creative idea to mechanize the movement of bristles of tooth brushes gave rise to a new product). Creative ideas can also help in bringing about improvements in existing products. The improvements may be in the form of value additions through including additional functional features, improving product reliability, simplifying the mode of operation etc. Creativity leaves ample scope in all these areas for product improvement.

(b) Generation of new ideas for process modification/improvements

Creative ideas can help in designing efficient manufacturing processes. Assembly line manufacturing which helps mass production was a new process modification introduced by Ford Motors, which revolutionized the manufacturing process of automobiles. Creativity can also be directed towards designing ways for the smooth flow of materials across the shop floor, for the reduction of wastages, for minimizing the inventory level etc. Creative ideas can also develop safer methods of production, reduced discharge of effluents, better utilization of by-products etc.(Coconut coir pith which is a by-product developed in the process of manufacturing coconut fibre was once considered a waste without any value. The moisture retention capacity of the coir pith was made use of to convert the coconut coir pith into an useful product, viz., compressed coir pith blocks, to be used in agricultural farms and in plant nurseries for retaining moisture and supporting the growth of plants/vegetations.)

(c) Generating ideas for business process improvement:

There is no dearth of scope for creativity in business process applications. New methods of marketing, identifying new uses for existing products, identifying methods for improving machinery efficiency, designing simple machines to handle specific processes etc., are some of the areas where creativity has a greater role to play.

All the above effects of creative thinking will help an organization in a big way.

4.2.4. Fostering Creativity in Organisations

Creativity is an asset for an organization. It is an intangible asset. It has a very great potential to transform an organization. Environmental factors like freedom to think / express, readiness and willingness to break away from established customs/patterns, playful attitude towards work attached with dedication and involvement etc., are some of the favourable conditions that stimulate creativity. Though mental disposition of individuals have a greater role to play in creativity, a supportive environment is very much required to bring out the hidden creative talents and to stimulate the employees to think creatively. Keeping these aspects in mind, the top management should see to it that a conducive and supportive environment is provided to the employees.

Some of the areas to be given thrust are discussed below:

- Avenues must be created to stimulate individual and group creativity.
- The employees should be encouraged to think differently and every idea should be received with due regard and recognition. No idea should be rejected to start with. Prima facie, some ideas might look too primitive or not possible of being implemented. But, if ideas expressed by employees are ignored it will spoil creativity. Every idea should be given due consideration and fair trial before deciding upon its acceptance/rejection.

- A reward system can be introduced for rewarding innovative and valuable ideas.
- The top management shall not be averse to meeting with failures in implementing new ideas. Failures are always learning experiences. The belief that the top management will not look down upon employees for failure of their ideas will create confidence in the minds of the employees and they will become free to think. Such free-thinking minds will be the breeding place for creative ideas.
- Lateral thinking shall be encouraged and the employees shall be trained in lateral thinking.

4.2.5. Group Creativity

Creative ideas can always be easily generated from a group. Group creativity includes those methods/techniques that can be used to stimulate interest among group members and make them think of new ideas. Brainstorming is the most commonly used technique for bringing about creativity in a group of people. There are two fundamental principles of brainstorming which are to be strictly adhered to if we want to make brainstorming an effective technique. The first principle is '*defer judgement*' and the second principle is '*quantity breeds quality*'. In a brainstorming session all ideas, however simple, trivial, irrelevant or unconnected they may appear to be shall be accepted. There shall be no screening of ideas. Initial criticism of original ideas should be avoided at any cost as this will kill the flow of ideas from the group. The second principle is a corollary of the first principle. When all ideas are accepted, the number of ideas increases and the number of potential ideas is a certain proportion of the total number of ideas. Further, increase in the number of ideas acts as a stimulus to improve upon the ideas already given, thereby increasing the worth of the ideas.

4.3. LINEAR THINKING VERSUS LATERAL THINKING

The term 'Lateral Thinking' was coined by Edward de Bono. Lateral thinking is a method of searching for solutions to problems/situations following unorthodox methods, by looking at things in a novel way. Lateral thinking looks at problem from an unexpected point of view. Normally, the human mind thinks in patterns. It tries to be logical in arriving at solutions to problems. Hence, in conventional thinking (i.e., Linear thinking), the thought process goes from one step to another till it arrives at the solution. At every step, the problem is analyzed and the relevant/right course of action is selected and others are ignored. Thus, the solution to a problem progresses sequentially from one step to another in a linear fashion. The human mind is so conditioned that it always looks forward unidirectional and does not look sideways to re-examine a problem/solution from an entirely different angle. While linear thinking attempts to solve problems by meeting them head-on, lateral thinking attempts to bypass the hurdles faced in the way, following a radically different approach.

Linear thinking	Lateral thinking
Linear thinking follows logical steps. What is considered as illogical is ignored.	Lateral thinking can be illogical or sometime intuitive.
Linear thinking arrives at solutions to issues in a sequence, following one logical step after the other.	Lateral thinking seeks solutions by thinking sideways and by jumping into new paths.
Since Linear thinking is uni-directional in its approach, it can be useful for bringing about improvements in existing products.	Since Lateral thinking is unconventional and non-orthodox in its approach, it leads to radical, different ideas which are useful for the creation of new products/ processes/services.
Linear thinking blocks creativity.	Lateral thinking supports creativity.

4.3.1. Certain Examples of Lateral Thinking

The following popular examples will make it clear the way human brain functions during lateral thinking.

(*a*) A black man, dressed fully in black is standing at a cross roads on a no-moon day, when the street lights are off. A black car without headlights moves towards him, but turns in time and moves past the man without hitting him. How did the driver manage to do so?

(Lateral thinking: It was the day time)

(*b*) If a plane crashes on the India-Pakistan border, where do they bury the survivors?

(Lateral thinking: Survivors are not buried, only the dead are buried)

(*c*) What can you hold in your right hand, but can't hold in your left hand?

(Lateral thinking: Your left hand)

(*d*) Ram's mother had three children. One is named April, another is named May. What is the third one named?

(Lateral thinking: Ram)

The above examples show the benefits of unconventional, illogical thinking in arriving at solutions to the given problems. Linear thinking will fail in such instances.

4.3.2. Techniques for Stimulating Lateral Thinking

There are many techniques designed to stimulate lateral thinking. All the techniques have the common premise of breaking the logical, conventional, systematic thought process and encouraging unconventional, random, illogical thought process so that mind can strike upon radically new ideas. Some of the techniques are discussed below:

(a) Random entry

This technique provides the participants with unconnected, irrelevant inputs with the objective of opening up new lines of thinking. This technique relies on the power of the human mind (as a self organizing system) to start thinking on new lines (new ideas) from seemingly random inputs. The random inputs given to the team can be words, pictures or even sounds chosen at random. The random inputs will not directly help in solving the problem at hand. It will help the mind think in new directions. The members should be asked to resist the temptation to think that the random word/ picture or any other random input has nothing to do with the problem at hand. The whole idea is that random associations will take people to unimagined domains and this will lead to path-breaking solutions.

There are many ways by which random inputs can be given. They are:

1. Selecting a word at random from a dictionary.
2. Selecting objects lying nearby at random.
3. Using a random list card and choosing an item from the card at random.

(b) Provocation and Movement

This technique (as other techniques also do) works by moving the thoughts out of the established patterns for solving problems. Provocations are unusual, stupid statements that state that something we have taken for granted about the problem at hand is not true. The statements are to be very stupid that they give a shock to the people and make their minds think beyond the routine way of thinking. Once a provocative statement is thrown open, it will generate ideas with the participants. All generated ideas are accepted without any judgment. The generation of ideas is known as the 'movement' phase since ideas start moving from the conventional pattern. Provocation gives the starting point for lateral thinking. The ideas generated during the provocation and movement process are likely to be fresh and original.

(c) Challenging ideas

This refers to asking why something is done the way it is currently being done. Problems, solutions and anything that lies in between can be challenged. Once a person challenges something, he starts thinking of alternatives.

(d) Disproving

This is similar to Provocation, but here any idea that is acceptable to all is challenged instead of restricting the scope to the problem at hand. Henrik Ibsen and John Kenneth Galbraith suggested that majority is always wrong. Irrespective of whether it is right or wrong their suggestion can make one think laterally. Any idea/concept that is acceptable to all (a 'goes-without-saying' concept) is chosen and it is opposed and questioned and an attempt is made to disprove it. In the process of attempting to disprove a generally accepted idea, new ideas open up and lateral thinking becomes possible.

(e) Metaphors and analogies

Metaphor is a figure of speech in which an impaired comparison is made between two unlike things that have something important in common.

Examples:

1. The school was a prison for him.
2. Let us be grateful to people who make us happy; they are the charming gardeners who make our souls blossom.

Analogy is a logical statement, demonstrating that if two things are alike in some ways, they will be similar in other ways also. Analogy is a tool for enhancing creativity.

Examples:

1. He is like a rock, (=He is strong and steadfast)
2. A gang of boys is like a gang of wolves.
3. Just as the earth revolves around the Sun, an electron revolves around the nucleus of an atom.

In using both metaphors and analogies, solution to the original problem is not directly attempted. Instead, it is arrived at by studying the metaphor/analogy.

The steps involved in the process are as below:

1. Remodel the problem.

   (the original problem is redefined into a similar but unrelated problem using the Metaphor)
2. Ignore the original problem and brainstorm to solve the metaphor/analogy.

3. Back-mapping the solution.

   (every idea generated to solve the metaphor/analogy is back-mapped and adapted as necessary for the original problem)

(f) Unconscious problem solving

The team members are made to dwell at length over the problem and then they are allowed to take a break. This method uses the sub-conscious mind to solve the problem. But the person must be ready to listen to his conscious mind and record the ideas as the ideas percolate into the conscious mind. Great thinkers are great relaxers. Einstein was a day-dreamer and he used to spend much of his time relaxing, by sailing on a lake. Emerson, another great thinker spent most his time fishing. Thus, good relaxation, followed by intensive thinking can open up the mysteries of the world.

(g) Problem reversal

According to Edward de Bono, the creative thinking expert, if we want to know what could be improved, we have to first make a detailed list of all the features that could possibly go wrong and from this list choose those ideas that are useful. This approach helps in coming up with ideas from a different perspective. Hence, the ideas developed will be creative and totally new. Suppose we want to improve the life of a dry cell battery. The original question to be answered is,'How to improve the life of a dry cell battery?' The original question is reversed and the reversed question may look like, 'How to reduce the life of dry cell battery?' For the reversed question, start developing ideas. After exhausting the ideas, reverse each of the ideas so that the reversed ideas will give answers to the original problem. From these reversed ideas, identify those ideas that are innovative, out-of-the box and useful.

4.4. DISCOVERY VERSUS INVENTION

Discovery is uncovering an existing truth. In discovery, something is revealed by an analysis of the observed world. Let something exists due to workings of nature, but is hidden; when the hidden thing is made known, a discovery happens. The word 'discover' reveals that the thing already exists, but under a cover, unknown to us. Once the cover is removed, we say that we have discovered.

Invention is not uncovering. It is a process of synthesis. Invention refers to the process of combining known rules, techniques, technologies etc., to produce something that has a greater value than the value of the sum of the parts that it is made of.

Scientists discover while engineers invent. Discovery can sometimes happen accidently. This is because, it already exists. The only thing is that it is not noticed. Accidental discovery is known by the term *serendipity*. But, for invention, one has to strive for. There can be no accidental inventions. Maybe, one may strive to achieve something and end up with achieving something else. But, without putting forth efforts, inventions are not possible.

Discovery pertains to natural occurrences while inventions pertain to man-made artifacts*, tools, processes etc. (*an artifact is an object intentionally produced by man for a certain purpose/use.)

Isaac Newton discovered the force of gravity. The force of gravity existed even before Newton noticed it. He only uncovered the natural law. Scissors, automobile, steam engine, electric bulb, radio, television etc., are inventions.

Note: The difference between invention and discovery is that you invent something that did not previously exist while you discover a real thing that is already existent.

4.5. INVENTION VERSUS INNOVATION

Innovation is the creation of a product or introduction of a process for the first time from out of an invention.

National Knowledge Commission, Govt. of India defines Innovation as under:

'Innovation' is defined as a process by which varying degrees of measurable value enhancement is planned and achieved, in any commercial activity. This process may be breakthrough or incremental, and it may occur systematically in a company or sporadically; it may be achieved by:

- introducing *new or improved goods or services* and/or
- implementing *new or improved operational processes* and/or
- implementing *new or improved organizational/ managerial processes*

in order to improve market share, competitiveness and quality, while reducing costs.

Invention forms the first stage of development of a new product or process based on scientific concepts/technological ideas. Most inventions remain as inventions and only a few of the inventions develop into innovations. An innovation is said to have taken place only when a new product or process that is invented is further refined in such a way that it is commercialized and is put into the market place for customers to choose and buy. (For example Michael Faraday invented Electro Magnetic Induction. Following the invention of the scientific principle of Electromagnetic Induction, many electrical gadgets were innovated.)

Technological innovation has become one of the most important drivers of success in a competitive business environment.

The differences between invention and innovation can be summarized as under:

	Invention	Innovation
1.	It is the creation of a new technology. The new technology may relate to either a product or a process or a service. (eg. Transistor is a product invented.)	It is the creation of a new product, process or service by making use of the invention.
2.	For a creation to be called as 'invention', the technology created should be a novel one.	Innovations need not be always based on novel ideas. Innovations can be on the basis of an invention that is totally new or an invention that is already known. Those innovations that make use of an existing technology and add new features continually fall under the category of 'Incremental Innovations.'
3.	All inventions may not be commercialized. Putting an invention into commercial application depends on the expected demand for the innovative product/process/service.	Innovations result into commercialization. This is because, the process of innovation is normally begun only after studying the commercial viability of the proposal and after getting convinced that the innovation will have market acceptance.
4.	Inventions occur as a result of human ingenuity and creative thinking. Hence, they can occur accidently. Inventions can also occur through trail and error process. It may also so happen that some inventions will occur in an unaccepted/unanticipated domain, while working in some other domain.	Innovations are always induced since innovations have a profit motive. The firms engaged in innovation make use of some inventions and strive to find out applications of the ideas for commercial exploitation.
5.	Inventions are autonomous in nature, i.e., they do not happen due to environmental impulse. Hence, there is no attribute of success/failure attached to inventions. Any invention that has something new in it is considered successful.	Innovations can be either successful or unsuccessful. Its success or failure depends on the level of market acceptance of the innovative product or process and the business prospects of the firm that introduces such products/processes.
6.	The scope of invention is limited to finding something new, something that did not exist earlier. Hence, inventions are mostly restricted to R&D Centers and are related to products and processes.	Innovation can be possible throughout an organization in all spheres of activities. Innovations are possible in marketing techniques, sales promotion, recruitment techniques, training of personnel etc., apart from innovations in products and processes.

4.6. TYPES OF INVENTIONS

Inventions can be broadly classified into the following two types:

(a) Autonomous Invention (or Spontaneous Invention)

(b) Induced Invention

Autonomous Invention

These inventions occur spontaneously, without response to any external/environmental impulse. They occur due to curiosity to excel in a field. The curiosity will come out in the form of inventions that are spontaneous. At times, inventions may also occur accidently, even without any curiosity to excel. Autonomous inventions may or may not immediately lead to production of innovative products. Carrying out innovations based on inventions that are autonomous depends on the likely commercial successfulness of the inventions. Hence, those autonomous inventions that are not carried forward for innovations will remain mostly unpatented.

Induced Invention

Induced inventions have a motive behind them. The motive may be economic gain or some other circumstances that exert a necessity to invent. For example, a firm may direct its efforts and resources towards inventions in order to invent new technologies so as to overcome the competition from other players in the field. A company that directs its efforts for finding the process of manufacturing a fuel that can become a substitute to fossil fuel is engaged in the process of invention. Another situation leading to induced inventions is the change in the customer tastes and preferences, change in market conditions etc. Also, when companies forecast a greater phase of technological growth or when they forecast the emergence of a new technology that would replace the existing technology, inventions may be induced to handle the situations that would arise in the future. When a technology that is currently in use is already at the fag-end of its life cycle and is expected to become obsolete in the short run, companies will be forced to invent. When companies want to capture new markets with new products or when they want to achieve technological supremacy in their field as a part of their technology strategy, the companies, under bare necessity, will encourage induced inventions in their product/process domains.

4.7. CHARACTERISTICS OF INNOVATIONS

Innovation is the successful implementation of new/creative ideas, resulting in the creation of a new product/service and/or carrying out improvements in existing products/service.

Characteristics of innovations are as under:

(*a*) Innovation is broader in scope than Research and Development. Research and

Development is an activity that will be funded by the organization. The objective of the R&D department is to make use of the funds and develop inventions. Innovation refers to converting inventions into innovative products/processes. Mere invention of scientific principles will not provide a firm with monetary benefits. Only when the invention is converted into an innovative product/process/service, the firm will stand benefited monetarily.

(*b*) Innovation occurs with the generation of new ideas

(*c*) Innovation is not just the generation of new/creative ideas. It is giving shape to the creative ideas and converting the ideas into tangible products/services.

(*d*) While the generation of creative ideas does not require any resources, innovation needs some resources to implement the creative ideas.

(*e*) Innovative ideas can emerge from many sources.

(*f*) For innovations to occur there must be proper linkages between the different sources. Individuals with creative ideas (who can be customers or others), firms, academic institutions, private research laboratories, Government funded research organizations are some of the sources that bring out innovations. These components need to interact with one another and a healthy and constructive interaction will lead to the creation of innovative products/services. (Refer Fig. 4.1)

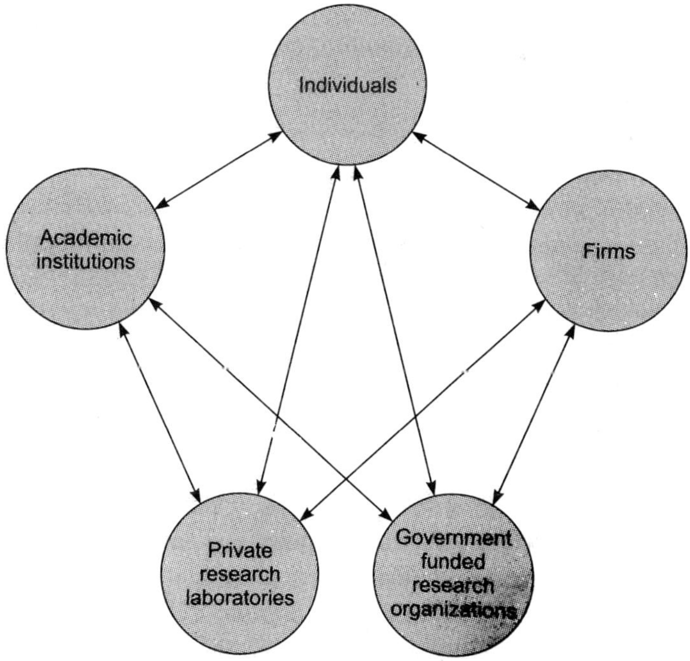

Fig. 4.1 Linkages between sources

(*g*) Innovation carries along with it a lot of risk and uncertainty. This is because, any innovation will be considered successful only if it is commercially successful and brings profit to the business enterprise. There is always a risk of innovative products/services being rejected by the market, leading to heavy losses for the business enterprise that has ventured upon such innovative products/services.

(*h*) Innovation has a profit motive. Innovation for the sake of innovation is meaningless. It is not like a scientific discovery that is done for the sake of understanding some of the laws of nature, without any profit motive.

(*i*) Innovation should offer some additional convenience to the people by way of a new/improved product or service and thereby offer additional earnings to the business enterprise as well.

(*j*) Since innovation will bring a new set of processes, new techniques/methods of production, it will induce organizational change. The organizational structure and culture will undergo a change that is necessary for implementing innovation. Such organizational changes may be resisted by the employees, who may want the *status-quo* to continue. Resistance to any change is inherent in every organization. Hence, the top management should devise ways and means for achieving the required organizational changes.

4.8. CHARACTERISTICS OF INNOVATIVE ORGANIZATIONS

Organizational structure should be conducive for innovation. It should be free from rigid hierarchy which will breed inefficiency. The organizational structure should be such that it coordinates all the organizational members into one team and motivates them towards achieving excellence. No doubt, it is the people who give strength to any organization. But, they will add strength to the organization only if they are kept motivated and kept in high morale and if their talents are correctly channelized. The characteristics required of innovative organizations are summarized below:

(*a*) Innovation is an activity that deserves top priority for a production oriented organization. Hence, the top management should be committed to innovation and should extend all possible support to the people involved in the process.

(*b*) Regular production activities can be planned ahead. Innovation cannot happen like regular production. Hence, strict/rigid planning will not be any use. The planning and control systems should be designed with a lot of flexibility.

(*c*) Innovation requires inputs from all functional domains. It is not the exclusive role of R&D department alone. For innovation to be successful, people from across all the departments should contribute. Hence, multifunctional teams should be formed wherever possible and wherever required.

(*d*) There should not be any interdepartmental or intradepartmental barriers for innovation. Such barriers normally creep in, in the absence of proper communication within the organization. An organization that wants to succeed in bringing out innovative ideas should ensure effective and smooth flow of communication throughout the organization. All the persons who occupy senior level positions should see to it that upward communication takes place in the organization without any hesitation and apprehension.

(*e*) A supportive organizational culture should prevail. The organization should have incentive/reward systems to encourage innovations, should recognize and respect the initiative of individuals, support employees in their career growth, accept genuine mistakes/errors, accept failures in the R&D efforts as part of the game.

(*f*) The organizational hierarchy should be very conducive, with lot of flexibility to accommodate the changing requirements.

(*g*) Innovative organizations are always futuristic and look for the future need of their customers. This will guide them in developing new products as well as in improving existing products in tune with customer expectations.

(*h*) They are always watchful of the competitors and keep track of the steps taken/strategies followed by the competitors and plan for suitable counter measures.

(*i*) Innovative organizations encourage all their employees to be part of the innovation process. Involving all the employees helps in two ways. The organization is likely to get very good ideas from unexpected quarters. Since all the employees are involved in innovative practices, implementing any plan of action will become easier due to the willing cooperation of all the employees.

(*j*) Innovative efforts will be suitably rewarded in the organization.

(*k*) They are ever ready to embrace new technology in order to improve their competitive advantage.

(*l*) Individual and team autonomy is an essential element that supports innovation. Innovative organizations will give individuals and teams clear goals and full autonomy to choose their own method of achieving the given goals. Such freedom creates a fertile breeding ground for innovation.

(*m*) Autonomy and freedom to innovate also will come up with mistakes. The individuals and teams may choose inefficient route to achieve the goals and may fail in the process. People learn from failures. An innovative organization will have a greater tolerance for failures and will have the firm conviction that failures are stepping stone for success and that organizations learns equally, if not more, from failures as they learn from successes.

4.9. TYPES OF INNOVATIONS

Innovations can be classified into different groups based on different criteria. They are discussed below:

4.9.1. Product Innovations *Versus* Process Innovations

Product innovations relate to what a firm produces. It is about a firm's tangible output. For example, CFL (Compact Fluorescent light) bulb is the innovation of a product. This technological innovation has offered energy efficient lighting bulbs to the consumers. Process innovations relate to how a firm produces its products. How a firm markets its products/services, will also fall under the category of process innovation. Thus, process innovation is about how a firm produces and delivers its products/services to its consumers. For example, the lithography method used to fabricate microchips was a process innovation. This process innovation is related to the process of manufacture and deals with a new way of producing a product. Assembly Line method of production introduced by Ford Motor Company between 1908 and 1913 is considered as a great process innovation that led to mass production. Apart from the manufacturing process, process innovations have their role to play in marketing, in logistics and all such areas where some process is involved. Delivery of custom-built computers to customers by Dell Corporation using efficient and transparent transport mechanism is a process innovation. In this system, the customers are able to track the parcels in real time as they are getting transported to their place.

Process innovations may require realigning of business especially for firms engaged in offering services. For example, a vehicle insurance company that makes its representatives visit its customers at their place and at their time of choice and offering on-the-spot assistance in processing premium amounts, in the assessment of damages, guiding the customers in lodging their claims, advising the customers on claim settlements etc., all fall under the category of process innovation. Since such process modifications will require a total change in the way an organization functions, it will lead to a lot of structural changes in the organization and business process may be required to be realigned.

4.9.2. Incremental Innovations *Versus* Radical Innovations

Incremental innovations refer to minor improvements made in products/services. It can be a small modification or addition to an existing product/process/service which enhances its value and thus helps the firm achieve competitive advantage. For example, a mobile phone with touch-screen in the place of push-button key-pad is a minor modification of the product which can be categorized as an incremental innovation. GPS system attached to a car is an addition to an existing product (car) that adds value to the product, which is an incremental innovation. Thus, incremental innovations bring about some improvement over something that already exists. For example, changing the design of the refrigerator by introducing two doors in the place of a single door, wherein a separate door is provided for the freezer-box portion apart from the main door is an incremental innovation. This arrangement improves efficiency. This is because of the reason that the freezer door is opened only very rarely while the main door is opened quite often. If there is a single door, whenever the door is opened, the entire inside of the refrigerator, including the freezer compartment that requires a greater degree of refrigeration is exposed to the atmosphere, which reduces the efficiency of refrigeration.

Radical innovations relate to technologies that are totally new and depart very much from the existing technologies.Radical innovations come with significant improvements in the product/operational features. They also come with a huge cost-reduction. However, they have a high degree of risk from the point of view of commercialization of the technology, since radical innovations embody new knowledge and customers may take time to recognize the utility of the new technology and build confidence and familiarity with the new products. Since risk and return go together, radical innovations, once accepted by the market will bring very attractive profits to the organization.

4.9.3. Breakthrough Innovations *Versus* Radical Innovations

Breakthrough innovations are innovations with new value propositions that expand the business into new markets and offer new advantages to the companies and to the customers. An innovation may be a radical one, but to be considered as a breakthrough innovation, the product/service should deliver a new value proposition, the product/service should outperform average products/services in their category in terms of sales velocity, should have sustained demand from the customers and should offer quantum benefits to the customers which the customers would not have otherwise got.

'Chik' shampoo of Cavinkare which was first offered to the consumers in sachet packs is an innovation which revolutionized the retail market. This is a breakthrough innovation that capitalized on the fortune at the bottom of the Pyramid, targeting the rural population of India. Though the innovation relates to the packaging and not to the product as such, the innovative idea of reaching out to the rural masses, offering them the convenience of usage and making use of their affordability when the product is sold in such small quantities, made the innovation really a breakthrough innovation.

Hewlett-Packard's inkjet printer which displaced the dot-matrix printing and expanded the scope for desk-top printing industry which gave the company the leadership position in the computer printer industry is an example of breakthrough innovation. Here, the innovation was in the form of product innovation.

Breakthrough innovations take the form of fulfilling an unsatisfied customer need. But, customers may not be at times, knowing whether they have an unsatisfied need' which a totally new product can satisfy. For example, when customers were using dot-matrix printers, they might not have been aware of any other technology that might offer them convenience and cost-effectiveness at the same time. But, by the time inkjet printers were introduced, they would have realized its advantages and the added value that the inkjet printers offered over dot-matrix printers. Thus, survey of consumer opinion may not always give pointers for breakthrough innovations. People will come to know about an improved product, only after using them. Apple's iPhone would not have been made possible relying only on customers feedback, because in the absence of such a product, the customers might not be in a position to visualize its importance and necessity for them. Research and Development activity has a greater role to play for bringing out such breakthrough products. Once the products are developed, they are pushed into the market and market will absorb the product instantaneously provided the product has the attributes of breakthrough innovation.

4.9.4. Radical Innovations *Versus* Disruptive Innovations

Radical innovation is an emerging technology that has substantial improvement over existing technologies and that offers scope for new applications. Radical innovations also have the potential to change the pattern of consumer behavior. Radical innovations have an order of magnitude improvement in performance over existing technologies. (Example: Credit Card, Container system of transport, Gamma Knife which is a radio surgical treatment for cancer that delivers a dose of Gamma radiation to the target area etc.)

Disruptive innovation changes the rules of business in such a way that the rules used for managing business till now are no more valid. Disruptive technology is a new technology that replaces established rules of business in a given domain. The difference between a new technology that is radical and a disruptive technology is that the disruptive technology will change the rules of business totally. Clayton Christensen introduced the term 'disruptive' in his book 'The Innovator's Dilemma'. Similar to radical innovations, disruptive innovations also change the way of doing things. But, disruptive innovations have the potential to disturb and alter the existing business model of the organization/industry. LCD TV, which replaced CRT-based TV, mobile phones which replaced land-line phones, transistor radios which replaced valve-based radios etc., are some of the examples of disruptive innovations.

Disruption is a business phenomenon and it need not be due to technology alone. A disruptive innovation may or may not represent a technical breakthrough. Major breakthrough innovations which are radical in nature may or may not be disruptive. On the other hand, even minor (or incremental) innovations can be disruptive.

The first characteristic of disruptive innovation is that in the initial stages, it provides comparatively lower performance as measured by the prevailing industry standards. It means that products that already exist in the market offer better performance than the disruptive products.

The second characteristic of disruptive innovation is that to start with it serves the market that is presently underserved by the existing products or not served at all.

The third characteristic of disruptive innovation is that it has a steeper growth trajectory than the growth trajectories of existing technologies, so that at a later stage, it can serve the higher end markets also.

Let us understand the operation of disruptive innovation with the help of a diagram. (Refer Fig. 4.2)

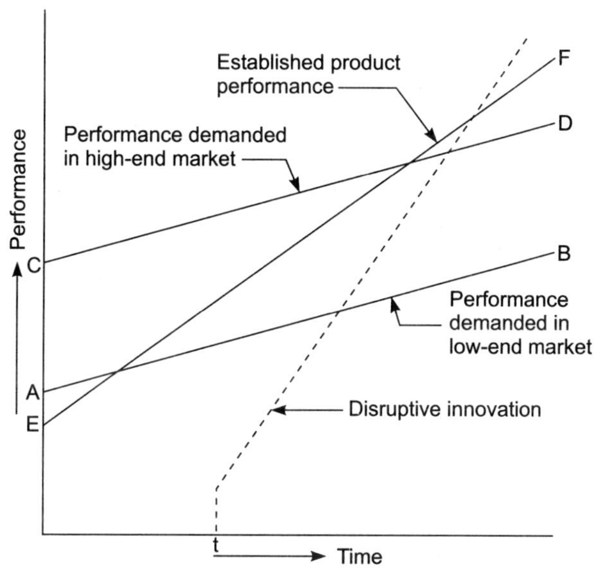

Fig. 4.2 Disruptive innovation

In every market there are low end and high end customers. When products are introduced in a market, the products can serve both the low end and high end markets. The expectations (or the performance demanded) by the customers of low end market are lower than the performance demanded by the customers in the high end market. In Fig. 4.2, the line – AB represents the performance demanded by the customers in the low-end market, while the line – CD represents the performance demanded by the customers in the high-end market. The line – EF represents the performance offered by the existing products. Comparing the lines – AB and EF, we understand that in the initial stages the performance offered by the existing products was below the expectation of even the low-end customers. Over a period of time, the performance has improved and the existing products started offering performance that is above the expectations of the low-end customers. By this time, the expectations of (or the performance demanded by) the high-end customers still remained above the level of performance offered by the existing products. After some time, the high-end customers are also satisfied since the product performance has reached up to their expectations and even surpassed their requirements. This is how the relationship between the performance offered by the products and the performance demanded by the market behaves in the normal run.

Consider the situation at the point of time 't'. By this time, the established products would have already started offering performance well above the expectations of the low-end customers. This means that the low-end customers would be paying substantially more for a product that has feature that they will never use. Here lies the gap. If a new product is introduced at this point of time, aimed at the low-end customers, that costs very much less (though the product will have features 'inferior' to the features available in the existing products), it will catch up with the low-end customers. Sometimes, such a product will also serve the requirements of those sectors of customers who were not able to afford to the existing products and wanted a much cheaper and simpler product. Innovating such a product is called disruptive innovation. Another important feature of disruptive innovation is that the phase of development will be too fast and its performance will outperform the existing products in a short span of time. A critical and distinguishing characteristic of disruptive innovation is that it will displace existing market leaders.

Thus, disruptive innovation produces a product/service that takes root initially in simple applications at the bottom of a market and then moves up in the market very fast, eventually displacing established players in the field.

(Example: Personal Computers — To start with the computing power and speed of PCs were very less as compared to the Mini and Mainframe computers. The Mini and Mainframe computers catered to the needs of home-users and small office users who could not afford to buy the existing versions in the market. In a short span of time, PCs which came as disruptive innovation improved their capacity and speed and captured a greater market share, substituting many high-end versions of computers.)

4.9.5. Architectural Innovations *Versus* Modular Innovations

The term 'architecture' refers to the ways in which components are integrated and linked together to form a product. It deals with linkage of a few modules (or components) and does not deal with the modules themselves. Modules (or sub-systems, or sub-assemblies) are capable of performing independently certain distinct functions. Architectural innovations occur by studying the way in which the different components are linked and reconfiguring the linkages between the components of existing products in a new way that improves the system efficiency. The individual modules (or components) remain untouched and they perform their distinct functions. Modular innovation involves introduction of some new technology in one or more of the modules (components), while leaving the linkages between the components remain untouched.

For example, ceiling fan has the following components: motor, bearings, shaft, and blades. They are linked in a specific fashion to produce the product 'ceiling fan'. When the components are retained, but their mode of linkage is altered in such a way to produce a 'Pedestal fan' (or a Table-fan or a wall-mounted fan), the type of innovation is architectural innovation.

The earliest innovation in pump industry was reciprocal pump which consists of a motor, a crank shaft, cam, cylinder, piston etc., The rotary motion of the motor is converted into reciprocating motion which creates vacuum in the cylinder and sucks water. The centrifugal pump that evolved subsequent to reciprocating pump has a motor, a shaft, an impeller, casing, discharge nozzle etc., In centrifugal pump, a new technology was introduced whereby suction of water takes place by the centrifugal force generated by the rotating impeller as against the reciprocating pump where the suction of water takes place during the suction stroke of the piston that moves inside the cylinder. The shift from reciprocating pump to centrifugal pump can be considered as a modular innovation. If we consider that a pump has two main components, viz., a motor (which is the prime mover) and a mechanism that receives energy from the prime mover, both in reciprocating and centrifugal pumps, the prime mover exists as it is while the pumping mechanism gets altered.

4.9.6. Open Innovations *Versus* Closed Innovations

The term 'open innovation' was coined by Chesbrough, who introduced the term in his book 'Open Innovation: The new imperative for creating and profiting for technology.' Open innovation refers to a situation wherein firms use both internal as well as external ideas in their innovative process. As against this, closed innovation refers to a situation wherein firms use only internal ideas and carry out the process of innovation under controlled conditions; the innovations made are closely guarded in order to attain advantage over competitors. During the earlier part of the twentieth century, companies attached greater importance to closed innovations by funding their R&D divisions heavily and directing their employees towards innovation. This model suffered a few major setbacks. First, those firms that could not allocate large funds for R&D activities were at a disadvantage. Second, all the successful research findings by a firm could not be converted into innovative products/processes since some of the research findings might not relate to the firm's core business area. Thus, the money spent and the success achieved in research activities could not be fully capitalized.

These drawbacks, strengthened by factors like increased mobility of skilled workers, external options for unused technologies, increased readiness to outsource technologies etc., had led to the growth of open innovations during the latter part of the twentieth century.

Under open innovation, firms do not hesitate to share their knowledge as well as to acquire knowledge from other firms. Firms that are successful in striking at some innovations, but are not in a position to use them (due to whatever reasons) go for

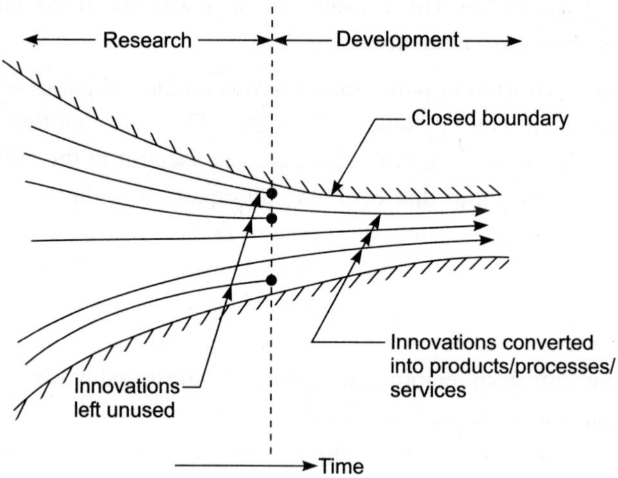

Fig. 4.3 Closed innovations

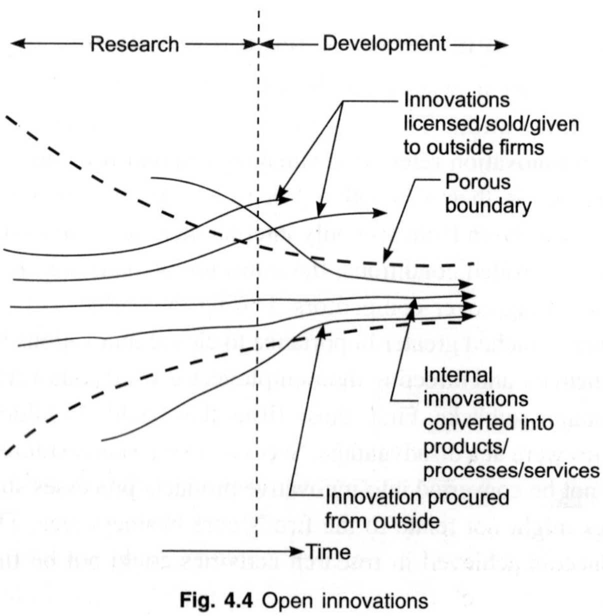

Fig. 4.4 Open innovations

licensing their innovations to other firms. Similarly, there are many firms that are ever willing to acquire technology from other firms if the technology is relevant to their business and if they are convinced that acquiring the technology would give them a competitive edge. Thus, open innovations provide a win-win situation to all the firms where all the efforts taken towards innovations reach the customers thereby benefiting the society at large. Figures 4.3 and 4.4 depict conceptual diagrams of closed and open innovations respectively.

4.10. PRODUCT INNOVATIONS VIS-À-VIS PROCESS INNOVATIONS

Product innovations and process innovations normally occur simultaneously. At times, an existing process can also be used to produce a new product. However, a new product often comes with a new process or at least with a modification of an existing process. Suppose a new innovative product is introduced, which makes use of a new process of manufacture. After the launch of the product, further innovations take place both in the product and in the process of manufacturing the product. While product innovations progress on the way to introduce additional product features/ improving upon the product functions/creating allied products etc., process innovations are often directed towards improving the effectiveness and efficiency of production. To start with, the rate of innovation is faster in respect of product than in process. The rate of product innovation reaches a peak and then starts to decline. By this time,

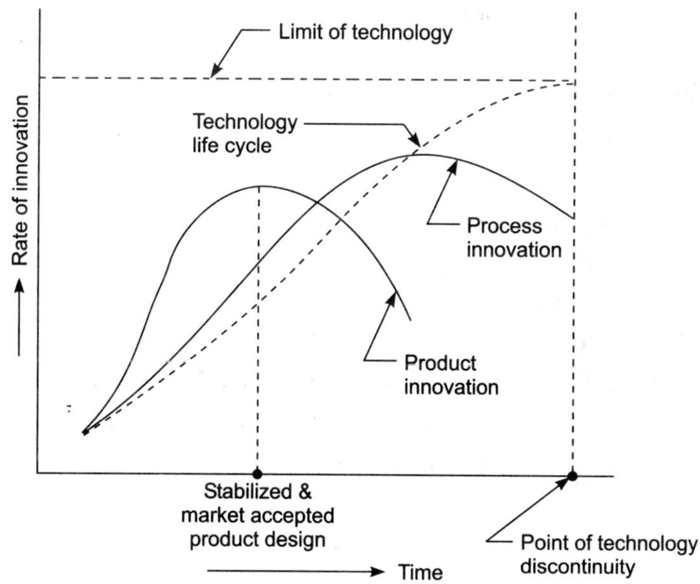

Fig. 4.5 Product & process innovations

a dominant product design emerges that the industry accepts as the standard. Further improvements in the product with the available level of process improvements will not be possible. However, process innovations can continue to occur even after the product innovations have ceased (Refer Fig. 4.5). The process innovation continues, which adds improvements in the product (by way of product refinements, lesser material consumptions, cost reductions, use of alternate materials etc.,) and this will continue until a new technology emerges and overtakes the existing technology and by this time, the product would have already become obsolete.

Referring to Fig. 4.5, it can be observed that both product and process innovations contribute to the growth of technology. The technology life cycle is represented by a smooth curve that gradually raises and reaches a flat profile at the right extreme end. A flat portion of the technology life cycle curve indicates that no further process innovation takes place. (By this time, the product innovation would have already reached its limit and stopped proceeding further.) Let us consider the technology life cycle curve shown in Fig. 4.5 as the curve representing a particular technology, say Technology-1. This technology has a limit (represented by the dotted line that is parallel to the X-axis and tangential to the technology life cycle curve). A new technology that is superior to Technology-1 will now takeover. This new technology (say, Technology-2) might have started evolving some time before Technology-1 reaches its limit. The progress rate of Technology-2 will be below that of Technology-1 to begin with; it will soon overtake Technology-1. A technology discontinuity is said to have occurred when Technology-1 has already reached its limit and Technology-2 has overtaken Technology-1. Beyond the point of technology discontinuity, Technology-1 would no longer be in existence.

4.11. RISKS ASSOCIATED WITH INNOVATIONS

All types of innovations always come with an element of risk. Some of the risks associated with innovations are discussed below:

(*a*) Technological innovations require allocation of substantial resources and hence firms that are starved of financial resources may not be able to take up innovation as a part of their regular activity.

(*b*) In spite of committing huge resources, innovations may not be always successful. (For example, the huge amounts spent by the world's largest research based pharmaceutical company Pfizer Inc. in R&D towards developing a cholesterol reducing drug as a cure for diabetics did not yield the expected results and the company had to swallow a huge loss in the process.)

(*c*) Even after successful innovations, huge funds are required for carrying forward the innovations. Funds apart, time and other efforts are required to be allocated for making innovations successful. In spite of all these efforts, there is a risk of the innovative products/services being not accepted by the market and this may result in huge losses to those firms that follow innovative practices.

(*d*) Innovations attempted should be in tune with the overall business strategies of the firm. If not, the innovations may not yield the desired results.

(*e*) A firm that is already in the market producing some products shall have to plan before reaching the market with new innovative products. The new products, if accepted by the market will result in decline of sales of the existing products of the firm, when the two products are substitutes or when the new product is an improved version of the existing product. This may affect the business prospects of the firm for a short tenure.

(*f*) Firms will find it difficult to convince employees about the benefits of innovation. The employees may hesitate to cooperate implementing the innovations on the apprehension that they may lose their position/status in the changed scenario. There will also be a resistance to accept the changes that will take place in the organizational hierarchy due to innovations. Unless there is active participation and whole-hearted cooperation of all the employees, the management may find it difficult to push through innovations.

(*g*) If the firm has erred in correctly assessing the life cycles of the different technologies and land up with innovating some product using a technology that is already in the state of maturity, the technology will be overtaken by a new technology within a short span of time, thus making the entire work, a futile exercise.

4.12. TECHNOLOGY-MARKET INTERACTION

There exists a strong, dynamic and mutually dependent relationship between technology and market. Technology serves the market. But, market should be ready to receive the technology. Only then, technology can serve the market. Hence, a firm that is involved in technology should be capable of assessing the market requirements in terms of technology and offer the market the type of technology that it looks forward to. Only then, there will be synergy and both the sides will stand benefitted. Offering a technology that is too costly may not find a market with the customers. Offering a technology that is outdated may also be not received well and this will take the firm towards difficult times in future. Offering a technology that is not user-friendly will also be not accepted by the market in spite of the technology having advanced features and being cost effective. After all, a consumer pays and buys a product or service for achieving the expected level of satisfaction from the use of the product/service. Hence, the product/service offered should be cost effective, user-friendly and technologically relevant and appropriate in order to find customer acceptance. To ensure this, firms should be in constant touch with the developments taking place in the market, should continuously assess the customer preferences and incorporate their findings and observations in the products/services that they offer, by using the relevant and suitable technology that will fulfill the requirements.

There are two linear models of technological innovations based on Technology-Market interaction. They are,

1. Technology push model
2. Market pull model

4.12.1. Technology Push Model

Technology push model is a technology-driven model. Suppose scientists come up with a good idea or discovery. The scientific discoveries made may not apparently indicate an application that can be commercialized. It is the turn of the Research & Development department to make use of the scientific discovery and design a product that is capable of satisfying some of the customer needs/wants. The R & D department will make prototypes for testing. After the testing phase is completed successfully, the job is handed over by the R & D department to the manufacturing department. Now, it is the duty of the manufacturing department to device methods to produce the product efficiently. After the manufacturing department succeeds, it becomes the responsibility of the marketing department to promote the product to the market. This model is given in Fig. 4.6.

'Technology push' describes a situation where an emerging technology or a new combination of existing technologies provides the required driving force for producing an innovative product/offering an innovative service. If the technology used has substantial advantages, the product will turn out to be a successful one and it will find its own market.

The scientific discovery may have taken place either within the company or outside the company. Figure 4.6 describes a model where the scientific discovery has taken place outside the company.

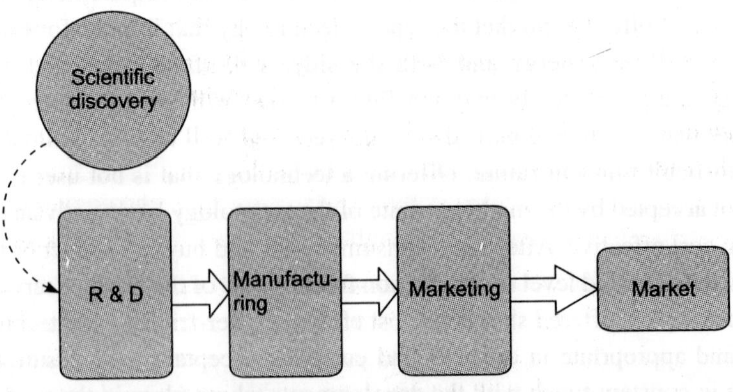

Fig. 4.6 Technology push model

Technology Push model will lead to the emergence of new products. If the technology is an emerging one, the new product designed may offer many new features to the customers. If the scientific discovery is radical, the products designed may offer many benefits to the consumers in terms of functional utility, new avenues of need/want satisfaction, cost effectiveness etc. However, the drawback of the model is that the firm may not know for sure how successful the product will be. Since the product takes shape from scientific discoveries, it may miss the 'market' element and the marketing department may have to work hard to push the concept and product into the market.

4.12.2. Market Pull Model

Market pull model is a customer need-driven model. This model is based on close interactions of the marketing department with customers. Marketing department will obtain feedbacks from customers on the need for new products/improvements in existing products and will feed the R&D department with necessary inputs based on customer feedbacks obtained. The R&D department will design the products/modifications to satisfy the customer requirements and after successful design and testing of the new product, will pass on the job to the manufacturing department. The manufacturing department will produce the product and pass it on to the market via marketing department. This model is given in Fig. 4.7.

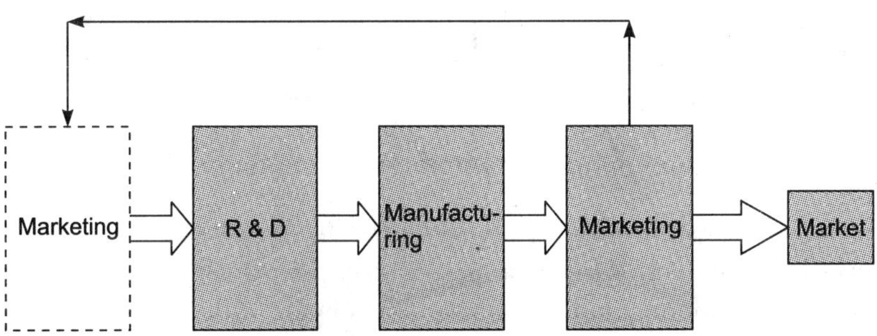

Fig. 4.7 Market pull model

Market Pull model is an effective way to connect technology with the market since the products are designed and manufactured in tune with the market requirements.

'Market pull' describes a situation where in the latent and unsatisfied customer needs are identified and the product/process innovations have their origin in these unsatisfied customer needs. The identification of customer needs occurs first, followed by the required developmental activities for producing the product/service.

In general, the technological developments that take place in consequence of Market Pull will be incremental in nature. The customers will have a tendency to ask for more in every product and hence may demand additional features in products which in turn will lead to incremental innovations. But, incremental innovations should not be looked upon as something with lesser importance. Over a period of time, many such increments will add up to give a product that is totally different from the originally introduced product. It is not that Market Pull Model will always lead to incremental innovations. If there is a strong demand from customers for some products and if no efficient and effective technology exists to produce products demanded by the customers, it may stimulate breakthrough innovations also.

4.12.3. Technology-push Innovation *Versus* Market-pull Innovation

(*a*) Technology-push innovation projects possess a greater level of market uncertainty. This is because of the reason that products are developed for utilizing the new technology that has been developed/ acquired. The importance goes to the technology rather than to the product. This is the reason for the market uncertainty of products brought out through technology-push factor. Market-pull approach is more certain about the market for the products since the products are designed in accordance with the market requirements. In this approach, the importance goes to the product rather than to the technology.

(*b*) The potential market applications for a technology-push strategy are essentially unknown, whereas the knowledge about the areas of need in a market-pull situation can be directly taken as the starting point for the potential applications.

(*c*) Technology-push approach makes extensive use of anticipatory and exploratory market research methods, whereas market-pull approach makes uses of market information and if required, will apply conclusive research for identifying the product requirements.

(*d*) Technology-push strategies generally strive for breakthrough innovations by investing heavily in R&D activities. Market-pull strategies normally lead to incremental innovations of products/processes with minimum/moderate additional investments.

(*e*) Technology-push strategies normally require a longer time period for implementation, usually in the range of 5 to 10 years. This is because of the reason that the strategy attempts to first identify areas of new technological innovations and then develop products/processes based on the identified technology. Market-pull strategy requires comparatively lesser time duration for implementation since the requirements for the technological innovations come from the market and as the innovations are usually small/marginal in nature.

4.13. SOURCES OF INNOVATIONS

Individuals

Individuals who contribute to innovations may be customers who use the products and services of a company. Since users are the persons who have first-hand knowledge about the product/service attributes, they know the additional/modified requirements and their ideas may lead to incremental innovations.

Manufacturing firms

Firms that are engaged in the production of products/offering of services may come up with both incremental as well as radical innovations through their R&D initiatives and also through motivated employees with creative ideas. Apart from manufacturing firms, those firms that supply raw materials, components, semi-finished parts etc., can also be instrumental in throwing up innovative ideas to the manufacturing firm.

Government funded research organizations

Government is a major player in the economy of any country and has a greater role to play in improving the technological capabilities of the country. Government sponsored research organizations play a major role in both fundamental and applied researches which can bring out many innovations.

Private research laboratories

Innovation will be a highly profitable proposition once it succeeds, especially when the innovation happens to be a radical/breakthrough one. Hence, many research laboratories in the private sector are engaged in innovations and their research findings become another source of innovations.

Academic institutions

Academic institutions have a large pool of knowledge workers and a still larger pool of students who have the capacity to come out with innovative ideas. What is required' is a close industry-institute interaction so that the academic institutions will understand the industry requirements and concentrate on innovating such products/ processes that will become commercially successful propositions. Without effective interaction between academic institutions and industry, the research findings of the academic institutions will lack industry relevance and will have very little impact.

4.14. GENERAL BARRIERS TO INNOVATION

Though the advantages of being an innovative organization is well known and the competitive advantages that innovation offers are proved beyond doubt, there still remains hurdles in the path to innovation as we find only a very little number of organizations that get benefited by innovation. There are barriers to innovation. The barriers are hidden in the sense that unless one makes an unbiased, in-depth analysis, these barriers will not be visible. They are quite evident, but still hidden. The following are some of the common barriers:

- The potential area of innovation may turn out to be one that will overpower the existing business. If this is the perception of an organization, then there will be a hesitation among many of the organizational members in going for the innovation. They will find comfort in doing what is already being done and that which has already been proved. Such a culture will be the greatest barrier.
- If the consumers of the product/service offered by the organization are such who do not demand anything superior, who are satisfied with the products/services being presently offered by the organization, the organization may not face any pressure to go for innovative products/services.
- Any innovation brings along with it a lot of changes. Changes are always accompanied by some sort of disturbance/readjustment which will involve an element of risk. Leaders/executives who by nature are risk-averse and who want to play safe will not be oriented towards innovation and organizations with such leaders can not pursue the path towards innovation.
- Complacency on the part of the employees at different level of an organization will play havoc and will pose threat for the very survival of the organization. This is because, complacency and resting on laurels will make an organization exposed to competition from strong players. But, the lesson will be learnt only when the survival becomes a question mark. By the time such a stage reaches, it will be difficult to overcome. Till such time, complacency on the part of the employees/ executives will act as a barrier for any initiative towards innovation.
- Every employee, every executive and every person who occupies different positions in the organizational hierarchy, will have his own area of competence, wherein they are better off when compared to many others. Everyone will try to focus their efforts and attention in the area of their strength so that they can improve their performance and relative importance among their peers. This attitude, which will be invariably present in most of the employees (unless they are sensitized about the ill effects that this will bring to the organization), will act as a barrier in attempting to do anything new that is not in the area of their competency. Innovation cannot flourish when such a culture prevails in an organization.

4.15. MYTHS ASSOCIATED WITH INNOVATION

Some of the myths associated with innovation are as under:

Break-through innovations start out as big ideas

There can be no rule as to how a break-through or radical innovation should be attempted. Many of the new ideas/innovations have their beginning in smaller ideas. Working on such smaller ideas can pave way for experimenting with some new initiatives that can ultimately lead to radical innovations. No idea can be considered small and ignored. If a company believes that it can arrive at break-through innovations by entrusting the job to a group of smart people and asking them to think hard and come out with innovative ideas that are new and worth investing in, the company may find the results discouraging.

Innovation is related only to products

This is a great misconception. The moment people talk/think about innovation, they think only about products. Hence, innovative thought process generally revolves around products. There is nothing wrong about relating innovations with products. But, products are not the only scope for innovations. Innovations are possible in every single aspect of the business. There can be innovations in the production process, in vertical integration of business (for example, in changing the way of purchase of raw material, in changing the way of delivering the end products to the customers etc.), in pricing of products, in changing the business model itself and many more. Restricting innovation only to products will act only as a limiting factor for a company in its journey towards innovations.

Innovations are risky propositions

As long as a company thinks that innovations are risky propositions, the company cannot assign innovation the place it deserves. It will only receive a secondary treatment and such a climate will not be conducive to innovation. No doubt, innovations have some element of risk in them. A product that is developed after spending huge time, effort and money may not be received by the market well. Such failures may occur once in a way. Such failures will show where the company has gone wrong. More often, innovation follows prudence. If the element of prudence is missing, the innovation may not click. Since risk is a function of investment multiplied by uncertainty, the risk can be minimized/eliminated if prudence is built into the innovative practices. Keeping aside innovative practices, considering them as risky is a misconception. Innovation backed by prudence will pay rich dividends in the long run.

Innovations cannot be taught

This misconception is due to the belief that innovative ideas can spurt only from a gifted few, who have the capacity to think laterally, differently and who have ingenuity. Identifying innovative opportunities depends on the ability to grasp the needs of customers, capacity to uncover the unrevealed, unspoken intensions/frustrations of customers and the ability to tap the areas that remain unexploited by the competitors. One can be trained to acquire these skills by which innovations can be made possible. The misconception that innovation cannot be taught arises from the wrong belief that innovation means radical, break-through innovations in the domain of new products. Even in this domain, people can be trained to think systematically so that innovative ideas can evolve. If a company believes strongly that innovations cannot be taught, then there is no need for any R&D department. But, every company that is in a business where technology has a role to play invariably has R&D department, which only goes to prove that innovations can be taught.

Innovation is not everybody's job

The belief that innovation is not everybody's job and that it is the role of the R&D department is a myth again. R&D department may come up with some product that is really new, radical and path-breaking. Such products may change the business scenario and may pay rich dividends to the company. But, such break-through innovations cannot be predicted with accuracy. Hence, along-side the path of break-through innovations, there must also be encouragement for incremental innovations and when all the employees are involved in the process of generating innovative ideas, it will yield tangible results.

Innovation is an expensive process

Industry statistics show that there is no correlation between successful innovations and the amount spent on them. 'More the expenditure, greater the number of successful innovations' is yet another misconception. The solution to inexpensive innovation lies in involving all the employees in the process of innovation. Innovation should become a work culture and all the employees should be motivated to contribute their part towards it. When all the employees are involved in the process and all of them understand that business innovation is part of their responsibility, then, innovation will not be expensive for an organization.

A great leader can make innovations happen

There is no denying the fact that great leaders spearhead organizations to great heights. Great leaders are required. But, merely choosing a great, talented leader and entrusting the work to him may not simply work. The on-going operations occupy the minds of the organizational members to a greater extent. The interactions between the on-going operations of an organization and the innovative processes that are to be carried out for making innovation a reality are too much involved requiring contributions from members across the cross section of organizational hierarchy. Hence, a supportive organization should prevail for the leader to spearhead it in the path of innovation.

4.16. OUTSOURCING TECHNOLOGY INNOVATION

With faster rate of technological growth and shorter product life cycles, only a few companies could afford to have in-house technology innovation facilities. In the present scenario of interdisciplinary growth of technology, a single company, acting alone cannot sustain technology advantage for a long time relying only on its own capital resources and creative talents. This has resulted in more and more companies seeking technology from outside. This trend has in turn given scope for the growth of companies whose main job is creation of new technology and selling/licensing the technology to prospective buyers. These technology innovators do not go for commercialization, as they lack the required financial resources, though they are stronger in terms of technology development. The existences of such companies who thrive only on R&D works have made outsourcing of technology innovation possible and even more cost-effective as compared to technology innovations made in-house.

Many organizations have been successful in achieving greater returns through outsourcing technology innovations and concentrating their efforts only on the areas of their core strength. Outsourcing technology innovations have come to the help of small businesses to compete with large companies in terms of bringing out innovative products.

4.17. KAIZEN

Kaizen is a Japanese word — 'kai' means change and 'zen' means good. Kaizen refers to "change for good". It is an ongoing process of improvement involving everyone — from the top management to the workers at the bottom line. Kaizen strategy is the single most important concept in Japanese management, which is key to Japanese competitive success. Kaizen is based on the logic of bringing continuous improvements internally from within the organization.

Toyota is well-known as one of the leading companies using Kaizen. In 1999, at one U.S. plant of Toyota, 7,000 employees submitted over 75,000 small suggestions/ideas of which 99% were accepted and implemented. This shows the power of Kaizen.

The continuous small improvements add up to major benefits resulting in greater productivity, improved quality, better safety, faster delivery, lower costs and greater customer satisfaction. These apart, employees working in Kaizen-based companies find their work more enjoyable resulting in higher employee morale, greater job satisfaction and lower employee turnover.

Kaizen involves every employee in making the change. The changes brought about are mostly small and incremental in nature. Kaizen focuses on identifying the problems at their source and solving them at their source so that the problems remain solved once for all. Kaizen is applied in all the activities of an organization. The principle behind Kaizen is that no day should be passed without adding something new. Kaizen is an on-going and never-ending process. Though Kaizen aims at continuous, incremental improvements, it cannot be exactly equated to incremental innovation.

4.17.1. Kaizen *versus* Incremental Innovation

Kaizen differs from incremental innovation in the following ways:

- Kaizen is a continuous process, while incremental innovations are one-time projects, though carried out continually at frequent intervals.
- Kaizen involves all employees in the organization. Every employee contributes something new in his area of work and does this continuously. Incremental innovations are carried out by the selected group of employees who are identified for the task.
- Kaizen, per se, may not require any additional investment (or, at the most may require very minimum investment), while incremental innovations require allocation of men and material resources of the required extent.
- Kaizen is a people oriented movement. The objective of Kaizen is to involve all the employees in the process of improving the organizational functions, processes and products. Incremental innovation is technology oriented and its objective is to add value through the use of technology.

4.18. REASONS FOR THE FAILURE OF INNOVATIONS

Failure is inevitable in the attempts made for innovation. An innovation is considered to have failed when it could not produce the product of acceptable quality and features or the process of acceptable performance. Even when the desired features/qualities of products/processes are achieved, if the products/processes turn out to be commercially unsuccessful, the innovation is still to be considered only as a failure. The causes for failure are many. Some of the causes are discussed below:

4.18.1. Poor Leadership

This is found to be the major cause for the failure of innovations. The success of a team depends on the vision and capability of the leader. A person who lacks leadership qualities may not be able to coordinate the efforts of the team members in achieving success. A leader is one who is having the vision to make a change while a manager is one who is required to cope up with the complexities of the change. Since successful innovations are possible only through right vision, proper coordination of resources and effective management of changes that take place consequent to innovation, if the person who heads the innovation team is not one with leadership qualities, the entire efforts will go waste.

4.18.2. Relying too Much on Internal Resources

There is an inherent tendency among leaders to rely more on internal resources (especially internal manpower), and hiring external manpower to the minimum extent possible. There are many psychological reasons for this which is hard to overcome unless the leader keeps away personal biases and prejudices. Leaders fall prey to this habit because of one or more of the following reasons:

Leaders are comfortable with personnel with whom they are familiar. When a person is hired from outside and if the person happens to occupy an influential position, it will put the person who is already heading a team that is involved in the process of innovation, in difficulty. He will have his own problems of readjusting himself to the changed environment. These things create a bias in favour of diverting internal personnel to the innovation team rather than seeking outside talents. There is nothing wrong in roping in an internal person provided he has the talents. But, the drawback is that people who have been with an organization for long fall into stereo-typed thinking and behaviour and it will be difficult for them to come out and indulge in out-of-the-box thinking. Other factors like the higher compensation package to be provided to external persons, the time required for scouting the right personnel from outside may also act as barriers for recruiting outside talents to be part of the innovation team.

4.18.3. Lack of Communication

Lack of communication among the team members involved in the process of innovation and also the absence of communication/misinterpretation of communication between the innovation team members and other members of the organization will pose hurdles in bringing out successful innovations.

4.18.4. Inappropriate R&D Efforts

R&D department is an important wing of any organization and it is instrumental in promoting innovations in an organization. Ineffective and improper management of R&D department will result in failure of innovation initiatives. The activities of the R&D department should in tune with the technology policy of the organization which in turn are guided by extensive market research and marketing research. For example, if the market research has identified an unfulfilled gap in the product range or an unattended customer requirement with respect a particular product, the R&D department should act to address these issues and its innovative efforts should be directed towards these areas. Only then, any innovation made by the R&D department will really add value to the products created out of innovation and the innovation will become a commercially successful one.

4.18.5. Organizational Change

Any innovation brings about an organizational change. The type of change depends upon the nature of the innovation. When the organization is not flexible enough to embrace the changes, efforts towards innovation may fail. For example, launching a new product may require certain changes in the composition and the hierarchical structure of the employees in the marketing department and other departments as well. These changes are to be incorporated and the employees shall be made to appreciate the necessity for change. If the employees do not appreciate the need for the required changes, they will put forth resistance to changes which will eventually spoil the efforts taken towards innovation.

4.18.6. Commercial Aspects

Failing to incorporate the voice of the customers in the product has been one of the main reasons for failure. A product innovated might have had exceptional features and might have been produced to perfection. But, it may not turn out to be a commercial success if the products do not gain customer acceptance. Companies should harness the wisdom of the crowd i.e., they should let the customers decide on their priorities before working on an innovative idea/product.

Another cause of concern is the behavioural changes required on the part of the consumers when they accept the new product. All new products tend to make a change in the behaviour of consumers in some way or the other. Consumers are obsessed with 'status-quo-bias' and they have a tendency to resist changes. The benefits that a new product will offer are often over-shadowed by the 'status-quo-bias' in the minds of the consumers and hence even a good, innovative product might fail to take off commercially. Hence, products are to be so designed that they demand least behavioural changes from the consumers. Such a step taken in the design stage of the product development will go a long way in making the innovation a commercially successful one.

4.18.7. Product-based Causes

A good product will sell itself. Hence, product innovations should be directed towards bringing out a good product. How to define the goodness of a product? There are certain product dimensions that can tell whether or not a product is good from the consumers' point of view.

First, the product should have a greater relative advantage over the existing products that it intends to replace. The relative advantage should be in terms of cost, functional utility, convenience of use, social acceptability etc. When innovation is directed either towards improving an existing product or producing a new product, this aspect is to be given priority. Without relative advantage from the customers' point of view, any innovation will be a failure.

Second, the impact of innovation, as evidenced by the benefits offered by the new product/service should be apparently visible to the consumers. This feature is called observability or visibility. Poor visibility will make the products unnoticed by consumers.

Third, the innovation should be simple and easily understandable by the consumers. The technology behind the product can be a high-end and complicated one, but when it comes to the product, the product features should be such that they do not pose any difficulty to the consumers in using the product. The product should be simple to use/ operate, however complicated the technology behind it may be.

Fourth, the innovation should be consistent with the values, customs, habits, beliefs and preferences of the potential consumers. Any innovation that ignores these aspects will finally turn out to be a commercial failure.

Last, but not the least, trialability is another factor that decides customer acceptance. Trialability is the degree to which a product can be tried for a limited period before it is adopted. Trialability is closely related to the concept of perceived risk. Medicines, soft drinks, cosmetics, cookies etc., are some of the products that can be given free for trial. Automobiles, GPS etc., can be given a test use before buying. Automatic Expresso Coffee making machines went well after trial by prospective buyers. But, some innovations are more difficult for trial. Such products, by virtue of their nature can rely more on observability than on trialability.

4.19. TECHNOLOGY TRANSFER

Technology Transfer is a process by which science and technology are transferred from one individual, company, group or country to another individual/company/group/ country. Technology Transfer takes place from the 'Source' to the 'Beneficiary'. The individual, company, group or country that owns and transfers the technology is known as the 'Source' and the recipient of the technology is the 'Beneficiary'. Technology Transfer is a continuous process. It is not a one-time activity. A company that has received a technology from another source must nurture the technology continuously so that the technology will be accepted and absorbed by the company. For nurturing the technology, the recipient organization should train its employees in the new technology. This will support the technology acquired. A technology that is not supported and nurtured will not offer the intended benefits and will become obsolete very quickly.

4.19.1. Types of Technology Transfer

(a) Direct Technology Transfer

Technology transfer usually occurs through a formal arrangement between the transferor and the recipient (or beneficiary). Technology Transfer may take place between one enterprise and another enterprise, one enterprise and Government, one Government and another Government or between one department of an enterprise and some other department of the same enterprise. Wherever the two parties to the Technology Transfer directly enter into formal arrangement between them, the transfer is called Direct Technology Transfer.

(b) Spin-off Technology Transfer

A 'spin-off' is a start-up company formed to commercialize a technology/an invention developed from the research work of a parent company. The reasons for setting up a separate 'spin-off' company may be based on financial, legal considerations and taxation related issues.

There is another kind of spin-off called university spin-off. Technological inventions developed in universities remain unutilized unless they are channelized into the industry in some form. University spin-off is a mechanism for achieving this. In most countries, the university can claim the Intellectual Property right over its inventions. They transfer their Intellectual Property to an interested corporation/company through a licensing arrangement to enable the transferee to exploit the benefits of the invention.

(c) Formal vs. Informal Technology Transfer

Under formal transfer of technology, the transferor and the recipient enter into a legally binding formal arrangement between them for the transfer of technology. The formal arrangement may be in the form of outright sale of technology by the transferor to the recipient or licensing of the technology with mutually agreed terms between the parties. Suppose a firm owns a superior technology. Another firm that opts to have this superior technology may acquire that firm so that it can make use of the technology. Such acquisitions of one firm by another with a view to having access to technology will also fall under the category of formal technology transfer. Apart from such formal arrangements/agreements, technology may also be transferred through informal methods. Some such informal methods of technology transfer are as under:

— A firm may acquire and employ main technical personnel from another firm.

— A firm desirous of acquiring a technology may do so making use of the published information relating to the technology concerned in print/electronic media.

— Seminars, Symposiums, research meets etc., may pave way for the informal transfer of technology through exchanges between the participants in such events.

— Academic institutions and research institutions may impart training/knowledge on the latest technology to interested people in order to disseminate the technology. Such opportunities may be made use of by firms for acquiring technology.

(d) Internal (or Intra-firm) Technology Transfer

This refers to the transfer of technology from one department of an organization to another department. Transfer of technology from the R&D wing to the manufacturing department will be considered as an internal transfer. Similarly, one department that is using an advanced technology may transfer the same to another department of the same organization that is using a lower level technology. A firm having production facilities at more than one locations may transfer technology from one location to another. All such transfers of technology that are internal to a firm are known as Internal or intra-firm technology transfer.

(e) External (or Inter-firm) Technology Transfer

This refers to the transfer of technology from one firm to another firm through a mutually agreed upon mode of transfer (like outright sale, licensing arrangement, franchising agreement etc.). External Technology Transfer takes place in view of the following reasons:

- A company may lack internal resources (men and material resources) for carrying out innovations. Such a company may find it easier and cheaper to buy a technology from another company that owns it.
- A company may have the required resources, but may be risk-averse. Such a company may prefer to buy an already proven technology instead of committing resources towards innovation that it considers risky.
- A company may feel buying a technology that is already proven may save time and money. By buying the technology, the company can go to the market quickly instead of developing the technology in-house and then going to the market, which will consume a lot of time.

- When competitors are progressing fast, a company will feel the pressure to come out with innovative products to meet the competition. In order to keep up with the competitors, a company may opt to buy a readily available technology, instead of spending time in developing a new technology afresh.
- Complex technological developments that take place continuously will require expertise/ core-competency in the relevant area. Developing Core competencies will take time and hence a company may opt to buy the technology.

(f) Cross Country Technology Transfer (or International Technology Transfer)

Technology can be transferred from one country to another. Generally this type of technology transfer takes place from industrially advanced and developed countries to developing/underdeveloped countries. Cross country technology transfer can take place through mutual transactions between the transferor and the transferee, by way of licensing, franchising or any other accepted mode. But, most of the cross country technology transfer takes place through the process of reverse engineering, cross-border movement of production methods and product designs, and movement of skilled workers across borders. Trade in capital goods between countries acts as an important source for technology transfer through reverse engineering.

(g) Cross Sector (or Cross-industry) Technology Transfer

This refers to the transfer of technology from one industrial sector to another for purposes not originally intended by the industry that developed the technology. Technology is common to many industries. But, the phase of technological development of the different industries differs to a greater extent. Hence, there is always a need to observe other industries and know the happenings there. This will help a firm to identify useful, cost-effective technologies in other industries that are capable of getting transferred. There lies great scope for transfer of technology from Chemical industry to Pharmaceutical industry, from Electronic industry to Healthcare industry, from Bio-tech industry to food industry etc. Making use of technologies used in space application technology for commercial use is an example for cross-industry transfer. Membrane separation systems that are commonly used in the treatment of waste water are used in dairy sector and soya-milk production units for separating higher molecular weight components from low molecular weight components which is a cross-sector Technology transfer. Chromatography is a technology used in Pharmaceutical industry for selective absorption of specific target molecules. This technology is adopted in food industry to isolate active components from grape juice, wine etc.

4.19.2. Channels for Technology Transfer

Technology transfer can take place smoothly only if proper channels are established. Once there are appropriate channels, technology being an intangible asset, can find its way easily from the transferor to the recipient through the channels. Some of the commonly used channels for Technology Transfer are as below:

(*a*) *General Channels*

These are the channels where information is made available in the public domain with limited or no restriction on the use. Seminars, conferences, workshops, trainings, publications, study visits, exchange of personnel between organizations etc., are some of the general channels through which technology transfer can take place.

(*b*) *Reverse Engineering Channels*

Reverse Engineering refers to examining a product in greater detail by dissecting them or practically taking them apart. When a receiver of technology is capable of breaking the code of the technology and producing a product on the strength of knowledge gained, by duplicating the product in some form, reverse engineering is a possible channel to achieve this. However, the company that attempts reverse engineering should have the required knowledge and expertise to do this and also there should not be any violation of Intellectual Property rights in doing so. Reverse Engineering is also being used as an invaluable tool by academics and students of different disciplines, who use this for the purpose of understanding the technology involved, without any intention of making a commercial use of it.

(*c*) *Licensing*

There are two parties to a licensing agreement. One party agrees to offer the right either to produce or sell a product to another party. The party who receives the right is the licensee and the party who offers the right is the licensor. Suppose a licensor offers a technology to a licensee. There can be an outright offer wherein the licensee pays a onetime amount to the licensor or there can be an initial lump sum payment followed by periodical payments by the licensee, as a percentage of the sales made every year.

(*d*) *Franchising*

There are two parties to a franchise agreement. The company that offers some business idea is the franchisor, and the company/person who buys is the franchisee. The franchisee conducts business as per the terms of the Franchise Agreement and under the franchisor's trademark. Since, for all purposes a customer views a franchisee as an extended arm of the franchisor, the franchisor normally gives detailed directions to the franchisee. The standards to be followed by the franchisee are incorporated in detail in the franchise agreement. Normally, the franchise agreement provides for the payment of royalty by the franchisee to the franchisor on a continuous basis apart from the initial franchise fee. When the franchisee is a new-comer to business, he gets the advantage of the brand name established by the franchisor and his guidance in carrying out the business. Hence, as a business proposition, the franchisee is not likely to face uncertainty in the market, but he/she may have to pay a slightly higher price for the supports extended by the franchisor.

(e) Turnkey Project

The company that offers a turnkey project takes the total responsibility for delivering the project. The project is designed, implemented, tested and handed over to the recipient in a ready-to-operate state. (The responsibility of the recipient is simply to turn the key on in order to put the project in operation.) The turnkey agreement may contain, apart from regular terms and conditions agreed upon between the parties, a provision for continued operational support by the project provider. In a way, turnkey project is akin to buying a plant/equipment with a warranty, but the scope of a turnkey agreement is very wide, covering the entire plant, its erection, commissioning, trail production etc.

(f) Foreign Direct Investment (FDI)

FDI acts as a channel for technology transfer since FDI is normally undertaken only in industries in which knowledge and technology are important. A MNC can set up its own wing or its subsidiary in the host country. Most countries of the world are receptive to FDI. They have enacted laws that provide a favourable treatment to FDI. Some countries offer various tax and monetary incentives to attract FDI. The desire to attract FDI has two reasons. FDI occurs when a MNC finds sufficient cost or technological advantage over the firms already operating in the host country, where it wants to invest. The cost/technical advantage should be sufficient enough that it offsets the higher cost of operating internationally. First, FDI brings in new investments into the country which in turn increases national income and employment. Second, FDI offers spill-over benefits to the local economy by way of technology diffusion, increased productivity, growth in exports etc.

(g) Joint Venture

In a joint venture, two or more firms join together and contribute equity fund for forming a new entity. A Joint Venture agreement between the parties will spell out the role of each of the parties like the financial contribution of each party, the technical collaboration between them, the profit/loss sharing ratio between them etc. International Joint Ventures are used to acquire technology from abroad. International Joint Ventures combine the properties of FDI and licensing of Intellectual Property.

(*h*) *Technology Incubation*

Technology incubation is a system where universities/academic institutes, industry and Government participate for the development and transfer of technology. In India The National Science and Technology Entrepreneurship Development Board (NSTEDB) has come out with two schemes for the development and transfer of technology, viz.,

(*i*) Technology Business Incubator (TBI) and

(*ii*) Science and Technology Entrepreneurship Park (STEP)

TBI is a managed workspace in a university/technical institution that offers low cost office facilities, business and professional services necessary for nurturing and supporting early stage growth of technologies and technology based enterprises. The facilities offered include resources for R&D, design, engineering, testing, communication/information services, business planning, managerial advice etc. TBIs nurture young firms, helping them to survive in their early stage.

The objectives of STEP as laid down by the NSTEDB are:

- To forge a close linkage between universities, academic and R&D institutions on one hand and industry on the other.
- To promote entrepreneurship among Science and Technology persons, many of whom were otherwise seeking jobs after their graduation.
- To provide R&D support to the Small-Scale Industry mostly through interaction with research institutions.
- To promote innovation based enterprises.

Facilities provided by STEP are:

- Precision tool room/Central workshop
- Prototype Development
- Testing and calibration facilities
- Computing facilities
- Databank/library/documentation facilities
- Telex/fax/Photocopying facilities
- Training & Technical support services
- Business facilitation services
- Quality assurance services
- Community utility services

The host institution of STEP (a university or technical institution) plays a key role to achieve synergic benefits by coordinating with the stake-holders.

4.19.3. Barriers to Technology Transfer

Barriers to intra-firm technology transfer:

(*a*) When there is no close interaction between the R&D department and the production department (which is normally the case, unless the top management takes a conscious effort to bring in synergy between the two departments), the R&D department will not understand the capability of the production department. The R&D department may go ahead unilaterally and arrive at certain plans which the production department may not be capable of implementing.

(*b*) Unless the production department is sensitized towards innovation, there will be resistance from the employees of the production department whenever the R&D department comes out with some innovative process/product. Giving shape to the aspirations of the R&D department may face a lot of hurdles.

(*c*) In the absence of perfect understanding between the R&D and the marketing departments, the new technologies developed/acquired by the R&D department may not match the expectations of the customers/ marketing department.

(*d*) An existing product that is doing well in the market may be required to be withdrawn and replaced by a new product (keeping the long term advantages in mind) and the R&D department might work on these lines. At times, there will be hesitation in stop producing the existing product and venturing upon a new product, especially when the existing product is enjoying customer support. Thus, the fear of the unknown and the logic of 'A bird in hand is worth two in the bush' may stall adopting the innovations made by the R&D department.

All the above factors will act against smooth transfer of technology within a firm.

Overcoming the intra-firm barriers:

(*a*) The R&D department shall be made to work in close coordination with production and marketing departments so that the activities of the R&D department can really bear fruits.

(*b*) The top management should take active part in technology transfer and should create a supportive organizational culture.

(*c*) Since technology transfer can be effective only if the need for the technology transfer is well understood by all the organizational members, there must be an effective communication system in the organization to disseminate information on the need for technology transfer and the methodology being followed by the organization for technology transfer.

(*d*) The top management should build multifunctional teams to be in charge of the process of technology transfer. Such multifunctional teams will be effective in two ways: it will help in speedy dissemination of information across the different teams and employees belonging to different departments could easily understand their respective roles in ensuring effective transfer of technology.

(*e*) Rotation of employees between production and R&D departments will help in their better understanding each others' strengths and limitations which in turn will help in smooth transfer of technology.

Barriers to inter-firm technology transfer:

(*a*) The technology transferor would like to take advantage of his position and would normally charge a heavy price to the transferee. The transferee may have to pay a heavy price in the form of royalties and know-how fees. At times, there can also be periodical payments to be made by the transferee to the transferor for issues like periodic maintenance charges, consultancy charges etc.

(*b*) Since the technology is acquired from another firm (which may be an indigenous firm or a foreign firm), the transferee is always at the mercy of the transferor and has to depend on his services even for minor issues. It may take a longer time for the transferee to get fully conversant with the technology and till such time the transferee has to depend on the transferor's support for smooth functioning of the unit.

(*c*) The core competencies of the transferor and the transferee may differ. The organizational culture of the two may also be different. These issues may create hurdles in the smooth transfer of technology.

(*d*) The transferor and the transferee usually enter into an agreement that contains stipulations binding both of them. Misunderstanding/misinterpretation of the conditions, violation of the conditions by any one of them will create lack of confidence and trust which may lead to confrontation and legal entanglements between them.

Overcoming the inter-firm barriers:

(*a*) There must be a thorough study and understanding of the core competencies of both the parties and the organizational cultures prevailing with both of them. Remedial measures should be thought of and implemented, like strengthening the technical expertise in specified areas, arranging cross-cultural trainings etc., in order to ensure that the technology transfer takes place smoothly.

(*b*) The transferee shall have an un-biased assessment of the appropriateness of technology proposed to be acquired and should get fully convinced that the technology transfer will be of benefit to the transferee firm and that the technology will be accepted by the employees and customers of the transferee firm.

(*c*) The success of inter-firm technology transfer lies in perfect mutual understanding of the terms and conditions of technology transfer by both the parties concerned. Hence, both the parties shall jointly draft the technology transfer agreement, understanding fully well all the covenants and without allowing any ambiguity.

(*d*) Both the parties shall ensure that there is effective communication within their respective organizations about the technology transfer and shall also communicate between themselves in clear terms. Doubts if any, should be cleared then and there and all such correspondences/clarifications should be properly documented in order to avoid any problem in the future.

4.20. REVERSE ENGINEERING

Reverse engineering is the process of analyzing a product, with a view to understanding the technology, the design features, the mode of operation, the materials used, the intricacies involved in the building of the product etc. This type of inquiry aids individuals in a constructive learning process. The process of disassembling/dismantling a product apart and studying the way in which the product works often proves to be an effective way to understand a technology, to build a new product making use of the technology, to make improvements in the technology, to modify/improve the product features etc. Reverse Engineering is opposite to 'Forward Engineering', which refers to building a product making use of engineering concepts. As against this, Reverse Engineering starts with final product and works backwards, thereby attempting to understand the design of the product, the technology involved, the specifications of materials used to build the product and the interrelationships between the different components of the product. Reverse engineering is widely practised in military services, where the captured weapons are disassembled and the intricacies of the design, the specifications, the materials used etc., are studied to have an understanding of the technology.

Stages involved in the process of reverse engineering

- Identification of the product, plant/machinery, component of a product/plant to be reverse engineered.
- Disassembling/dismantling the product, plant/machinery, component to be reverse engineered and studying how the product/plant/component has been designed and assembled; understanding the technology involved.

- Gathering all relevant technological data by observing the product/component/plant.
- Building a new product; the new product can be a replica of the original product or an improved version and introducing the new product in the market.

It may be noted that apart from understanding the design, technology involved, mode of construction etc., of a product, reverse engineering can also be used to identify the defects, if any, found in an existing product/component/plant/machine etc., and to devise the ways to rectify the defects.

Before attempting to undertake reverse engineering, it must be thought of whether getting license from the original manufacturer is a better option than reverse engineering. This is because, reverse engineering will be a time consuming process and hundred percent success cannot be guaranteed. At times, getting a license from the original manufacturer may be a cheaper option than reverse engineering.

Whether reverse engineering is a legally valid process and whether it will amount to infringement of intellectual property rights is a difficult question to be answered. It has been held by Court [Kewanee Oil Co. v. Bicron Corp., 416 U.S. 470, 476 (1974)] that reverse engineering is a fair and honest means of starting with the unknown product and working backward to divine the process which aided in its development or manufacture. However, it will be always advisable to get an expert legal opinion on the matter when one wants to make commercial use of the findings of reverse engineering.

4.21. VALUE ANALYSIS AND VALUE ENGINEERING

The Society of American Value Engineers (SAVE) defines Value Analysis as under:

Value Analysis is the systematic application of recognized techniques which identify the function of a product or service, establish a monetary value for that function and provide the necessary function reliably at the lowest overall cost.

Value Analysis is an organized approach that aims to identify unnecessary costs associated with a product/system/service and efficiently eliminate them without affecting the quality and functional reliability.

For understanding Value Analysis and Value Engineering, we shall first define the term 'value'.

$$\begin{aligned}\text{Value} &= \text{Performance} \div \text{Cost}\\ &= \text{What does a function do?} \div \text{How much does it cost?}\end{aligned}$$

The performance of a product is the measure of its functional features and properties that make the product suitable for a specific purpose. The purpose of value Analysis is to identify unnecessary performance characteristics and remove them, thereby reducing the cost, without affecting the satisfaction level of the customer.

Value Analysis and Value Engineering are the two terms that are used interchangeably. Though both Value Analysis and value Engineering attempt to identify unnecessary costs with a view to eliminating them, there exists a subtle difference between the two. The difference between the two lies in the time and the stage at which the techniques are applied. While Value Analysis is applied for an existing product, Value Engineering applies the same rules to a new product. Value Analysis is carried out with the objective of improving the value of an existing product. It is a *remedial process* whereby the unnecessary costs already incurred in a product are identified and removed/reduced. Value Engineering is applied at the design stage with the objective of ensuring that bad/unwanted features are not included in the product. Value Engineering is a *preventive process.* Value Engineering, when carried out at the initial stages of a product can reduce the cost of production substantially.

Uses of value analysis

- Value Analysis reduces the cost of a product.
- It helps employees to have a better understanding of the jobs that they do in the organization.
- Employees become more cost-conscious and value-oriented.
- It creates a conducive climate for the emergence of innovative ideas.
- Implementing changes becomes easier, since employees become aware of the benefits of Value Analysis and do not offer any resistance to changes that are carried out for the benefit of the organization.

The following situations in an organization indicate the immediate need for carrying out Value Analysis:

- There is continuous decline in the sales of the Company's products.
- Rate of return on investment shows a falling trend.
- Competitors offer their products at a relatively lower price to the customers.
- The company defaults in meeting delivery dates.
- Competitors come up with new and improved designs for the products.
- Processing and tooling costs go up steeply.

An item/product that does not satisfy a function intended by the user is of no use to the user. Hence, the objective of any business proposition is to identify the functions expected to be fulfilled by an item (or a product, or a project) and to arrive at the best way of accomplishing it. The best way is the way that the user considers best for him/her. Here comes the need to produce the item (or product or project) that satisfies the expectations of the user at the lowest cost, at the expected level of quality and at the shortest possible time. When these three objectives (viz., cost, quality and time objectives) are met, the item will obviously offer greater value to the user for the money spent by the user.

The stages involved in value engineering are:

- define and understand the nature of the problem
- generate alternative ideas as to how the problem may be solved
- evaluate the feasibility of the generated ideas
- fully develop and test the ideas judged to be the most suitable
- decide upon the best solution.

How to measure value?

Value can be measured using Value Index. Value Index (VI) is the ratio of Function Worth to Function Cost.

$$VI = FW / FC$$

where,

FW = Function Worth

FC = Function Cost

VI can take a maximum value of 1.00. When the value of VI is less, it indicates that there is good scope for value improvement.

FW is the lowest cost that is required to perform a function or a group of functions. FW is arrived at by comparing the relative costs of alternative methods of performing the function. When VI obtains the maximum value of 1.00, it indicates that FW = FC, which is an ideal situation.

FC is the cost to perform the function under consideration. When only one function is performed by an item, the cost of the item is considered as the cost of the function. When an item performs more than one function, FC is to be distributed among all the functions on pro-rata basis, based on some acceptable logic.

4.22. NATIONAL KNOWLEDGE COMMISSION'S REPORT ON THE STATUS OF INNOVATIONS IN INDIAN INDUSTRY

National Knowledge Commission's report released in June 2007 discusses in detail about the status of innovations in Indian industry.

Some of the findings of the report are summarized below:

(*a*) Indian economy is growing at the rate of 6% to 8% every year. Exports from India are growing at the Cumulative Annual Growth rate (CAGR) of 30%. Many Indian firms are competing with international firms and international brands. This has been made possible by a favourable environment, improvement in capital and labour productivity, innovative business practices, continued innovations in products/processes etc. Indian firms have become more and more competitive and have started producing improved products and services at lower costs. Innovation is emerging as a key driver for the growth of Indian economy.

(*b*) About 42% of the large firms and 17% of the Small and Medium Enterprises (SMEs) have introduced 'new to world' innovations during the course of business in the last five years. Percentage of revenue earned from products and services has registered increase.

(*c*) Nearly 50% of the large firms and SMEs attribute more than 25% of change in the following factors to innovation:
- reduction in costs
- increase in market share
- increase in competitiveness
- increase in profitability

(*d*) For large firms, innovation has the most significant impact on competitiveness while for SMEs, innovation has the most significant impact on increase in market share.

(*e*) 17% of the large firms rank Innovation as the top strategic priority and 75% rank it among the top 3 priorities.

(*f*) All the large firms firmly believe that innovation has gained importance as being *critical to growth and competitiveness* since the start of economic liberalization in India. All the large firms agree (of which nearly half strongly agree) that they cannot survive and grow without *investment in Innovation.*

(*g*) An overwhelming 96% of large firms in the sample covered by the study foresee that Innovation spending will be increasing over the next 3–5 years.

(*h*) For large firms, Innovation is most highly concentrated in operations, sales and marketing. More than half of the increase in market share, competitiveness, profitability and reduction in costs due to Innovation has occurred in SMEs due to three types of Innovation — new products, new processes and new services.

(*i*) 37.3% of large firms have introduced Breakthrough Innovation, while 76.4% have introduced incremental Innovation, which may be an indication that large firms in India are still in the mindset of incremental Innovation as compared with breakthrough Innovation.

(*j*) The average timeframe (from idea generation to market) of Innovation projects for half of the large firms is 1 – 3 years. Innovation projects in manufacturing firms have longer gestation period than in services.

(*k*) SMEs have greater Innovation Intensity than large firms. (Innovation Intensity is defined as the percentage of revenue derived from products/services which are less than 3 years old.)

(*l*) Innovation Intensity for privately and publicly owned firms is significantly higher than that of Government owned firms.

(*m*) Firms with majority foreign ownership have greater Innovation Intensity than those with majority Indian ownership.

(*n*) Innovation Intensity for MNCs is significantly higher than for non-MNCs while there is little difference in the percentage of 'Highly Innovative' firms among MNCs and non-MNCs.

(*o*) Internal processes for innovation such as maintaining a specific innovation department, allocating funds, rewarding innovative employees, forecasting probabilities of success, formalizing processes and systematic attempts, maintaining physical locations for innovation and constituting cross functional teams all lead to firms being more innovative.

(*p*) Firms in industries where innovations are patented, with more patent filings and use of IPR consultants are more innovative.

(*q*) Firms partnering with Government agencies, collaborating with universities and R&D labs tend to be more innovative.

(*r*) Firms with their primary market in India have higher Innovation Intensity than those with primary markets abroad. On the other hand, a greater proportion of firms with their primary market abroad have introduced more 'new to world' innovations as compared with firms with their primary market in India.

4.22.1. Barriers to Innovation Faced by Indian Industries as Evidenced by the Study Conducted National Knowledge Commission

The following are the barriers to innovation faced by Indian firms as per the National Knowledge Commission report, 2007.

(*a*) External barriers:

The most important external barrier to innovation, as perceived by both large firms and SMEs, is skill shortage due to the lack of emphasis on industrial innovation, problem-solving, design, experimentation etc., in the education curricula.

Other prominent external barriers are lack of effective collaboration with research in universities and R&D institutions, excessive Government regulations as well as insufficient pricing power to derive value from Innovations.

(*b*) Internal barriers:

The most important internal barriers as perceived by large firms are lack of organizational focus on innovation as a strategy for growth and competitiveness, inefficient knowledge management systems within the company, and poor understanding of customer needs and market dynamics.

For SMEs, prominent internal barriers are skill shortages due to lack of effective in-house training programmes, inability to move beyond the first successful innovation and develop a sustainable model for continuous Innovation as well as poor understanding of customer needs and market dynamics.

4.23. INTRAPRENEURSHIP

The word 'intra' means 'within'. Intrapreneur refers to the person who is an employee of an organization and who thinks like an entrepreneur, seeking out opportunities to benefit the organization in which he/she is employed. Intrapreneurs have their focus on innovation and creativity and transform a dream or idea into a profitable venture. However, they work within the organizational environment and follow the goals of the organization. Thus, entrepreneurs are 'inside entrepreneurs'.

Intrapreneurship relates to unleashing the entrepreneurial energies in the employees in large organizations, so that the employees operate with an entrepreneurial mindset which will lead to 'reinvention' of the organization. A person who acts with an 'employee mind-set' cannot become an intrapreneur. An intrapreneur will have the perspective of 'psychological owner' of the company in which he works, rather than assuming the role of a mere employee. Intrapreneurship is also known as 'Corporate entrepreneurship'. Sharma and Chrisman in their book 'Entrepreneurship Theory and Practice' define corporate entrepreneurship as a process whereby an individual or a group of individuals in association with an existing organization create a new organization or instigate renewal or innovation within that organization. Encouraging intrapreneurship among the employees has become all the more important since this remains an untapped area that can contribute a lot to rejuvenate the organization. It enables employees (at all levels) to unleash their passion that more often results in generating new avenues for business growth. Hence, tapping the entrepreneurial potential in all the employees, which is a great task for the management, will offer rich dividends to the organization and will also keep the employees highly motivated and satisfied in their work. However, for this to happen, the top management should understand the potential benefits of intrapreneurship to the organization and should create conducive environment for the growth of intrapreneurship.

Cost reduction, increased customer focus, incremental innovations in products/ processes, new product development are some of the areas where intrapreneurs have a great scope for contribution. Apart from this, they can also offer their contribution towards radical/breakthrough innovations, in coordination with the R&D wing of the organization. Intrapreneurial innovations act as growth engines to organizations.

For intrapreneurship to flourish in an organization, there are some requirements/favourable conditions to be present. These are discussed below:

(*a*) *Barrier-free internal communications*

Internal communication is the live wire with the help of which an organization makes it known to all its employees about anything that happens inside the organization. Organizational structures, policies and practices should be such that they promote internal communication. A good internal communication system will make the employees understand the customer requirements, the areas that are redundant as far as satisfying the organizational objectives are concerned, the resources that are underutilized, the areas where there is ample scope for improvement etc., and this will help them understand the areas that are to be concentrated for improving the organizational performance. It will build confidence in the minds of the employees and employees will come forward to share their views and contribute for the betterment of the organization.

(*b*) *Free access to customer views*

An organization exists to fulfill customer needs. Hence, what customers feel about the company and its products/services is a vital input. There must be a system in place to receive customer information and customer feedback so that the organization can reorient itself towards meeting the customer requirements. This will help employees to acquire intrapreneurial spirit and put forth their work in their areas of preference.

(*c*) *Rewarding ideas*

Innovative ideas should be rewarded by the management, irrespective of whether the ideas are/can be converted into products/product features or not. Recognition for creativity is a must for motivating the employees and for bringing out their passion for intrapreneurship. No doubt, it is the organization that takes the risk when a new product is introduced. The organization will be rewarded by the market if the product turns out to be a success. If the product fails, it may bring great losses to the organization. But any organization that gives priority to innovation, acts with the firm belief that one successful innovation will wipe away the ill effects of many failures. If an employee puts forth his efforts and come up with an idea that does not click, still the management should not fail to reward the employee for the simple reason that his contribution has not taken off well. If not rewarded, it will dampen the intrapreunerial spirit of the employee. Moreover, any reward is not going to cost much for the organization. It is the mind-set of the top management that matters than the money involved.

(d) Accepting failures/mistakes

As long as an employee is sincere in his attempt, clear in his objective to contribute his maximum to the betterment of the organization, the employee should not be punished/ignored for the failures that have confronted the organization and for losses that have been inflicted upon the organization due to failed attempts. Failures are part of the game. No one can succeed always. The management should have the heart to accept genuine failures and encourage/motivate the employees concerned to proceed further in their direction, keeping in view the causes for the earlier failures and overcoming them with shrewd determination.

(e) Engaging employees at all levels

Innovative ideas can come from any employee. Across the board, the culture of intrapreneurship should be implanted and grown at all levels. No employee should be left behind. This will build the confidence levels of the employees and will also strengthen internal communication in the organization.

(f) Training the employees on intrapreneurship

There must be enough opportunities for the employees to vent out their entrepreneurial passion. The only thing required to be done is that the employees should be made aware of the fact that the management will be in support of intrapreneurs in their attempt to bring out their entrepreneurial talents. This training is more of a confidence building measure and making the employees feel free about sharing their views/ideas without any apprehensions or hesitations.

(g) Developing an intrapreneurial process

Creating awareness among the employees about intrapreneurship, embedding and nurturing an intrapreneurial culture in the organization etc., are the prerequisites for converting those employees with entrepreneurial shills into intrapreneurs. However, for smoothing out the transition and to offer continued support to these breed of employees, there must be a system in place in the organization that guides intrapreneurial initiatives into realities. This can be achieved by introducing an intrapreneurial process that is thorough, fool-proof, user-friendly, timely and free from the clutches of bureaucracy. Once such a process is established, it will pave way for the emergence of many intrapreneurs from among the employees.

4.24. MANAGEMENT OF INNOVATION

Innovation management has become an important part of the operations of many businesses. This is because of the fact that business firms are under constant pressure to innovate to sustain themselves. Gone are the days when innovations were managed in an adhoc way.

For efficiently managing innovation, the management has to plan and act systematically. The following are some of the areas to be concentrated for managing innovations better:

- The technology strategy of the organization should be framed in such a way that it integrates with the overall business strategy of the organization. Technology should be part of the business strategy. Technology should not be thought of, as a separate entity, after finalizing the business plan. It has been established that firms that have not integrated technology into their business strategy have not been able to derive full benefits out of their technology. If there is no integration, the firms may be landing upon an inappropriate technology, purchase and implement a wrong technology, purchase a technology at the wrong time or may not be able to implement a technology properly, all of these leading to poor return on the investments made on technology.
- New product development time should be kept to the minimum. It should be ensured that new product development does not get delayed due to want of resources. The objective should be to reduce the concept-to-commercialization time so that a company can take a business concept to the market at the earliest. Any delay will cost heavily as the company may lose the first-mover advantage, if some other competitor comes up with the same/similar product earlier.
- Technology transfer should be handled meticulously. Technology transfer is a strategic decision. Both acquiring a technology and selling a technology fall under the domain of technology transfer. The legal conditions subject to which the technology transfer is effected needs to be studied scrupulously and advice/opinion of legal experts shall be obtained to protect one's position. The tradeoff between developing a technology and buying a technology shall be assessed carefully and correctly and a suitable decision should be arrived at. Similar to buying a technology, equal care should be taken in selling a technology and the mode of selling (outright sale/licensing/franchising etc.,) shall be decided from a strategic point of view.
- When an innovation programme demands men and material resources from across many departments, such interdisciplinary projects will be associated with a lot of complexities in managing the resources. The organizational structure should be conducive for smooth function of the organization as well as effective and efficient functioning of the innovation programmes. A project based organization structure can be thought of for handling major innovation initiatives.

- Every organization will be gifted with certain exceptionally talented people. Such talents may be present at any level in the hierarchy. The management should identify such talents and groom them properly in the area of Research & Development, which will go a long way in building a core team of knowledgeable and committed professionals who can lead the organization in the technology front.
- The organization should develop a supportive culture for innovation and individual initiatives should be adequately rewarded and encouraged.
- When the size of the organization grows, it will become difficult to integrate the different divisions and unify their actions towards innovations. Under such situations, a Cross Functional Team can be formed, drawing personnel from different functional departments and entrusting the team with the responsibility of achieving better coordination and integration between manufacturing, R&D and marketing departments. This will help achieve synergy and improve the effectiveness of innovation efforts.
- Free flow of communication is important for innovations to happen. Barriers to communication exist at different levels which filter vital information from flowing upwards. This prevents the top management from knowing the ground realities and the strengths and weakness of the organization with regard to innovations. The top management should identify the barriers and eliminate them, thereby ensuring that open and free communication happens in the organization without any hurdles. An honest conversation between the organizational members will throw open the issues for discussion and this will pave way for capitalizing on the organization's strengths towards innovations.

Review Questions

1. Explain the role of Research and Development activities in an organization in Technology Generation.
2. Define the term 'Creativity'. What are its characteristics?
3. Give a brief account of 'Creativity Gap'.
4. Explain the role of creativity in organizational growth.
5. What are the steps to be taken to foster creativity in organizations?
6. Distinguish between Lateral thinking and Linear thinking.
7. Explain the techniques for stimulating Lateral thinking.
8. Distinguish between discovery and invention.

9. Distinguish between invention and innovation.
10. What are the two types of inventions? Explain them in brief.
11. Define Innovation. What are the characteristics of innovation?
12. What are the characteristics of innovative organizations?
13. Explain the different types of innovations.
14. Distinguish between Product Innovation and Process Innovation.
15. Enumerate the risks associated with innovation.
16. Explain the process of innovation at the enterprise level, with the help of Technology Push Model and Market Pull Model.
17. What is meant by 'Break-through' innovation?
18. Describe the various sources of innovation.
19. What are the myths associated with innovation?
20. What is meant by 'Kaizen'? Distinguish between 'Kaizen' and incremental innovation.
21. Identify some of the causes that may lead to failure of innovations.
22. Define 'Technology Transfer'. Explain the different types of Technology Transfer.
23. Explain the different channels through which Technology Transfer can be effected.
24. Explain the barriers to Technology Transfers and the ways to overcome these barriers.
25. What is 'Reverse Engineering'? What are the stages involved in the process of Reverse Engineering?
26. Define 'Value Analysis' and 'Value Engineering' and briefly explain the process of Value Engineering.
27. Give a detailed account of the status of innovations in Indian industry.
28. Define intrapreneurship. Explain the conditions favourable for the growth of intrapreneurship in an organization.
29. What are the aspects to be considered in the management of innovation?

Technology Absorption and Technology Diffusion

5 CHAPTER

5.1. TECHNOLOGY ABSORPTION

This refers to acquisition of a technology followed by its assimilation. Technology acquisition is obtaining a new technology in the form of know-how, a product or a process by a firm. Technology acquisition aims only at acquiring a technology, whereby the firm that has acquired the technology will become the owner of the technology. A firm is said to have absorbed a technology if it has made use of the technology acquired and has reaped benefits out of it. A technology acquired by a firm will not bring any benefit to the firm unless the acquired technology is put into use. Thus, while the focus of technology acquisition is only to acquire a technology, the focus of technology absorption is to make beneficial use of the technology. By acquiring a technology, a firm can gain technological advantage over competing firms, but the firm can convert it into competitive business advantage only by absorbing the acquired technology. The acquired technology may be used as it is or the firm that has acquired the technology may carry out further modifications/developments and then make use of the technology. Thus, the term 'Technology absorption' refers to the acquisition of a technology, carrying out developments in the acquired technology and putting the technology into some beneficial use.

When a new technology (or for that matter anything new) is introduced in an organization, the employees seek to get answers for the two questions, viz., 'How useful is this for me?' and 'How easy is it to use?' The employees' perceptions to these two aspects will create a favourable or an unfavourable disposition towards the technology being introduced. Thus, perceived usefulness and perceived ease of use are the two factors that lead to acceptance or rejection of a technology. Only, if the perceptions among the employees are in favour of the new technology it will be easily absorbed into the organization. Otherwise, it will require a great effort on the part of the top management to absorb a new technology in an organization.

5.2. TECHNOLOGY ADOPTION

When a technology is absorbed as it is, without changing any of the parameters of the technology, it is referred to as Technology adoption. According to Rogers, technology users go through five stages before they can adopt a new technology, viz., (1) awareness (2) interest (3) evaluation and (4) Trail. The technology adoption process is depicted in Fig. 5.1.

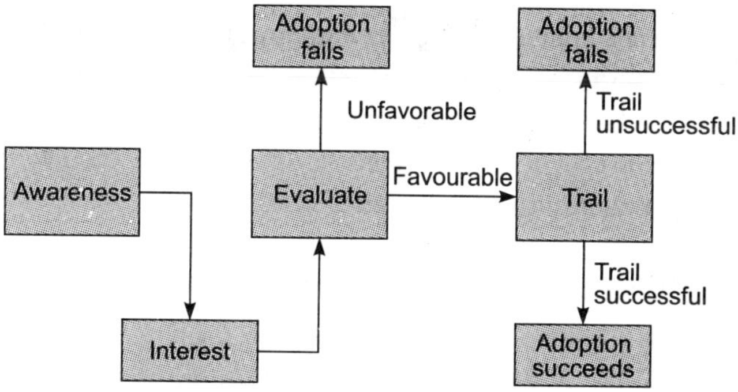

Fig. 5.1 Technology adoption process

5.3. TECHNOLOGY ADAPTATION

When a technology is absorbed by modifying (or altering/changing) some of the parameters of the acquired technology, it is referred to as Technology adaptation.

Need for technology adaptation

Technology adaptation will be necessitated under the following circumstances:

- A technology acquired may not be exactly suitable for the market/customers that a firm caters to. Based on the customer requirements, certain parameters of the acquired technology may be required to be modified so that the products/services will attract market acceptance.
- The firm that has acquired a technology may be required to invest on plant and machinery and on other resources which may require a huge financial outlay. The firm may opt to make use of the existing set of plant and machinery and other resources wherever possible in order to reduce the capital investment. This attempt will also require modification of certain parameters of the acquired technology.
- A technology may involve the use of certain bought out parts/components to be included in the final product. If the parts/components to be bought out are not available, the firm may have to plan for it suitably and do the required modifications in the acquired technology.

- A technology acquired may be one that does not comply with the statutory requirements. For example, there can be restrictions on the quality of the effluents produced in the production process. Such restrictions may warrant modification of the acquired technology.
- The technology acquired may, at times, not suit the local conditions in terms of techno economic factors. For example, machines produced in a country where the cost of labour is higher as compared to the cost of electricity will have such features that minimizes manpower requirement for operating the plant and maximizes the level of automation. When such a technology is acquired by a firm in another country where the cost labour is comparatively cheaper and the cost of electric power is comparatively costlier, the technology needs to be modified to suit the local conditions.

5.4. MANAGEMENT OF TECHNOLOGY ABSORPTION

Every organization that has plans to acquire and absorb a technology shall plan for absorbing the technology within the shortest possible time. A firm decides to acquire a technology only after a detailed study and after getting fully convinced that the technology proposed to be acquired and absorbed will give the firm a competitive edge.

Having convinced about the advantages of going for the acquisition of a technology, early absorption will help the firm reap the benefits early. Hence, a firm should identify the likely impediments in the process of technology absorption and should plan for early absorption. At times, it may so happen that a firm may prefer to postpone technology absorption for sometime due to the following reasons:

- Employees may offer resistance for introducing latest technologies, fearing adverse effects on them. The firm may take time to educate the employees and to make the conditions conducive for implementing the new technology. New technology absorption may adversely affect the existing business/ operations of the firm. For example, the sales of existing products may get adversely affected if new, improved products are introduced in the market. It could be beneficial for the firm to first exhaust the sale of existing stock of products before releasing the new products into the market. This may delay to some extent the early absorption of technology.
- Resource constraint may be one of the reasons for the delayed absorption of technology. A firm may not have adequate funds to invest in new/additional equipments; there may be shortage of skilled man power; time may be required to train the employees in tune with the requirements of implementing a new technology.
- Lack of direction, preoccupation with other activities, lack of initiative from the top management, delay in finalization of the terms of technology transfer

agreements etc., are some of the reasons for the delayed absorption of technology.

5.4.1. Delayed Technology Absorption and Its Consequences

Delayed absorption of technology will have the following adverse effects:

- For a firm that delays technology absorption, reaping of the benefits of technology will also get delayed.
- Delayed technology absorption means delayed entry into the market (with the products of latest technology). This time gap may sometime prove very detrimental if some other company which was working parallel on the same technology enters the market first. Under such conditions, the firm that has delayed its technology absorption will find it difficult to penetrate the market.
- Delayed absorption of technology will lead to increased cost. In order to ensure that the technology absorption takes place at the appropriate time, the firm should plan in advance, anticipate the likely hurdles that it may face on its way to technology absorption and should have remedial measures in hand to tackle the hurdles. Effective communication, well thought-out plan, development of time schedule for completion of the different activities involved in the process of technology absorption, unambiguous and clear-cut agreements with transferors of technology incorporating provisions for all eventualities, training the workers in the new technology area and making them receptive to the new technology, hiring the required number of skilled employees (with specific skill sets required for the job) wherever necessary etc., are some of the factors that deserve attention of the top management if it wants to avoid delay in technology absorption.

5.4.2. Steps to be Taken for Avoiding Delay in Technology Absorption

- Employees' active participation is a prerequisite for efficient absorption of technology in an organization. It is only the employees who are going to make technology absorption a reality. Hence, all the employees at the different levels of the organization must be involved in the process right from the beginning. They must be made party to the discussions/deliberations and decisions on acquiring a new technology. When the employees are convinced that a new technology acquired by the organization is for the benefit of the organization as well as for their individual benefit, the absorption process will be smooth and fast.
- When a technology acquired is a new/sophisticated one and when the required skilled man power for effectively embedding the technology in the organization

is not available, absorption will get delayed. The management shall identify the deficiency in skill level if any and hire personnel of required skill and knowledge and also train the existing employees adequately.

- In any technology acquisition process, it is the top management that is more convinced about the long term advantages to the organization of acquiring the technology. Hence, the top management shall be committed to technology absorption and should take the lead in guiding the entire organization towards that goal.
- The progress of technology absorption shall be continuously monitored and periodical reviews of the progress shall be conducted at different levels in the organization. Hurdles noticed, if any, shall be removed immediately.
- Continuous monitoring and periodical reviews will be effective only if time-bound targets are fixed for the different stages of absorption and the actual progress is compared with the targeted progress.
- Technology absorption will come across many hurdles in the process since it involves close coordination of personnel from across many departments. Hence, to ease out the process, multifunctional teams shall be formed and entrusted with the task of facilitating the technological absorption process.
- Technology absorption brings about a lot of changes in an organization. Change management can be effective only if there is an effective communication system in place in the organization.

5.5. TECHNOLOGY DIFFUSION

Technology diffusion refers to the spread of a new technology amongst the potential market and its absorption by the users, whereby the users get new products/processes/services that are based on the new technology. Technology diffusion may take place from a current user to a potential user, from the owner of the technology to the user, from one region to another, from one industry to another, from one country to another etc. Since a new technology paves way for innovations, diffusion of a new technology across various industries/markets leads to finding out new usages or new applications of the technology by innovating new products/processes/services. Hence, the term 'Innovation-diffusion' is also sometimes used in the place of Technology-diffusion.

According to Rogers, technology diffusion is a process during which an innovation is communicated among members over time.

There is a subtle difference between adoption and diffusion of technology. While technology adoption is an individual process, technology diffusion is a group phenomenon and it is the sum total of technology adoption of several individuals/firms over a period of time.

5.5.1. Factors Influencing Technology Diffusion

There are many factors that influence the diffusion of technology and the rate at which technology gets diffused. Some of them are discussed below:

(a) Perceived benefits of the innovation

If the benefits of the innovation are obviously visible, its adoption will be easier and quicker. The rate of diffusion will also be faster if the users perceive greater benefits from the new technology than what they get from the existing technology. It may be noted that it is not just the supremacy of a new technology over an existing technology that matters. What is more relevant is the users' perception of the benefits that the new technology might offer. Only when the users believe that switching over to the new technology will be to their advantage, they will go further with acquisition and absorption of the new technology. Thus, diffusion of an innovation and the rate at which it gets diffused depend on the perception of the technology in the minds of the users.

(b) Complexity of the technology

If a technology/innovation is complex and it creates an impression among the users that it will be difficult to be put into use, its acceptance will be slower.

(c) Trailability

Trailability refers to the ease with which an innovation can be tested/experimented. If a user finds it easier to test/experiment with a new innovation, he/she is more likely to adopt it since the technology will give him/her the required confidence to adopt it.

(d) Observability

An innovation should be 'visible' to others in order to be accepted by them. An innovation that is more visible will prompt quicker communication among peers and like-minded individuals which in turn will create a condition favourable for adoption.

(e) Ease of use

The success of an innovation lies in offering products that are easy to use/services that are easy to be offered and obtained. Ease of use will encourage adoption.

(f) Level of risk involved

The perceived level of risk should be minimum. In spite of promising returns on investment, ease of use, better trailability and better observability, an innovation that comes with a higher level of risk will not find adequate number of adopters. People will follow a 'wait and watch' approach in adopting such types of high-risk innovations.

Theory of technology diffusion explains how, why and at what rate a new technology spreads through the potential users. Evert Rogers, professor of rural sociology advocated his theory of technology diffusion in 1962. He defined technology diffusion as the process by which an innovation is communicated through certain channels over time among the members of a social system.

According to Rogers, *'Innovations that are perceived by individuals as having greater relative advantage, compatibility and less complexity and that can be tried and observed will be adopted more rapidly than other innovations.'*

5.5.2 S-Curves in Technology Diffusion

When the cumulative number of adopters of a technology are plotted against time, we get a 'S-Curve' of technology diffusion. The curve takes '-S- shape since the diffusion/ adoption in the initial stages is slow because the users are unfamiliar with a technology when it is first introduced in the market. With the passage of time, the technology is better understood by the users and they become more useful to them, facilitating adoption. Further, with the passage of time, organizations learn better ways of doing things and with organizational learning, coupled with improved scale of operation, the price of products fall down, all these leading to faster rate of adoption. Hence, the rate of diffusion/adoption increases with the passage of time. However, after some time, the market gets saturated and the rate of diffusion/adoption slows down. This results in a 'S-curve'. (Refer Fig. 5.2)

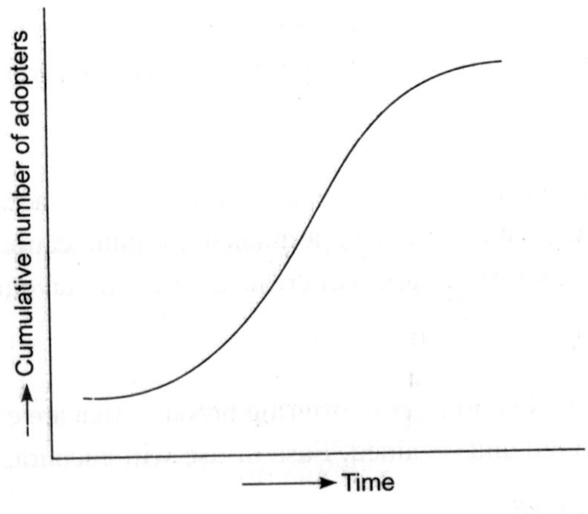

Fig. 5.2 Technology adoption pattern (S-curve)

Everett M Rogers' theory of product diffusion (or technology diffusion)

S-curve of technology diffusion is often explained as a process of different categories of people adopting a new technology at different points of time. The category of adopters proposed by Everett M Rogers has become widely established in marketing literature. This model classifies customers according to how quickly they adopt a new product. According to this model, there are five categories of customers and each category is defined by some internal personality trait. The five categories of customers are:

- Innovators
- Early adopters
- Early majority
- Late majority
- Laggards

Innovators are those who first adopt an innovation. They are younger in age, better educated and more informed. They have the courage to take risk and are prepared to purchase the product before it is tried and tested. They are found to form part of about 2.50% of the total number of adopters.

On the other extreme are laggards. They are risk averse and are skeptic about any technological advancement. They have limited education. They will not enter the market until a product is well advanced in its life cycle. They form about 16% of the adopters.

'Early adopters' are the second fastest category of adopters. They also have a greater financial liquidity. They occupy higher social status, are well educated and better exposed to business environment. They form about 13.50% of the total number of adopters. They possess the status of opinion leaders by virtue of their social and financial status. For marketers who market a new product, influence of early adopters is crucial in gaining market share. Early adopters give the required momentum for the product to penetrate the market. They go for purchase after investigating the product in depth.

The 'early majority' category adopts innovations after getting themselves fully convinced about the benefits of the innovation and in the process of seeking to justify their decision to adopt, they spend more time than the early adopters. They rely on recommendations from early adopters who have experience with the product. Also, their rate of technology adoption is slower as compared to innovators and early adopters. They form about 34.00% of the total number of adopters.

The 'late majority' category of adopters approaches innovation with a sense of skepticism. They take a longer time to get convinced about the usefulness of the innovation. They also tend to show a lower rate of adoption. They are motivated only by proven technology. They wait for early majority to use, get convinced and approve the product before they opt for buying the product. They read product reviews and get fully convinced before buying. They normally come from families with mediocre social status and they do not act as opinion leaders. However, they are in contact with 'early majority' category and with others in 'late majority' category. They form about 34.00% of the total number of adopters.

Laggards belong to the low income group and are the last to adopt an innovation that has already been proven in the market. They will buy a product only when they believe that they are maximizing value for their purchase. They will wait and watch till such time the price has fallen to such a level, which, in their opinion, gives them maximum value for their money. They form about 16% of the adopters. By the time the laggards go for buying, newer technologies would enter the market.

The phase of diffusion takes the form of a bell-shapped curve when plotted, taking the time span on the X-axis and the number of adopters on the Y-axis; the shape of the curve becomes S-shaped, when the cumulative number of adopters is plotted on the Y- axis. (Refer Fig. 5. 3 below)

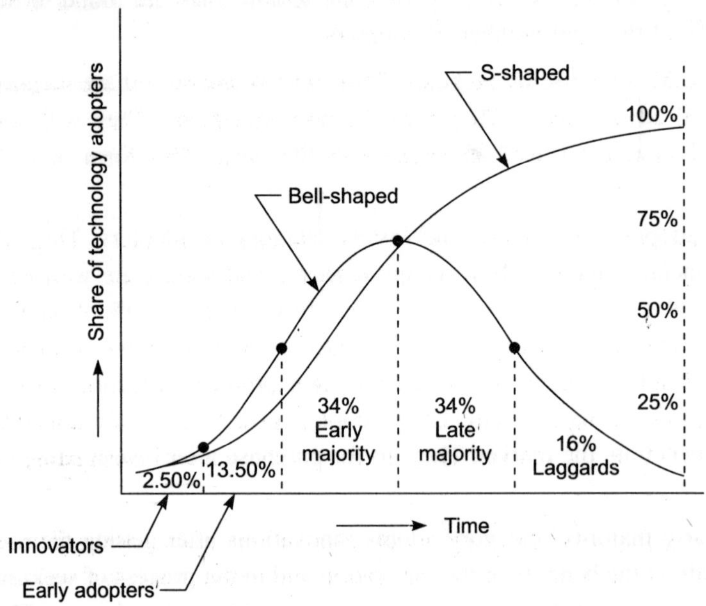

Fig. 5.3 Technology diffusion curve with adopter categories

5.6. TECHNOLOGY CYCLES

The 'S-curve' model of technology diffusion has been widely accepted and it has proved its validity over a period of time. This model points to the fact that technological change is cyclical in nature. When a technology S-curve reaches its limit, it indicates that the technology has fully matured and further improvement becomes stagnant. This is the time when new technologies emerge and replace the existing technologies.

Such new technologies which overtake existing technologies totally change the nature of competition in the industry (Refer Fig. 5.4). Emergence of new technologies brings new industry leaders while those who are complacent in updating their technology/adopting new technology lose out in the process. This process was named '*creative destruction*' by the renowned economist Joseph Schumpeter. He, in his work 'Capitalism, Socialism and Democracy' (1942), coined the term *creative destruction* and defined it as the process of industrial mutation that incessantly revolutionizes the economic structure from within, incessantly destroying the old one, incessantly creating a new one. Schumpeter argues that the process of creative destruction is the essential fact about capitalism. When creative destruction occurs, a new technology kills technology/technologies that is/are older. The emergence of Personal computers (led by Microsoft and Intel) destroyed many companies that were manufacturing mainframe computers. Though the evolution of such new technologies ushers in a state of disturbance, uncertainty and turbulence, it always proves to be a welcome change since the new technologies open up many vistas for innovation.

Referring to Fig. 5.4 we observe that in the initial phases, the efforts invested in a new technology may reap lower returns than the returns offered by the existing technologies. Hence, in the initial phases, there will be reluctance on the part of entrepreneurs to switch over from an existing to a new technology. But, after sometime, the new technology will prove its worth and its performance (and hence returns) for a given level of effort will be greater than that of the existing technology.

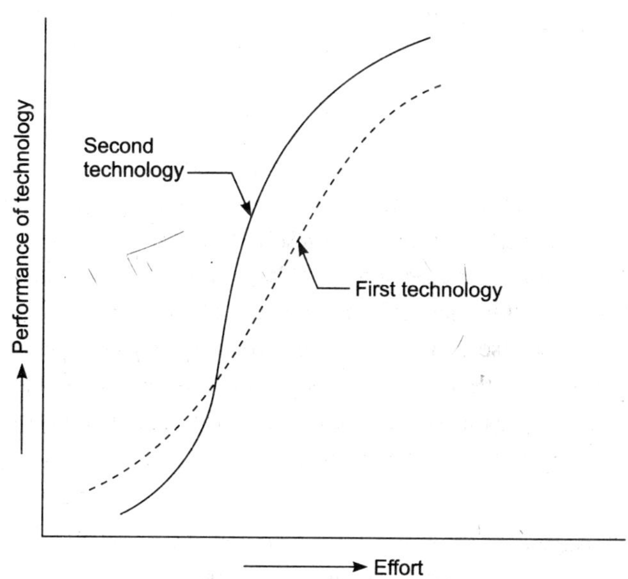

Fig. 5.4 New technology overtaking existing technology

The speed at which a new technology (that is superior to an existing technology) overtakes an existing technology depends on factors like the complexity of the knowledge underlying the new technology, the initial investment required to switch over to the new technology, the availability of required technical man power and technology resources. From the point of view of the innovator of the new technology, if he/she wants to improve the phase of adoption, he/she has to ensure that the users are not taken back due to the complexities involved in the technology.

5.7. DOMINANT DESIGN

The concept of Dominant design was introduced by William J. Abernathy and James M. Utterback in 1975. When a technology emerges, in the initial phase (which they called as *fluid phase*) there will be a lot of uncertainty both in the technology and in the market for the product. The products, though satisfies the needs of certain niche markets, will suffer from drawbacks like lesser reliability, crude form of design and exorbitant cost. The competing firms will introduce a number of alternative designs with improved design features, increased reliability and reduced cost. Incremental improvements in the design will be carried out continuously based on the market feedback. Eventually, the consumers and the producers arrive at a consensus on the desired product attributes and a dominant design emerges which becomes a de facto industry standard. A dominant design is one that suits almost all of the customer requirements/expectations. Abernathy and Utterback define dominant design as under:

'In many new product categories, the market accepts a particular product's design as one that defines the specifications for the entire product category; such a design is referred to as the dominant design.'

The dominant design gets stabilized and it establishes a stable architecture for the technology and this brings about standardization of products. Once a dominant design has been established for a product, the emphasis of competing firms shifts to process innovations and incremental innovations which will add further value to the products. The incremental innovations are attempted only to improve upon those components of the product that are within the stable architecture already arrived at. Utterback and Abernathy termed this phase as *specific phase,* because any innovation done during this phase are all specific to the dominant design. Since the dominant design is the one that is established and accepted as the industry standard, all competitors will be under obligation to stick to this design if they want to capture a reasonably good market share.

Prior to the emergence of the dominant design, firms are constantly experimenting. Till such time the dominant design emerges, design modifications will still be going on and hence firms cannot reap the benefits of economies of scale. By the time the dominant design emerges, there will be a large number of firms competing with one another, trying to make a breakthrough. Once a dominant design has emerged, some firms exploit the possible economies of scale. This creates entry barriers for other firms in the industry.

According to Utterback and Suarez (1993), the competitive effects of economies of scale becomes essential only after the emergence of a dominant design, when competition begins to take place on the basis of cost and scale in addition to product features and performance.

The dynamics of the marketplace gets modified once a dominant design emerges. The study of dominant designs in each category of products is very relevant and important for marketing managers since the dynamics of the marketplace is the basis for the formulation of marketing strategies.

5.8. DIFFUSION COMMUNICATION CHANNEL

There are two prominent channels of communication through which innovations (or technologies) get communicated and diffused. They are mass media channels and word-of-mouth communication. Word-of-mouth communication progresses very slowly to start with. With the passage of time, the rate at which the innovation/technology spreads will pick up. The number of adopters of a new technology/innovation on the basis of word-of-mouth communication, when plotted against time will take the shape of a bell-shaped curve. The rate of adoption will be slow to start with, but will gradually increase with the passage of time, will reach a peak and then will start falling. By the time the rate of diffusion has reached its peak, the technology would have become more prevalent and technology adopters would perceive lesser and lesser importance due to which the rate of adoption will gradually fall down, thus forming a bell-shaped curve.

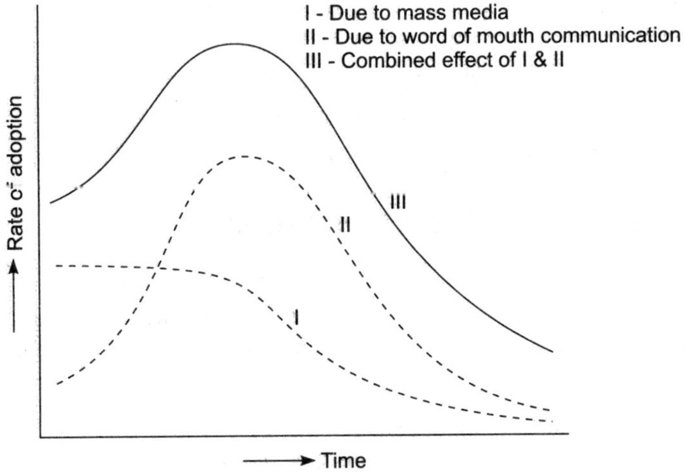

Fig. 5.5 Adoption-communication channel relationship

The influence of mass media in spreading technology will be great to begin with. This is because of the fact that mass media can have a wider reach instantaneously. However, the rate of adoption will fairly remain the same over a period of time and will then start falling down, after the technology loses its prominence.(Refer Fig. 5.5)

5.9. DIFFERENCES BETWEEN TECHNOLOGY ABSORPTION AND TECHNOLOGY DIFFUSION

Having understood the mechanism and nature of technology absorption and technology diffusion, we are now able to distinguish between the two.

- Technology absorption relates to a single unit/firm. It is concerned with making use of a newly acquired technology by a firm/company within its organization and within its associated concerns/affiliates. Thus, the scope of technology absorption is narrower and restricted to one entity. Technology diffusion is a broader concept and it relates to the spread and absorption of technology beyond the boundaries of a single firm. It embraces the total industry and thus it is wider in scope, as compared to technology absorption.
- By absorbing a new technology, a firm achieves specific technological and competitive business advantages. By diffusion of technology, the technology gets absorbed by all firms in an industry. Thus, due to diffusion of technology, all the firms that absorbed the technology stand benefitted and this leads to an overall increase in the stock of technological knowledge possessed by a nation.
- When a technology is absorbed by a firm, it acquires the technology from a source (the transferor) and assimilates the technology within the firm. In this process, the flow of technology is from the transferor to the transferee. The transferee stands benefitted by virtue of gaining technical and business advantages due to absorption of the technology. When more and more firms absorb a technology and come out with products of their own, certain firms that are committed to technology may come out with minor improvements over the acquired technology. Thus, technology diffusion also gives the original innovator an opportunity to learn from the followers and imitators.

5.10. BENEFITS OF TECHNOLOGY DIFFUSION

Technology diffusion benefits all players in an economy. With a faster phase of technology diffusion, more and more industries/business firms adopt/adapt new technologies with the result competition increases. Competition among business firms brings down prices of products/services which benefits the consumers. Competition also leads to quality improvements of products/services, which in turn bring benefits to consumers. Thus, consumers are able to get their money's worth and stand better placed. This in turn leads to increase in demand for products and services from the consumers, which facilitates mass production. Mass production further reduces the price to the consumers and at the same time enables the business firms to earn additional profits in terms of additional gross earnings. With the availability of technology based products and services at reasonable price and with the overall economic growth taking place, the standard of living of the people in the community improves. Thus, people in all sectors of the economy and the country as a whole benefit due to diffusion of technology.

5.11. MANAGEMENT OF TECHNOLOGY DIFFUSION

To begin with, an innovator firm enjoys a greater competitive advantage. When the technology starts diffusing, the competitive advantage enjoyed by the innovator firm gradually gets eroded. When the diffusion of technology, more and more firms start using the technology. Applications of the new technology in diverse fields get introduced and over a period of time, the technology becomes generic in nature. The many technology followers who have joined the stream acquire expertise and pose serious threats to the original innovator firm. The technology followers, being large in number, bring out many incremental innovations in the technology and start dominating the market. In order to handle such situations, an innovator firm should have a proper technology management system in place. The innovator firm should keep a close watch over the developments in the market and should at least match, if not overcome the subsequent technological developments. It is also essential that the innovator firm follows an open-ended approach for technology up-gradation/innovation and should not hesitate to learn from other existing/competing firms.

5.12. INDIAN TELECOM SECTOR — GROWTH THROUGH FASTER DIFFUSION

(Source: Data published by the Department of Telecommunications, Govt. of India and Dun & Broadstreet India report on Indian telecom Industry.)

The Indian Telecommunications industry is one of the fastest growing in the world. The Indian Government was committed to provide thrust to this sector, as providing easy, effective and cheaper mode of communication to the masses is bound to stimulate economic growth of the country in many ways. The telecommunication policies announced by the Government of India and the regulatory framework implemented by the Telecom Regulatory Authority of India (TRAI) provided a very conducive environment for the telecom service providers. This has made this sector very competitive, and consumers were able to get the services at a comparatively very cheaper tariff and also the accessibility of the services improved substantially. The total number of telephones has increased from about 430 million in March 2009 to about 926 million in December 2011. Substantial reduction in tariff rates due to stiff competition among the service providers and increased network coverage acted as catalysts for the growth of this sector.

Pre-Liberalisation Scenario

In the 1880s telecommunication services were merged with the postal system and came under the monopoly of the Department of Post and Telegraph. Till 1983, the Indian telecom sector was entirely under the ownership of the Government. In 1984, the private sector was allowed to take up only the manufacture of telecommunication equipments. In the same year, the Government of India set up an autonomous body, the Centre for Development of Telematics (C-DOT) with the objective of developing R&D activities in the telecom sector. It was set up to develop the state-of-the-art telecommunication technology to meet the needs of the Indian telecommunication network.

In 1985, there came the first breakthrough in the management of the telecom sector when the Government bifurcated the Department of Post and Telegraph and set up two separate departments, viz., the Department of Post and the Department of Telecommunication (DoT). The DoT was established as a wholly-owned Government operator for the entire telecom service operation in India. The responsibility for managing the planning, installation, maintenance, management, and operations of telecom services was entrusted with the DoT.

In 1986, the Government of India set up two new public sector corporations viz., MTNL (Mahanagar Telephone Nigam Limited) and VSNL (Videsh Sanchaar Nigam Limited) under DoT. MTNL was established to look after the operation of basic telephony services in the metros of Mumbai and New Delhi. VSNL was set up to operate, develop and accelerate international telecom services in India. The power to formulate telecom policies and regulation of the policies were retained by the DoT.

In 1989, the Telecom Commission was set up as an executive body to assist the DoT in policy regulation, licensing, wireless spectrum management, administrative monitoring of PSUs, research and development and standardisation/validation of equipment etc.

Liberalisation Policy 1991

In 1991, India came out with the new economic policy of liberalisation. The policy aimed at improving viability, competitiveness and efficiency of the Indian economy in the international market and also for enhancement and growth of international trade. To attain the objectives of new economic policy, the need for a telecom service of world class quality was felt essential.

In 1992, the telecom sector was deregulated with the Government unbundling the domestic basic services and the domestic value-added services (VAS) and allowing private sector participation in provision of value added system such as cellular and paging services.

National Telecom Policy 1994 (NTP-94)

The National Telecom Policy was announced in 1994. The policy was aimed at improving India's competitiveness in the global market and provided a base for rapid growth in exports.

The main objectives of NTP-1994 were:

- to ensure telecommunication is within the reach of all, i.e., to ensure availability of telephone on demand as early as possible
- to achieve universal service covering all villages, i.e., enable all people to access certain basic telecom services at affordable and reasonable prices
- to ensure world-class telecom services; to remove consumer complaints, resolve disputes and encourage public interface and provide a wide permissible range of services to meet the customer requirements and expectations at reasonable prices
- to ensure that India emerges as a major manufacturing base and major exporter of telecom equipments
- to protect the defence and security interests of the nation.

The NTP-94 policy eventually facilitated the emergence of Internet services in India on the back of established basic telephony communication network. This policy also paved way for the entry of the private sector in telephone services. The private sector participation in the sector was carried out in a phased manner. Initially the private sector was allowed in the value added services, and thereafter, it was allowed in the fixed telephone services. Subsequently, VSAT(Very Small Aperture Terminal — a type of two way satellite that transmits both narrow and broadband data to satellites in orbit) services were liberalized for private sector participation to provide data services to closed user groups.

Establishment of TRAI (Telecom Regulatory Authority of India)

The TRAI was established in 1997 to regulate telecom services, for fixation/ revision of tariffs, and also to fulfil the commitments made when India joined the World Trade Organisation (WTO) in 1995. With the establishment of TRAI, the regulatory function of telecom sector was entrusted with TRAI while the policy-making and operation functions remained with the DoT.

The functions allotted to the TRAI are:

(*a*) Recommending the need and timing for introduction of new service provider
(*b*) Protecting the interest of customers of telecom services
(*c*) Settling disputes between service providers
(*d*) Recommending the terms and conditions of license to a service provider
(*e*) Rendering advice to the Central government on matters relating to the development of telecommunication technology and any other matter applicable to the telecommunication industry in general.

New Telecom Policy 1999 (NTP-99)

Though the entry of the private sector in the field of telecommunication was made possible by the NTP-94, there were concerns raised by the private operators and investors about the viability as the revenue realized by them were very much below the targeted revenue. Hence, the Government of India decided to come up with a new telecom policy. Further, in order to achieve India's vision of becoming an IT superpower along with developing a world-class telecom infrastructure in the country, there was a need to develop a new telecom policy framework. Accordingly, the NTP 1999 was framed with the following objectives and targets:

- Providing affordable and effective communication for citizens was at the core of the vision and goal of the new telecom policy
- Providing a balance between provision of universal service to all uncovered areas including rural areas, and the provision of high-level services capable of meeting the needs of the economy
- Encouraging the development of telecommunication facilities in remote, hilly and tribal areas of the nation
- Facilitating India's journey to becoming an IT superpower by creating a modern and efficient telecommunication infrastructure taking into account the convergence of IT, media, telecom and consumer electronics
- Converting PCOs, wherever justified, into public telephone information centres having multimedia capability such as ISDN (Integrated Services Digital Network) services, remote database access, Government and community information systems etc., to bring about a competitive environment in both urban and rural areas by providing equal opportunities and level playing field for all players
- Providing a thrust to build world-class manufacturing capabilities and also strengthening research and development efforts in the country
- Achieving efficiency and transparency in spectrum management

- Protecting the defence and security interests of the country
- Enabling Indian telecom companies to become global players.

To achieve the above objectives of NTP 1999, the following specific targets were fixed:

- Make available, telephone on demand by 2002 and achieve a teledensity of 7% by 2005 and 15% by 2010
- Encourage development of telecom in rural areas by developing a suitable tariff structure so that it becomes more affordable and by also making rural communication mandatory tor all fixed service players and thus achieve a rural teledensity of 4% by 2010 and provide reliable transmission media in all rural areas.

Developments after 2000

The following major developments took place on the policy front of telecom sector after the year 2000.

- Establishment of Bharat Sanchar Nigam Ltd (BSNL) in the year 2000. [*BSNL took over the business of providing of telecom services and network management from the erstwhile Central Government Departments of Telecom Services (DTS) and Telecom Operations (DTO), with effect from 1st October 2000 on going concern basis. BSNL makes focused efforts & planned initiatives to bridge the rural-urban digital divide in ICT sector and it operates across India except New Delhi & Mumbai.*]
- Opening up of National Long Distance (NLD) and International Long Distance (ILD) services to competition in the year 2000.
- Privatisation of VSNL and the termination of monopoly of VSNL in the year 2012.
- Introduction of Unified Access Licensing (UASL) regime in the year 2003.[*Under this regime, both basic service operators and cellular carriers gained freedom to offer basic and/or cellular mobile services using any technology and this had ensured a fair competitive market for the service providers.*]
- Interconnection Usage Charges Regime in the year 2003.[*The TRAI implemented the Telecommunication Interconnection Usage Charges (IUC) Regulation during 2003 to fix the terms and conditions of interconnectivity between service providers, to ensure effective interconnection between different service providers and to regulate arrangements among service providers for sharing their revenue derived from providing telecommunication services.*]

- Announcement of Broadband policy in the year 2004. [*In December 2003, penetration of broadband and internet services in India was very low at 0.02% and 0.4% respectively. Hence, the Government of India announced the Broadband Policy on 2004 on the basis of TRAI recommendations to facilitate greater levels of penetration. The policy estimated the internet subscribers to grow to 40 million and broadband subscribers to grow to 20 million by 2010, which would include subscribers using various technologies. The Broadband Policy Framework virtualised creation of infrastructure through various access technologies, which could contribute to growth and could coexist. The policy aimed at creation of an environment for promoting knowledge-based society. It was also realised that improving broadband connectivity would bring about major implications such as creation of e-governance, online education, telemedicine networks and connectivity for rural knowledge centres, greater integration into the world economy through international voice and videoconferencing, lower prices for NLD and ILD etc. The new broadband policy encouraged creation and growth of infrastructure through various access technologies that can mutually coexist such as optical fibre technologies, digital subscriber lines on copper loop, cable TV network, satellite, and terrestrial wireless technologies etc.*]
- Enhancement of Foreign Direct Investment limit in telecom sector from 40% to 74% in the year 2005.
- Permitting mobile number portability in the year 2008. [*Mobile Number Portability (MNP) enables subscribers to change their operators while retaining their number. This not only gives more choice to customers but also leads operators to further improve their services to retain their customers. The DoT issued guidelines for MNP service license on August 1, 2008.*]
- Telecommunication Interconnection Usage Charges (Tenth Amendment) Regulations, in the year 2009. [*Interconnection is very important for the service providers and users. A variety of access networks —fixed and mobile, national long distance network and international long distance networks have to interconnect with each other to make local, national and international calls possible. In order to have seamless end-to-end service, it is imperative to have an effective interconnection usage charges (IUC) regime in place. The regulation aimed to cover arrangements among service providers for payment of IUC for telecommunication services, covering basic service, which included WLL(M) services(mobile wireless in local loop), cellular mobile service providers and long distance operators throughout India.*]

	No. of Telecom subscribers (in million)			Growth (%)	Teledensity*	Ratio of mobile to fixed
	Fixed	**Mobile**	**Total**			
1991	5.07		5.07		0.60	
1992	5.81		5.81	14.60	0.67	
1993	6.80		6.80	17.04	0.77	
1994	8.03		8.03	18.09	0.89	
1995	9.80		9.80	22.04	1.07	
1996	11.98		11.98	22.24	1.26	
1997	14.54	0.34	14.88	24.21	1.56	0.02
1998	17.80	0.88	18.68	25.54	1.94	0.05
1999	21.59	1.20	22.79	22.00	2.33	0.06
2000	26.51	1.88	28.39	24.57	2.86	0.07
2001	32.44	3.58	36.02	26.88	3.58	0.11
2002	41.48	13.00	54.48	51.25	4.30	0.31
2003	42.58	33.58	76.16	39.79	5.10	0.79
2004	45.00	50.00	95.00	24.74	7.04	1.11
2005	49.00	76.00	125.00	31.58	10.66	1.55
2006	40.43	149.50	189.93	51.94	17.16	3.70
2007	40.77	177.79	218.56	15.07	18.22	4.36
2008	39.41	261.08	300.49	45.96	26.22	6.62
2009	37.96	391.76	429.73	43.01	36.98	10.32
2010	36.96	584.32	621.28	44.57	52.74	15.81
2011	34.73	811.60	846.33	36.22	70.89	23.37
2012	32.17	919.17	951.34	12.41	78.66	28.57

**Number of telephone connections in use for every 100 individuals living in that area.* [The advent of wireless technology has led to the tremendous growth in teledensity in the country.]

The Indian telecom sector has proved to be an international success story. The sector has witnessed a spectacular growth after 1991. There was a situation during the 1980s when an applicant had to wait for about three years to obtain a telephone connection. In a span of less than two decades the situation has changed totally and telephone companies have now started wooing customers. This has been made possible due to effective diffusion management on the part of the Government of India which introduced conducive polices, collaborated with scientific agencies and pushed through a telecom revolution through sustained effort. The Government of India gave thrust to telecom sector since it has been recognized world over that telecom services is an important tool for the socio-economic development of a nation and for ensuring rapid growth and modernization of various sectors of the economy. As seen from the above policy initiatives of the Government, it is evident that the Indian telecom sector has witnessed the most fundamental structural and institutional reforms since 1991 that has led to effective diffusion of the latest technologies in the country. Despite the economic growth taking place in the country, India continues to find it difficult to channelize its resources towards activities that directly lead to economic development, since there are many other areas that demand a share of the Government's financial support. Hence, the Government had little to do to increase the number of land line telephone connections since more than half of India's rural population does not have even access to electricity. Hence, the Government had to necessarily rely on mobile technology. Market oriented regulation that encouraged competition in terms of both the number of competitors and the breadth of services that they can offer has played an important role, which in turn had a cyclic effect of attracting the service providers, eventually leading to a effective and faster diffusion in the sector.

Review Questions

1. Define the following terms : (*a*)Technology acquisition (*b*) Technology absorption (*c*) Technology adoption (*d*) Technology adaptation.
2. Explain the need for Technology adaptation.
3. What are the factors to be considered in the management of Technology absorption?
4. What are the consequences of delayed technology absorption? Enumerate the steps that companies must take to speed up the process of technology absorption.
5. Define 'Technology Diffusion'. What are the factors that influence Technology Diffusion?
6. Explain Everett M Rogers' Theory of Technology Diffusion (or Explain the S-Curve of technology diffusion.).
7. Explain 'Technology Cycles'. What, according to Schumpeter, is creative destruction?
8. Define the term 'Dominant design'. Explain the behaviour of market dynamics before and after the emergence of Dominant design.
9. What are the two main channels of communication through which technology diffusion takes place? Describe the phase of diffusion over time through these two channels.

10. Distinguish between Technology Absorption and Technology Diffusion.
11. How does Technology Diffusion benefit an economy?
12. Enumerate a few important aspects that need to be considered in managing Technology Diffusion.
13. "Indian Telecom Industry witnessed a faster phase of diffusion in Telecom sector due to the coordinated efforts of the Government of India, Scientific agencies and Service providers supported by the huge unfulfilled demand in the industry" —Support this statement with an analysis of the Indian Telecom sector.

Business Strategy and Technology Strategy

6

CHAPTER

6.1. STRATEGY AND STRATEGIC MANAGEMENT

The term 'Strategy' is derived from the Greek word *strategos* which means generalship. In other words, it refers to the direction of military force. In business parlance, the term strategy refers to the determination of long term objectives of an organization and the adoption of courses of actions to achieve the objectives and execution of the planned actions by allocation of the required resources. It is the organization's basic plan that expresses the policies, methods and courses of action for translating the objectives into results.

Strategic Management is the process by which an organization formulates its objectives and manages to achieve the objectives. While planning is only about programming, strategizing is about discovering and programming.

According to William F. Glueck, Strategic Management is a stream of decisions and actions which leads to the development of an effective strategy or a set of strategies to help achieve corporate objectives.

According to Arthur Sharplin, Strategic Management is the formulation and implementation of plans and carrying out activities relating to the matters which are of vital, pervasive or continuing importance to the total organization.

Ignor Ansoff defines Strategic Management as a systematic approach to a major and increasingly important responsibility of general management: to position and relate the firm to its environment in a way which will assure its continued success and make it secure from surprises.

Thus, strategic management is the deciding upon the long term goals and objectives of an enterprise and adopting the required courses of actions and allocation of required resources that are necessary to achieve the goals and objectives. In other words, it is the set of activities related to the formulation and implementation of strategies to achieve the organizational objectives.

The operating decisions of a firm are oriented towards improving the profitability of the current operations of the firm and hence these decisions aim at improving the efficiency of the firm's resource conversion process. (example: decisions relating to production scheduling, pricing, marketing, inventory management etc.)

As against operating decisions, strategic decisions relate to fundamental questions like what business the firm should be in and how it should conduct its business. They have a long term perspective. They are non repetitive in nature and are taken by the top management. These decisions are concerned with the allocation of the total resources at the disposal of the firm among its product — market opportunities.

6.1.1. Functions of Strategic Management

- Planning for the future by developing the organizational objectives.
- Developing an organizational structure that can fulfill the organizational objectives and developing effective information system.
- Motivating the employees and getting the cooperation of all the employees and different members of the organization.
- Using necessary control systems to ensure that the organization functions in such a way that it meets its objectives.
- Providing leadership for the long term survival of the organization.

6.1.2. Process of Strategic Management

Strategic Management is a continuous process. It involves the following phases:

I. Strategy Planning (also called 'strategizing')
   (*a*) Environmental scanning
   (*b*) Defining the vision, mission and objectives of the business
   (*c*) Identification of the strategic alternatives
   (*d*) Formulating the right strategy

II. Strategy Implementation and

III. Strategy Evaluation and Control

I. *Strategy Planning*

(*a*) *Environmental scanning:*

Environmental scanning refers to the acquisition and use of information gathered from sources external to the company. Every organization operates in a social system. The environment offered by the social system consists of many factors like the society, the competitors, the peers, the legal framework in which business has to operate, the political structure, the technology, the psychological and cultural framework of the people etc., An organization constantly interacts with its environment, i.e., with the various factors that constitute the environment.

Scanning the environment helps to achieve the following:

- To understand the influence of external forces on the organization.
- To assess the threats and opportunities, so that proactive actions can be taken to avoid surprise shocks. Environmental threat is a challenge to an organization. The challenge is posed by conditions in the environment that are unfavourable to the organization. Unless the environmental threats are identified and the organization takes proactive steps to counter the effects of such threats, it will cost heavily on the organization. Identifying the opportunities offered by the environment and exploiting them using the internal strengths of the organization will help a company gain competitive advantage. Environmental scanning entails gathering both factual as well as subjective information on the business environment in which a company is operating or planning to enter. Thus, environmental scanning helps to improve the accuracy of planning efforts.

Though environmental scanning is the prime duty of the top management, large companies assign the task of scanning to one or more employees. Scanning can be proactive or reactive. A reactive scanning is an adhoc scanning done in response to a crisis/problem faced by the organization. Proactive scanning is a continuous process that is carried out to get a continuous flow of new ideas, so that the company can plan its future courses of actions.

(b) Defining the Vision, Mission and Objectives of the business

Vision: According to Miller and Dess, vision is a category of intensions that are broad, all-inclusive and forward thinking.

Vision statement answers the question 'What do we want to become?' It is the long term perspective of the business. Vision statement gives the direction to the organization and without a vision, a business will wander aimlessly and efforts will get diverted and wasted. Vision statement identifies what the organization intends to be in the future. Vision statement moves the organization towards a greater purpose. When an organization finds it difficult to get a clear answer for an issue and at situations requiring critical decisions to be taken, vision statements will be of help.

Requirements of a vision statement:

- It must be short, simple, to the point, unambiguous and powerful.
- It must provide a clear direction without leaving scope for misinterpretation.

- It must inspire the stake holders and should have an emotional impact.

Vision statement of Tata Motors:

"To be the best in the manner in which we operate, best in the products we deliver and best in our value system and ethics."

Vision statement of Reliance Industries Ltd.,:

"Through sustainable measures, create value for the nation, enhance quality of the life across the entire socio economic spectrum and help spearhead India as a global leader in the domains where we operate."

Vision Statement of McDonald's:

"We are committed to doing what is right. To being a good neighbour and partner in the community; To conduct our business with the environment in mind."

As seen from the above vision statements, we find that they give a clear direction that the company should follow in the long run. All the business strategies that a company takes should be aligned with the company's vision.

Mission: Mission statement answers the questions, 'What are the things to be done? and 'How are things to be done?' in order to reach the vision.

According to Thompson, mission is the essential purpose of the organization, concerning particularly why it is in existence, the nature of businesses it is in and the consumers it seeks to serve and satisfy.

Mission statements should be simple, clear, precise and feasible. Mission statements are more specific than vision statements and they establish broad guidelines of how the firm will achieve its vision over a period of time.

Mission statement of Indian Institute of Bankers and Finance

" To develop professionally qualified and competent bankers primarily through a process of training, examination and continuing professional development programmes."

Though Mission statement gives shape to the vision, they still do not provide tangible goals and objectives that must be met to achieve a firm's broader purpose. Hence, we make use of goals and objectives. Goals are no doubt the end results of a planned activity. The term 'goal' is sometimes getting confused with the term 'objective'. Sometimes, they are used interchangeably. However, there is a subtle difference between objective and goals. Objectives are open-ended attributes that an organization strives to achieve in the future. Goals are close-ended attributes that an organization strives to reach and are expressed in specific terms. For example, 'achieving increased market share' can be an objective while 'increasing the existing market share by 20% in the next year and increasing the market share by another 20% in the subsequent year' can be a goal.

(*c*) *Identification of the strategic alternatives*

An organization always interacts with its environment. The organization will have its own strengths and weaknesses. The environment may provide certain opportunities or pose certain threats to the organization. Based on the strengths and weaknesses of an organization, there can be various alternative strategies that can be thought of when the organization interacts with its environment. To begin with, all possible strategies are to be identified. Out of the many alternative strategies, a few of them may be more promising than the others. These promising strategies are to be separated out for further analysis.

(*d*) *Formulation the right strategy*

From out of the promising strategies, the one that is found most suitable should be identified. In identifying the most suited strategy, it must be borne in mind that the most suited strategy need not be the best strategy. A strategy may be the best among the alternative strategies. But, if the strategy is not in tune with the organizational objectives, it can not be the right choice. Thus, the chosen strategy should be one that falls in line with the organizational objectives.

II. *Strategy Implementation*

After the right strategy is identified, it must be properly implemented. Correct implementation of a chosen strategy depends on many factors. For example, the organizational structure must suit the chosen strategy. If the organization structure is not conducive, it must be suitable modified before implementing the strategy. There must be an effective leadership for effective implementation of any strategy. There must be an effective communication system in place in the organization. Functional policies should be developed in tune with the strategy. Available resources must be efficiently allocated to ensure smooth implementation of the strategy.

III. *Strategy Evaluation and Control*

The purpose of strategic evaluation is to verify the effectiveness of the strategy in achieving the organizational objectives/goals. Evaluation is done by comparing the actual performance of the organization with the goals. Control follows evaluation.

This is the last phase of the strategic management process. But, it is an on-going process. Strategy implementation must be continuously monitored for its effective implementation. Only when there is continuous monitoring and evaluation, suitable course of action can be taken when something goes wrong.

Thus, strategic management is a dynamic process and new actions are initiated whenever there is any change in any of the factors that affect the strategy.

6.2. TECHNOLOGY STRATEGY

Technology strategy is the plan of action aiming at attaining the technological goals of an organization.

Technology strategy at the national level

Before studying the technology strategy of an organization, let us have some discussion on the technology strategy of a nation. Can a country have a technology strategy?. The answer is a strong 'yes'. Since the economies in the world compete on the basis of technology and as technology has been recognized as the major wealth creation tool, it is mandatory that every country should have a technology strategy of its own. This will guide the industries in the economy in the right direction. The national technology strategy will indicate the direction in which the different industrial sectors in the economy are expected to progress. Technology strategy at the national level is formed by taking into account, the nation's priorities, the technological resources and competencies available within the country, the future technological goals aimed at, the financial and man-power resources available, the status of technological development that have taken place/are taking place outside the country, the technological gap between the country and the rest of the world etc.

The technology strategy of a nation can take two directions:

(*a*) It can be oriented towards development of technology indigenously, supporting and encouraging the indigenous strength in technology, acquiring advanced technologies from abroad, with maximum participation of indigenous talents and resources.

(*b*) It can take a proactive role and embrace new technology wherever it is available and bring it into the country, by way of technology transfer by Transnational and Multinational corporations. Such a strategy will invite FDIs in the sectors where technology is required by the country, thereby helping the diffusion of technology in the strategically important sectors and encouraging technology diffusion.

A country can also identify different sectors of the economy and pursue different technology strategies for the different sectors depending on the requirement.

Technology strategy at the enterprise level

The technology strategies of firms operating in a country are guided by the technology strategy of the country. As far as possible, individual firms operating in a country should align their technology strategy in line with the national priorities as this will provide a supportive environment.

The purpose of Technology Strategy is to attain a sustainable technical advantage thereby giving the firm a competitive edge in its business.

The distinct technological advantages possessed by the firm, the products/services that the firm can produce/offer making use of the technology available with the firm, the expectations of the customers, the technology status of existing players who are already in the field producing similar/near-similar products/services, strategies followed by them/likely to be followed by them etc., are to be given due consideration before formulating the Technology strategy.

In general, the steps involved in the formulation of Technology Strategy are as under:

(*a*) Identify all distinct technologies that are prevalent in the chosen field.

(*b*) Identify those technologies in other industries engaged in similar activity, or those technologies that are in the process of development in research labs/ institutes.

(*c*) Assess the direction of change that is likely to take lace in respect of key technologies.

(*d*) Assess the firm's relative technical strengths and capabilities and the scope for product/process improvements.

(*e*) Work out the cost-benefit aspects of making improvements in products/ processes.

(*f*) Select a Technology strategy after assessing the relevance/importance of all important technologies vis-à-vis the technological requirements, modifications/ improvements aimed at.

6.2.1. Components of Technology Strategy of a Firm

(*a*) *Identifying the industry*

The industry in which a firm opts to compete is a major deciding factor in the technology strategy. The present technological developments in the industrial sector will define the level of technology required by the firm. In general, a firm has to either start its operations with the latest technology being in use in the sector or has to plan for acquiring a still better/advanced technology in the start-up stage itself.

(*b*) *Industry forecasting*

Industry forecasting aims at gaining an understanding of the forces that are likely to affect the industry over long run and their influence in deciding the direction in which the industry is likely to develop. Since many economic forces affect an industry at a macro level, their effect will be felt at the micro level, i.e., at the level of individual business enterprises. Hence, if an individual business enterprise is blind to the happenings at the macro level, it will find the going tough. For example, the Multi Fibre Arrangement (MFA) governed the world trade in textiles and garments from

1974. The MFA imposed restrictions on the export of textiles and garments from the developing countries to the developed countries, by fixing 'quotas'. The MFA regime existed for 25 years, until 1994 when the Uruguay Round of Multilateral Trade Negotiations resulted in the Agreement on Textiles and Clothing (ATC). The ATC sought to phase out all quota restrictions in four phases spread over a period of 10 years. The first three partial phase-outs were in January 1995, January 1998 and January 2002 and the final one on January 2005. Since, there would be no quota restrictions for the export of textiles and garments from India (being a developing country) to any part of the world from 1st January, 2005, Indian textile industry got a boost; but, at the same time, Indian textile industry was under pressure to face the competition from international players and was under compulsion to produce quality products to compete in the international market. Sensing this situation, Government of India came out with a scheme of assistance to the textile industry by announcing a scheme called 'Technology Up-gradation Funds Scheme' and the scheme was meant to provide term loan to the Textile industry at international interest rates, in order to help them modernize their production facilities.

The following segments of Textile and Jute industry were covered under the scheme:

(*a*) Cotton ginning and pressing

(*b*) Textile industry covering:

- Silk reeling and twisting
- Wool scouring and combing and carpet industry
- Synthetic filament yarn texturising, crimping and twisting
- Spinning
- Viscose Staple Fibre (VSF) and Viscose Filament Yarn (VFY)
- Weaving, knitting and fabric embroidery
- Technical textiles including non-wovens,
- Garment/design studio/made-up manufacturing
- Processing of fibres, yarns, fabrics, garments and made-ups

(*c*) Jute industry

By the announcement of the Technology Up-gradation Funds Scheme, the above sectors of textile and jute industry were able to get funds at very cheaper rates for modernization of their industry by way of purchasing machines with latest technology. A business firm operating in this sector would have got benefited only if it was aware of the scheme of assistance extended by the Government of India.

(c) *Technology positioning*

A firm has to place itself in a strategic position within its industry, with regard to technology. The technology to be chosen by the firm is the one that the firm believes as the best for it. The firm has to decide on how the chosen technology will give it the required technological competitive advantage.

In Technology positioning, a firm has to choose the technology that it considers is the best suited for it. Before taking this decision, the firm has to decide whether it wants to be a Technology Leader or a Technology Follower. This is a strategic decision to be made considering the pros and cons of the decisions.

For one firm, assuming the 'Technology Leader' position may be best suited while for another firm 'Technology Follower' position may be the best one. It depends on a number of factors like the financial, technical and man-power resources available with firm and the risk-taking capacity of the firm.

The advantage of a Technology Follower is that the follower will be required to invest substantially lower costs for adoption of a technology instead of incurring a huge cost for creating a technological change. Further, any error/mistakes that are irreversible will affect the first-mover (or Technology Leader). Hence, the Technology leader had to face the cost of such irreversible errors. The technology follower plays safe and can avoid such irreversible mistakes.

(d) Assessing technological availability and sourcing of technology

These activities are often entrusted with the R&D wing of the firm. The required technologies can be identified and sourced from within the organization or from outside the organization or by a combination of both approaches. A Technology Audit will help to identify the technologies possessed by the firm and their standard. It will also throw light on the capacity of the firm to develop certain technologies that are required but are not available from external sources/are very costly when procured from external sources. The pros and cons of having internal source/external source/a combination of these sources for acquiring a technology should be assessed and a suitable decision is to be taken. Joint Venture, strategic alliances, Collaborative research are some of the means through which external and internal technological resources will be combined to acquire the required technology.

In assessing the availability of technology, a firm should not be merely guided by the narrow vision of finding the technology that is cheaper by cost. In fact, there can be synergic benefits between the technologies that are already with the firm and the technology newly acquired by the firm. The synergy can be achieved by correctly identifying the technology to be acquired new, keeping in consideration the type and nature of technologies already available with the firm.

(e) Embedding the technology into the firm

Once an ideally suited technology is identified, the technology should be embedded into the organization. Mere acquisition of technology is not enough. By acquisition, a firm will come into possession of the technology. But only when the technology is put into right use, the firm will derive the benefits of the technology. For achieving this, the technology should be absorbed into the organization and all those concerned who will be required to use the technology should be made fully conversant with the technology. The management should also see to it that the technology is made available to the right person at the right time. For achieving this, there must be a perfect Knowledge Management system in place in the organization. A technology acquired but kept unused will soon be forgotten and will cost heavily on the organization.

Another aspect of embedding technology in an organization is that, in the process of technology generation, technology transfer and technology implementation, it should be ensured that technology leakage does not take place. Technology should be protected through appropriate IPR (Intellectual Property Rights) protection mechanism.

(f) Technology exploitation

Exploitation of technology refers to making better use of technology. If a company owns a technology in which it is the market leader and if the technology has multiple uses, the best way to exploit the technology might be licensing the technology. This option will involve very little financial commitment on the part of the licensing company. Licensing a technology to one or more companies will help diffuse the technology. Technologies that have a wide range of applications are best suited for licensing since the rate of diffusion will be much faster and the licensing company can earn a good return in the form of licensing fee.

If the technology is one that has been newly developed by a company, the company has to first prove the technology through internal applications. The company has to first make use of the technology to produce its own products, in order to prove its worth. Once the technology gets stabilized and proven, it becomes capable of being licensed/transferred/sold etc.

Technology exploitation should be done as early as possible. This will help the technology to get market penetration faster. Faster diffusion of technology (through the process of licensing or any other means) will act as a deterrent for competition from attempts to develop similar technologies/products by competitors since they will find it riskier to develop and introduce a technology in the market when a similar/near similar technology has already established itself and diffused well. Thus, early exploitation of technology will keep the competitors away.

(g) Continuous improvement

Continuous improvement/up-gradation of technology is a pre-condition to remain technically competitive. Apart from keeping a watch on the technological developments taking place in the industry and taking steps to continuously update the technology, a firm has to have a strong thrust for continuous internal development of technology. This should be made a culture of the organization and continuous product, process and technological improvements should become a way of life in the firm and every employee should be made to realize that it is technology that drives the organization and the organizational culture should voluntarily involve every employee to continuously contribute for the technological development.

6.3. LINKING BUSINESS AND TECHNOLOGY STRATEGY

Business Strategy and Technology Strategy are like two sides of the same coin. They are to be closely linked. Technology Strategy should be formulated within the scope of the Business Strategy. Business Strategy and Technology strategy should be correctly linked and they should not attempt to take the organization in two different directions. Failure to integrate Business Strategy and Technology strategy has been found to be the major contributing factor for the decline in the business competencies of many firms.

The first pre-requisite for achieving effective linkage of Business and Technology strategies is that both the sides (i.e., the Business side and the Technological side) should agree on common priorities. Difficulties normally arise because of wrong perception. The business side may perceive that technology is a sub-set of business while the technologists may believe that business is a sub-set of technology. But, the reality is that, both are important and both have their relevance. Either is worthless without the other. The management should be able to align the business and technology strategies in the same direction to focus on achieving the organizational objectives.

The purpose of business strategy is to gain a sustainable economic advantage for the business while the purpose of technology strategy is to gain a sustainable technical advantage. A close look at this statement will reveal that the technology strategy, by providing technical advantage gives the business firm a competitive edge which goes to supplement the business strategy. Thus, these two strategies are interwined.

The business strategists and the technology strategists should work together and identify common ground for formulating their strategies. Some of the issues to be considered by both the sides before formulating their strategies are as under.

(*a*) The core business area of the firm

(*b*) The core competency of the firm

(*c*) Products/services that need to be improved upon

(*d*) New products/services that are to be produced/offered

(*e*) Relevance and importance of technology to the business of the firm

(*f*) Major business strategies of the firm

(*g*) Business strategies that require the use of technology

(*h*) The strategic advantages that the technology/technologies can provide to the business (*i*) The technologies that need to be given importance/thrust

(*j*) The technologies that can be developed in-house/to be acquired from outside for attaining competitive advantage.

(*k*) The sources of availability of technology and the preferred mode of acquisition

(*l*) The financial commitment required for developing/acquiring the proposed technology.

(*m*) The cost-benefit aspects of new technologies that are to be developed/acquired

Product-Technology matrix:

This is a tool for depicting the relationship between the products/services proposed to be produced/offered by a company and the technologies required for each of the products/services. This tool can also be used for the products/services that are already being produced/offered by the company. The matrix is constructed as below: (refer Fig. 6.1)

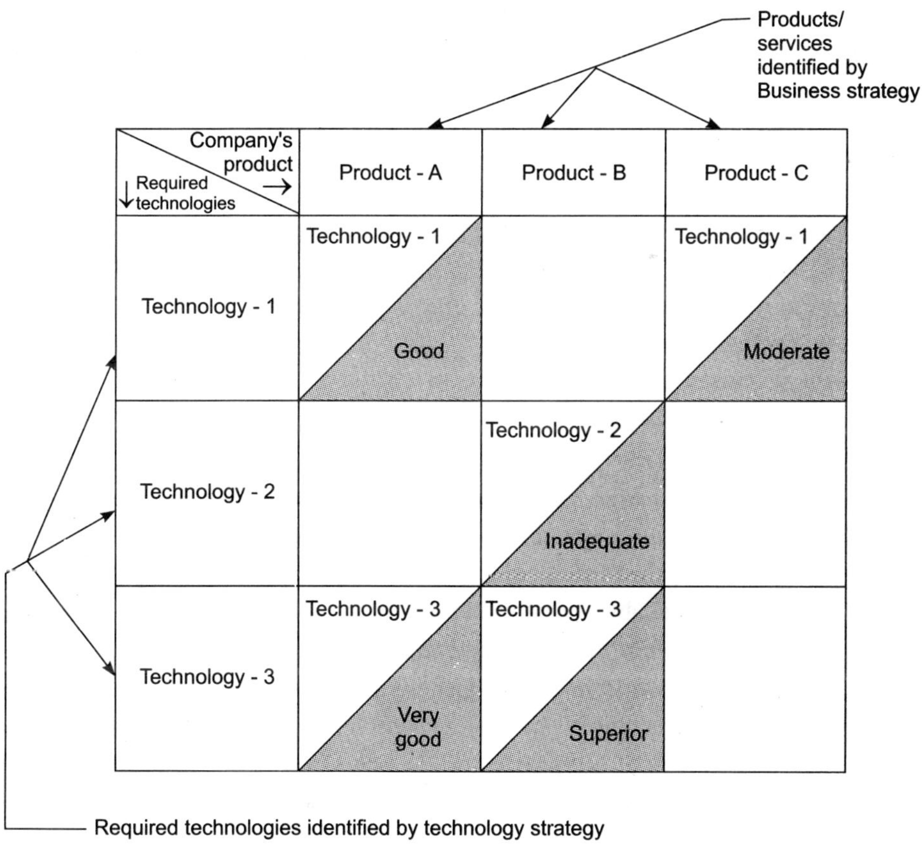

Fig. 6.1 Product-technology matrix

1. Identify the products proposed to be manufactured by the company. This is arrived at by exploring the business strategy of the company. Mark these products in the top row of the matrix.
2. Identify all the different technologies that are required for the production of products identified and mark all these technologies in the first column of the matrix.
3. Assess the status of technologies owned/possessed by the company and indicate the status in the cell that lies at the interaction of a 'Product Column' and a 'Required technology row' [Referring to Fig. 6.1, if the company has a 'Good' strength in terms of Technology-1 which is required for manufacturing Product-A, in the cell that lies at the intersection of Product-A column and Technology-1 row, it is marked as 'GOOD'. The same technology (Technology-1) is also required for Product-C. But, Product-A and Product-C are different products. Though the Technology-1 is considered 'GOOD' for Product-1, it is considered as 'MODERATE" for Product-C', because the technology is more suited for Product-A than for Product-C. Under the column Product-C, except the first cell all other cells are left blank. This indicates that Product-C requires only one technology. The available technology (technology-1) can be made use of for the production of Product-C; but this technology is not the best fit for Product-C as its status as for as Product-C is concerned is rated as 'MODERATE". This shows that are better technologies available for the production of Product-C. An observation of the remaining cells in the matrix, as given in Fig. 6.1 shows that Product-A and Product-B require two different technologies while Product-C requires only one technology.]
4. Study the product-technology matrix and decide on the following:
   - Which are the technologies already possessed by the company that are required for the production of products that are identified by the business strategy and what are the relative strengths of the company with respect to these technologies already owned by the company?
   - Which are the technologies that are not available with the company or that are available, but they are not the superior technologies, so that the company needs to acquire/outsource these technologies?
   - Which are the technologies that are available with the company and are superior in nature so that the company can also lend these technologies to other interested companies outside, apart from using them for their own production, thereby making better use of the available technology?

6.3.1. Decision Matrix Technique

Strategic decisions often involve weighing the strengths and weaknesses of different attributes attached to the problem to be tackled. When two attributes are to be considered jointly to arrive at a decision, a decision-matrix will be of use. This will aid in arriving at a rational decision though there will be an element of subjectivity in the assessment of the quality of the different attributes.

For example, when a company wants to acquire a new technology and if a few versions of the new technology are available, the company may have to come to a decision to choose any one of the available technologies. Suppose a few versions of a particular technology are available for acquisition with different price and quality parameters. The available technologies can be fitted in a Price-Quality decision matrix. Since there are only two decision variables (viz., price and quality standard), if we have two price bands and two quality bands (viz., high price and low price and high quality and low quality), the available technologies can be depicted in a (2 × 2) matrix, called decision-matrix. (Refer Fig. 6.2)

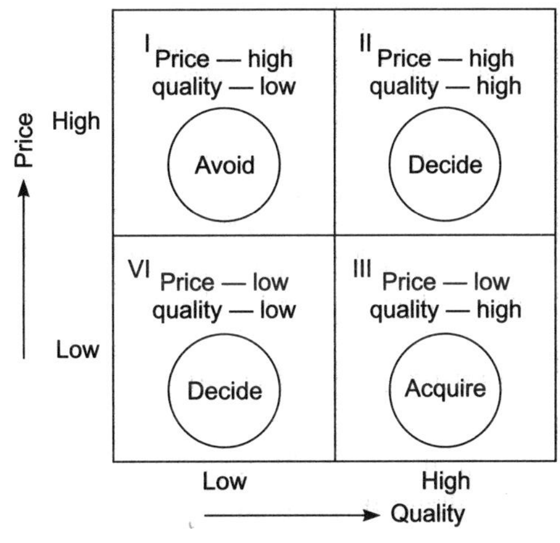

Fig. 6.2 Price-Quality decision matrix

If a particular technology falls in Cell-III, it is a technology that is available at a low price, but its quality is high. Hence, any technology that falls in cell-III are worth acquiring. Similarly, a technology that falls in Cell-I has a low quality, but comes with a high price. Hence, this technology can better be avoided. The technologies that fall in Cells-II and IV need further study before deciding upon acceptance or rejection. For a technology for which quality is of prime consideration and price is not an issue, a technology that falls in Cell-II can be considered for acquisition, provided there is no technology that falls in Cell-I is available. (This is because, if a technology that falls in Cell-I is available, that technology will be available at a lower price, without compromising on the quality.) Similarly, for a situation for which price is of prime importance and a low quality is not of concern, a technology that falls in Cell-IV can be considered, provided there is no technology that falls in Cell-III is available.

6.3.2. Coordinate Positioning Method

In Decision Matrix method, we can only assign two values for each attributes. For example, for the attribute of price, we can only have two values, viz., 'high' and 'low'. When we want to choose from a large number of options to be evaluated to arrive at an optimum choice and when we want to assign values to the attributes on a continuous scale (instead of discrete values like 'high' and 'low'), it can be better done by coordinate positioning method. This method allows us to assign values to each attribute on a continuous scale ('highest' to 'lowest', ''best' to 'worst' etc.,) The two attributes are represented on the two coordinates. Suppose price and quality are the two attributes. Let the X-coordinate represents one attribute, say 'price'. The attribute 'price' will have a continuous scale from 'lowest' to 'highest' on the X-coordinate. If the Y-coordinate represents the attribute 'quality' from 'lowest' to 'highest' value on a continuous scale, these two attributes can be positioned on the X-Y plane. (Refer Fig. 6.3)

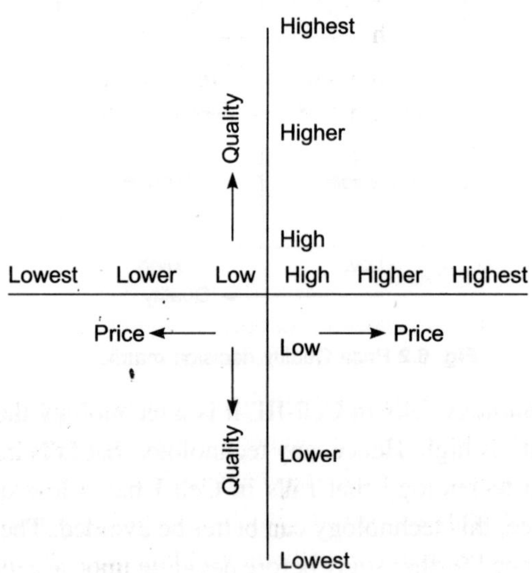

Fig. 6.3 Coordinate positioning method

The different options available can be placed at their appropriate positions in the X-Y plane. (Refer Fig. 6.4)

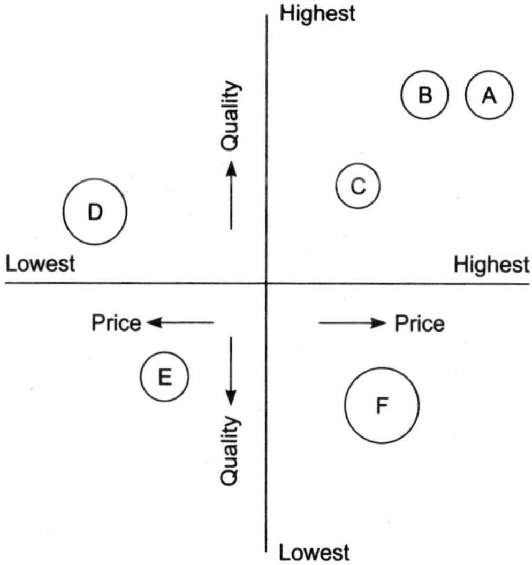

Fig. 6.4 Coordination positioning method

A → Highest Quality & Highest Price

B → Highest Quality & Higher Price

[Of the above two, B is better than A.]

C → Higher Quality & Higher Price

[When we want to choose between B & C, the relative importance of quality/price needs consideration. When lower price is the prime consideration, the choice will be 'C' while when quality is of consideration, the ideal choice will be 'B'.]

6.3.3. (M X N) Matrix Method

Suppose there are two attributes that are attached to a technology/business decision. For example, acquiring a new technology may involve assessment of the technology with regard to its level of advancement and its cost of acquisition. Entering into a licensing/franchising agreement may be another strategic decision which may involve cost and technological considerations. In the Decision Matrix method, we could assign only two values for the attributes (viz., high or low). In the Coordinate positioning method, we could position the different technologies/business options on a X-Y plane on a continuous scale with regard to two attributes, (say, with regard to cost and technology). However, after positioning the different options available on a X-Y plane, we can only make a relative assessment on their comparative merits, by physically observing their position in the X-Y plane. Instead, if we want to assign quantitative value to the different levels of the two attributes, we could have a quantitative assessment of the different combinations of the two attributes (cost and quality). (M X N) Matrix method will be of use for this approach.

In (M X N) Matrix method, we can assign values to the two attributes by measuring the attributes on a 3-point or 5-point likert scale. If we use a 3-point scale, we can assign values as under:

Attribute	Low	Medium	High
Cost	3	2	1
Technology status	1	2	3

[**Note:** When the cost is low, it is beneficial to the acquiring company. Hence it is given a higher value of '3'. When the technology status is high, it is beneficial to the acquiring company. Hence, it is given a higher value of '3']

When we consider the combination of Cost and Technology status, the values for each attribute can be added. But, out of the two attributes, one attribute may have a greater influence. For example, for one company technology status may be the prime criterion and cost may come next. For another company, cost may come first and the company can even compromise on technology to some extent if there is a cost advantage. Hence, depending upon the relative importance attached to the two attributes, weights can be assigned. A company that considers technology as an important attribute can assign a higher weight to technology than to cost. For example, if it assigns a weight of 0.75 (2/3) to technology, the remaining weight of 0.25 (1/3) goes to cost. For such an assumption, the values of the individual cells are as below:

The values indicated inside each cell refers to the relative values of technologies that will fit into the respective cells.

Cost / Level of Technology	Low	Medium	High
Low	[3 × 0.25 + 1 × 0.75] = **1.50**	[2 × 0.25 + 1 × 0.75] = **1.25**	[1 × 0.25 + 1 × 0.75] = **1.00**
Medium	[3 × 0.25 + 2 × 0.75] = **2.25**	[2 × 0.25 + 2 × 0.75] = **2.00**	[1 × 0.25 + 3 × 0.75] = **2.50**
High	[3 × 0.25 + 3 × 0.75] = **3.00**	[2 × 0.25 + 2 × 0.75] = **2.00**	[1 × 0.25 + 3 × 0.75] = **2.50**

Suppose we want to make a choice between three different technologies. They can be depicted in the matrix in the appropriate boxes after taking into account their cost and technology level. The technology that corresponds to the cell of maximum value is the technology to be chosen. Suppose we depict three technologies viz., technology-A, technology-B and technology-C, which, according to their cost and technology status combination fit into the three cells as shown below.

Cost / Level of Technology	Low	Medium	High
Low			
Medium	Technology-A **(2.25)**	Technology-B **(2.00)**	
High		Technology-C **(2.00)**	

Out of the three technologies, Technology-A scores better while the other two technologies are equally rated. Hence, the first choice is Technology-A. [Note: This decision is based on assigning two-third weight to technology and one-third weight to cost. The choice can vary if different weights are assigned to the attributes.]

6.4. CORE COMPETENCY

Core competencies are collective sets of knowledge, skills and technologies that a company possesses and applies to add value to its customers. According to Prahalad and Hamel, Core Competency refers to a harmonized combination of multiple resources and skills that distinguish a firm in the market place. For example, a company that is strong in technology may have strong technical competency in the areas like design and development capabilities, industrial engineering, software development, quality management etc., while a company that is strong in marketing may have strong marketing competency in the areas like pricing, sales & distribution, product mix, product management etc.

A company can improve its competitive abilities by becoming a learning organization and continuously updating knowledge in its area of core competency and offering new/improved products/services which can not be easily duplicated by competitors.

It is very vital for the management to identify the organization's core competencies and build upon it. Core competencies are usually converted into core products/services.

Core Competency is not just core technical competency. A company that has high level of abilities in certain areas can combine and harmonize these abilities which can make the company gain expertise in a certain key business attribute. Then, this key business attribute in which the company excels is considered as its Core Competency. Since achieving Core Competency involves coordinating and synchronizing expertise in many related areas of business, it becomes very difficult to imitate.

Characteristics of core competency

- Core Competency is that competency based on which a company can be differentiated easily from its competitors. Core Competency will uniquely identify an organization.
- Since Core Competency is the result of harmonization of many areas where a company has additional expertise, a company will be found to exhibit its core competency in a range of products in which it has its presence.
- Core Competency possessed by a company can not be easily imitated. Though Core Competency of a company will be visible as a single business attribute in which the company is found to possess unparallel expertise, at the background there will be many interrelated activities that make it possible for the company to excel in one attribute. Hence, it can not be easily imitated by others. It will require years of dedicated work and mobilization of special resources, making it very difficult to imitate the core competency possessed by a company.
- Core Competency, apart from giving an edge to a company, will be beneficial to the customers of the company as it makes a significant contribution to the end products offered by the organization. With unique products having special features, accessing a wide variety of markets becomes easy for the company.

[The Core Competency of Hindustan Unilever Company Limited is the strong, well-spread out distributor network; the Core Competency of Maruti Suzuki India Limited is the well developed sales and service net work.]

6.4.1. Core Technical Competency

Though a company can have core competency in any area, core competency in technical area (i.e., Core technical competency) is more important in the present scenario of business competition that depends more on technology. Core Technical competency can cross market boundaries and can provide basis for significant product superiority. The following are some of the special attributes of core technical competency:

- Core technical competency is more difficult to imitate.
- It offers greater value to customers.

– It is extendable to new products; since many different products may require the same technology, the core competency in one technology area can be extended to many different products in the product portfolio of the company.
– It offers a greater competitive advantage.

Potential Core Technical Competency (PCTC)

A company may have potential technical knowledge and skill that remains unexploited. PCTC has all the attributes of core competency except that they have not been developed by the company to a level of excellence. They indicate the company's failure to develop fully their key areas of technical expertise. A technology strategy will attempt to identify the PCTC of a company so that suitable strategies can be formed to exploit the unexploited potential.

Desired Core Technical Competency (DCTC)

These are the critical technical competencies that are currently missing from the organization. DCTC may be apparently visible or may be hidden. For example, if it is found that some of the competitors are already in possession and are using certain technical expertise that are absent in a given organization, it indicates a DCTC for the organization. This DCTC will be apparently visible. Sometimes, a technology may be emerging in an industry that is very relevant for an organization's activity, but the technology is yet to be acquired/developed by the organization. This is also a DCTC, but it remains hidden and will soon come to the surface once the technology is perfected and it emerges successfully.

A company's strategic core technical competencies are the complete set of technical competencies that have been targeted for future development and exploitation and they comprise of a mix of existing, potential and desired technical competencies.

6.4.2. Technology and Core Competency

The technology that a company makes use of can be broadly classified into three groups, viz.,

1. Distinctive technology
2. Basic technology
3. External technology.

Distinctive Technology

Distinctive technology is the technology that gives competitive advantage to a firm based on core competency. Business firms are required to protect the distinctive technology, nourish it and capitalize on it in order to enjoy sustained technological advantage over competitors.

Basic Technology

This is the technology that is available to all organizations. These technologies do not give any distinct advantage to a firm. But, they are required for the normal production operations.

External Technology

These are those technologies that are more economically supplied by an outside vendor. If a firm goes for acquistion of this technology, it will prove to be costlier. Hence, a firm can rely on outside vendors and concentrate its efforts on other technologies where it has a competitive edge. However, if this technology is some thing that is very vital for the very survival of the firm, efforts are to be focused to arrive at cost-effective methods of acquiring the technology, since this alone will help the firm in the long run.

6.5. SWOT ANALYSIS — USE OF SWOT MATRIX IN THE FORMULATION OF A COMPETITIVE BUSINESS STRATEGY

SWOT analysis is carried out by business firms to understand the internal and external environments. In the term SWOT, 'S' stands for 'Strength' and 'W' stands for 'Weaknesses'. These two aspects relate to the internal environment of the firm. The letter 'O' stands for 'Opportunities' and 'T' stands for 'Threats'. These two aspects relate to the external environment. SWOT analysis is carried out to identify the internal strengths and weaknesses and matching them with the opportunities and threats coming from the external environment. SWOT analysis will help to formulate an effective business strategy. An effective business strategy will be one that makes use of the internal strengths and capitalizes on the external opportunities and at the same time neutralizes the external threat by minimizing/reducing/eliminating the internal weaknesses. Thus, SWOT analysis gives a broader framework for formulating appropriate business strategies.

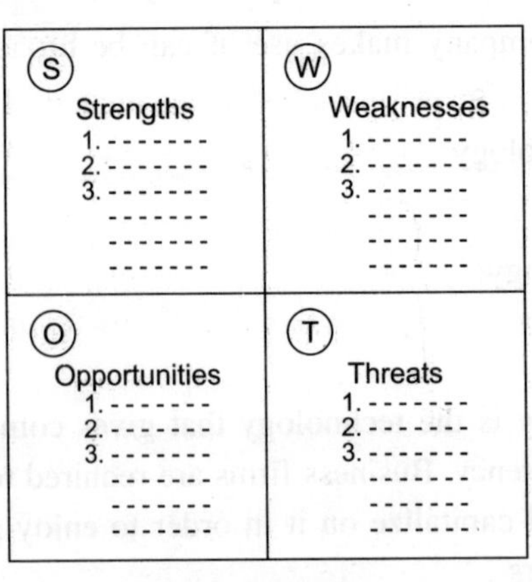

Fig.6.5 SWOT Matrix

In a SWOT matrix, the S, W, O and T factors are written in the corresponding cells, which give a snap-shot view of the internal and external environments of a firm. (Refer Fig. 6.5)

For identifying the possible business strategies, the SWOT matrix is modified and reconstructed in such a way that it gives four more cells (S-O, W-O, S-T and T-W) for indicating the possible business strategies. (Refer Fig. 6.6)

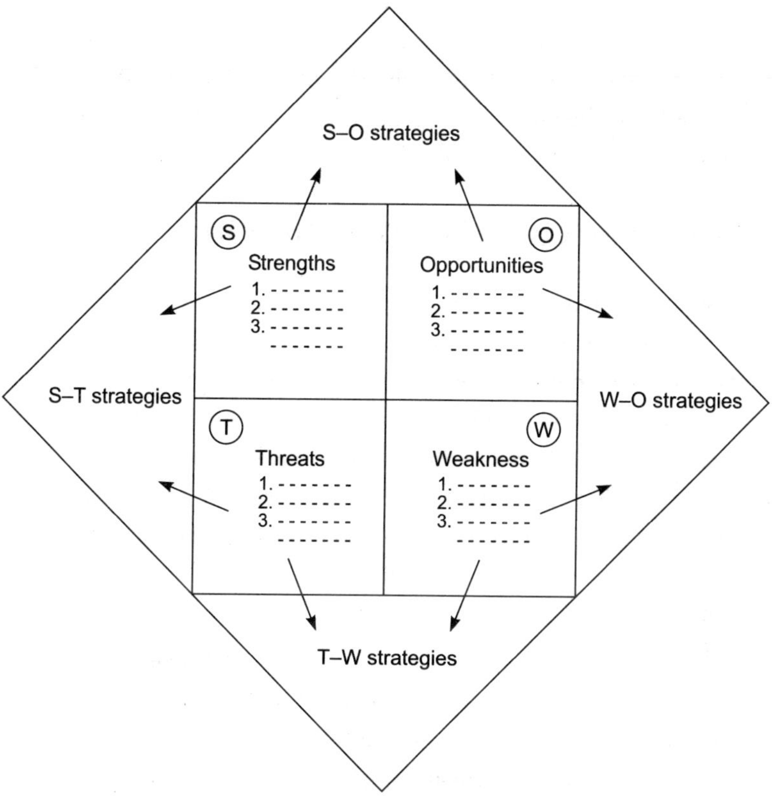

Fig. 6.6 SWOT Interaction matrix for business strategy

The S-O cell in the matrix (the cell that is common to strengths and opportunities) indicates the possible strategies that the firm can follow to achieve its business objectives. All possible strategies that make use of the internal strengths of the firm and that exploit the external opportunities are thought of and recorded in S-O cell.

Similarly, the strategies that can be used to overcome the external threats by making use of the internal strengths are thought of and recorded in cell S-T.

The strategies that can be followed to overcome internal weaknesses by making use of the external opportunities are indicated on W-O cell; the strategies that minimize internal weaknesses and avoid external threats are recorded in cell T-W.

After all the possible business strategies are identified and recorded in the four cells, the most effective and implementable strategies are chosen from out of this list of strategies identified.

Though business strategies can be formulated keeping the vision, mission and objectives of a firm, identification of possible business strategies using SWOT matrix will be more systematic and will provide an opportunity to exhaust all possible strategies. Formulating business strategies without using SWOT matrix will lack direction and may not give the desired results.

6.6. VERTICALLY INTEGRATED CORPORATION

In any business firm, whether it is a manufacturing or a service firm, there are many different technologies that are owned/possessed by the firm pertaining to the different organizational functions. For example, a manufacturing firm may possess technology related to its products, technology related to production, technology related to marketing its products etc. Some firms may either own or have control over all the required technologies. Some other firms may own or have control over only a few of the required technologies. The choice depends upon many factors and the ideal choice may differ from one firm to another, depending on the firm's core competency, internal strength, strength of other players etc.

A firm is said to be a vertically integrated one if it either owns or has control over all or most of the technologies that are required for the production and marketing activities. Oil multinationals like Exxon, Mobil, Royal Dutch Shell etc., are good examples of companies that are vertically integrated. They control the entire chain of Oil industry starting from locating of Oil deposits, drilling, extracting crude oil, transporting to the processing plant, refining of petroleum products and distributing the product to the end-users through a network of dealers.

Suppose a company acquires a product technology. This means that the company has the know-how to manufacture the product. For a manufacturing company, this will be the first stage. If the company simply acquires the product technology, but manufactures the product using the manufacturing facilities of other companies, either by way of getting things done on job-order basis or through a licensing arrangement etc., the company's technology integration status is at very low. It owns only one technology (viz., product technology) but depends on other players for the rest of the technologies. When this company wants to integrate further, it can go for acquiring the production technology. If there are a number of technologies required for production, the company can acquire all or only a few of the required production technologies depending upon option that is best suited under the given conditions. Suppose the company has acquired all the required production technologies. Now, the company, apart from owing the know-how, also owns the manufacturing facilities. This represents the first stage of integration. By now, for marketing the products, the company has to depend on some other company that possesses the required technology for marketing. If the company wants to further integrate upstream, it can acquire the marketing technology also. Now, the company has product, production and marketing technologies in-house and this is a higher degree of integration.

The decision to integrate further or not at any stage depends on how critical the technology is to the company. In the above example that we have discussed, if the company has already acquired the product and production technologies and is now in a situation to decide on whether to acquire marketing technology or not, this decision is a strategic business decision and depends on factors like the importance of marketing to the company, the competency/resources available at the disposal of the company for taking up marketing activity, the strength of other agents who are specialized in marketing and who can take up marketing of the company's products etc., Another aspect to be considered is the component of non-value added cost that gets added to the product cost by the time it reaches the end user. For example, marketing, distribution and retailing represents about 20% to 30% of the value of a car, depending upon the length of the supply chain. Direct sale through internet can reduce the non value added cost substantially. The following two diagrams (Figs. 6.7 and 6.8) indicate the decision choices that can be made under two different situations.

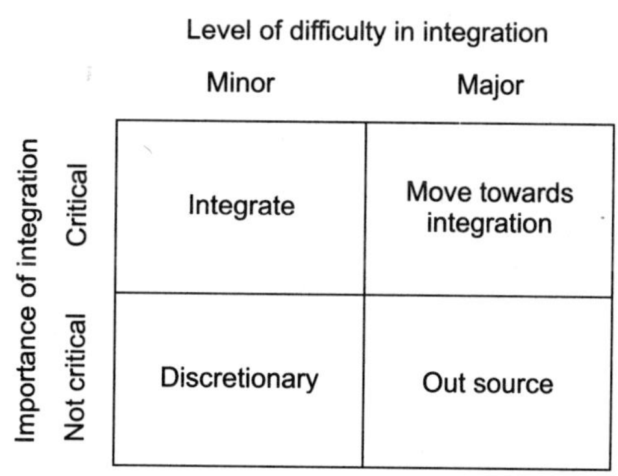

Fig. 6.7 Importance vs. Difficulty in integration

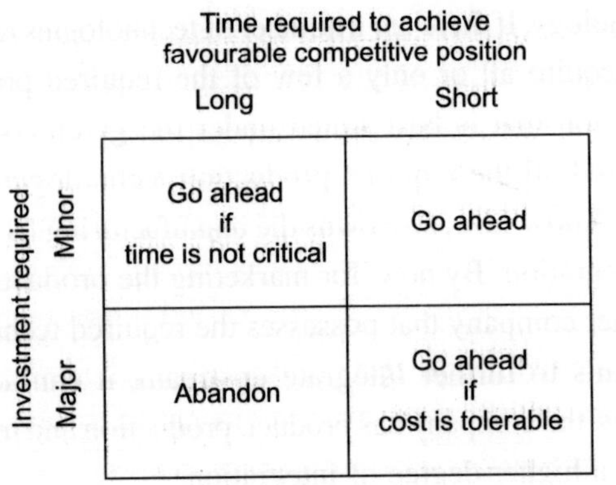

Fig. 6.8 Investment vs. Time required for integration

6.7. STMS (STRATEGIC TECHNOLOGY MANAGEMENT SYSTEM) LIFE CYCLE MANAGEMENT

STMS life cycle would show where a company's product/service lies in the cycle. The STMS life cycle consists of the following phases:

- Technology creation
- Technology monitoring
- Technology assessment
- Technology transfer
- Technology acceptance
- Technology utilisation
- Technology maturity
- Technology decline.

The cycle repeats after technology decline phase where a new technology overtakes an existing technology that got outdated. Successful companies have a close watch over the STMS life cycle and whenever a technology reaches maturity phases, the companies realize that it poses a threat in terms of technology and if not acted upon at this stage, the existing technology might soon slip into a decline phase. Since the successful companies have a close monitoring of the phases of technological life cycle, they do not allow their product to become obsolete or outdated and take corrective measures to overcome such situations.

6.8. SUSTAINABLE COMPETITIVE ADVANTAGE

A firm is said to possess competitive advantage in an area, if the firm performs better in that area than any other firm. The better performance of the firm should result into adding some value to its product/service that attracts customers. If the element of customer attraction and customer acceptance is missing, it can not be said that the firm has achieved competitive advantage, though the firm may be performing differently from other firms in the industry. It is the addition of extra values to the product/service that customers desire which makes a firm enjoy competitive advantage.

For technology oriented firms, their competitive advantage lies in exploiting technology, integrating human resources and offering products/services that have unique features that are desired by the customers, but not available in any of the competitors' products. It is not just enough if the technology is very impressive. The technology should result in a product/product feature that is acceptable and offers value to customers. A technology that does not satisfy customer expectations will not be of help in attaining competitive advantage.

It is not enough if a firm has just gained competitive advantage by forming the right strategy of product development/product improvement. The competitive advantage gained is to be sustained in the long run. When the phase of technological development increases and when the level of competition between firms get stiffened, firms will be finding it increasingly difficult to maintain competitive advantage for a longer period of time. In the fast changing world of technology, maintaining competitive advantage even for a period of one or two years has become a difficult task. Hence, to sustain the competitive advantage, a firm has to strive hard continuously. Continuous value creation/value addition can be possible only with concerted efforts and following a right technology strategy.

Value addition should become a watch-word for every department and every employee in the organization. R&D wing has a crucial role to play in attaining sustainable competitive advantage. The R&D department should see to it that it supports value addition in every possible manner.

Technology audit should be focused towards improving the technological competency of the firm in such a way that the firm has the required financial and human resources to implement value addition practices over its products/services on an on-going basis.

Bench marking is another best practice that a firm should follow to support value addition. In bench marking, the firm seeks out the best products/best processes in other firms and sets them as reference for improving its quality standards to the bench mark level. The firms also seek to find out as to how the other firms in the market achieve product/process quality standards and attempt to either imitate or improve upon in order to produce a product/service of equal or better quality.

6.9. CHARACTERISTICS OF COMPANIES THAT MANAGE TECHNOLOGY SUCCESSFULLY

Companies that have been found successfully managing their technology have been found to possess some common characteristics. Some of them are discussed below. It is not that every successful company (in terms of managing technology successfully) will possess all these characteristics. It depends on the nature of the market, type of the product being manufactured by the company, status of technology and many other related factors. However, in general it can be said that the following are some of the key performance factors possessed by companies that are found to be technologically sound.

(a) Favourable corporate culture

A favourable and supportive organizational culture will orient every employee in the organization in the direction of technology development and improvement. Every employee, starting from the top CEO to the lower level shop-floor employee will believe that technology alone can take their company ahead of others. In a company where such a culture prevails, technology will not remain as the sole responsibility of the R&D department. Every employee will contribute his share towards technology improvement. Such a conducive organizational culture can not be created overnight. It will be the result of continuous education, training and brain-storming, thus making every employee sensitive to the need for technology development in the organization.

Successful management of technology is found to depend upon the attitude and belief of the employees at all levels rather than on the technology itself. Thus, organizational culture that supports technology is more important. When a culture that regards technology as the life force that supports the organization prevails, it will be visible throughout the company starting from the CEO at the top to the bottom-most employee in the hierarchy. Employees in all levels/cadres will be receptive to innovative and creative ideas. Successful ideas will be adequately rewarded. People with extraordinary talent to generate innovative business ideas will be given opportunity to man higher positions in the organizational hierarchy. When such a culture prevails, technology is not restricted to a few persons/departments in the organization, but becomes a way of life in the organization.

(b) Supportive top management

It is found that the top management of successful companies recognize the importance of technology and necessity for strategically managing technology. Being aware of the importance of achieving and retaining technological supremacy, the top management is always on toes to ensure that the organization is not left behind in terms of technology. They closely follow the developments taking place in technology domain and take steps to align their organization in tune with the latest technology, by acquiring the required resources and by training the human resources to become competent enough to handle technology related issues. The top management provides the required moral and financial support for innovations, encourages creative ideas, ensures frequent and useful brain-storming and interactive sessions of key employees on the contemporary trends in technology and the need/scope to adopt latest technology etc., In addition, the top management encourages innovations across the organization by motivating all the employees and making them to participate in the technology mission of the organization. The top management and the key managers/decision makers in the domain of technology management are watchful of the developments taking place and involve themselves in frequent reviews/discussions to strengthen their technology status.

(c) Revived R&D department

In technologically successful organizations, R&D department is no more considered as a conventional research laboratory. It is integrated with the shop floor. R&D initiatives take shape from the shop floors, with the involvement of customers and employees. R&D departments are made to function as strategic units and their success is measured by the number of innovative products successfully introduced in the market by the R&D department and the number of innovative features introduced in existing products. R&D department does not act in isolation, but acts in total coordination with other functional departments of the organization. R&D department also takes active part in identifying and arranging strategic alliances by virtue of their knowledge and expertise in technology related areas. Strategic alliance for collaborative research is an area where R&D departments are actively involved. R&D departments also act as nodal agencies in studying the technologies available in other parts of the world, in identifying the technology that will improve the competitive edge of the company and in transferring the required technology to the company.

(d) Strategic alliances

Companies that are successful in managing technology are found to attach greater importance for strategic alliances. The strategic alliances may take the shape of mergers and acquisitions, joint ventures, franchising, licensing, technology/know-how tie-ups, collaborative research etc., In a fast changing world of technology, strategic alliances have a major impact in attaining technological competitiveness. While devising a strategy for strategic alliance, an organization shall assess its core technological competency and should identify the core technologies which it should develop internally and identify other technology areas where the organization can go for strategic alliances. Successful organizations are found to follow such practices meticulously.

(e) Competitive analysis

Competitive analysis is an on-going process. Companies that manage their technology successfully are found to carry out competitive analysis on a continuous basis. They identify their main competitors, analyze their products, processes and business strategies and adopt those practices where the competitors are found to have an edge. In studying competitors' products, reverse engineering is widely followed. Successful companies constantly pose questions like 'Who are our competitors?', 'What are the strengths of our competitors?', 'What are the technologies possessed by our competitors?', 'What are our strengths/weaknesses vis-à-vis our competitors?', 'What are the strategies likely to be followed by our competitors?', 'What are the strategies to be followed by us to counter the strategies of our competitors?' etc., and the search for answers to such questions in order to overcome competition and establish technological advantage over competitors.

(f) Technology audits

Technology audits help companies to ascertain the status of technology within the company and to compare it with the status of technology possessed by competitors. This indicates the direction in which the company has to move in terms of technology in order to remain competitive and not left behind. Successful companies are found to take up technology audit seriously as a strategic tool and not as a mere routine.

(g) Closer customer interfaces

Companies that are successful are known for maintaining good rapport and strong interactions with their customers. They identify the customer expectations quickly through effective customer interface and bring about the required technological improvements in the products/processes that satisfy the customer requirements. Their close association with customers enable them develop proprietary technology that produces products matching customer requirements and thus the companies achieve distinct advantage which will be difficult for competitors to match.

Review Questions

1. Define the Terms 'Strategy' and 'Strategic Management' and explain the process of Strategic Management.
2. Explain 'Technology Strategy' and discuss about Technology Strategy at the national level and at the enterprise level.
3. Explain the components of Technology strategy in detail.
4. What is the relationship between Business strategy and Technology strategy?

5. Explain the use of the following techniques in taking rational business/ technology decisions:
(*a*) Decision matrix method,
(*b*) Coordinate positioning method,
(*c*) (M X N) matrix method.
6. Define the term 'Core Competency'. What are the characteristics of Core Competency?
7. Explain the importance of Core Technical Competency.
8. Explain the use of SWOT matrix in the formulation of competitive Business Strategy.
9. Define the term 'Vertically integrated corporation'. Explain the steps to be followed in taking a stand for or against vertical integration.
10. Indicate the steps involved in Strategic Technology Management System (STMS).
11. How can a company plan for achieving sustainable competitive advantage?
12. Explain the characteristics of companies that are found to manage technology successfully.

Organizational Structure, Organizational Learning and Leadership

7 CHAPTER

7.1. HUMAN RESOURCE FOR MANAGING TECHNOLOGY

In the process of managing technology, people with technical knowledge/skill represent the most important asset of an organization. This is a critical asset. Continuous flow of new ideas relating to technology will emerge only from this pool of employees. It is this pool of employees who are going to convert the technology plans and technology strategies of the organization into reality. Hence, no organization which depends on technology can afford to ignore this asset. Technology based organizations survive only on the basis of creativity and innovative ideas of scientists and engineers and the technical skills of employees who convert the innovative ideas into products. Having understood the importance of technical manpower, an organization should optimize the output of this category of employees and utilize their knowledge, talent and skills effectively. Mismanagement or underutilization of scientific and engineering talent will lead to negative consequences as far as the development and sustenance of the organization is concerned.

Some of the areas to be concentrated for effective utilization of scientific and engineering talent are discussed below:

(*a*) Right person for the right job is the formula for hiring personnel for any department of an organization. This assumes greater importance when it comes to hiring technical personnel, especially when hiring personnel for R&D activities. R&D department being an important department in the technology profile of an organization, it should be manned by competent persons.

(*b*) Persons with specialized scientific and technical knowledge are the backbone of a technology-based organization. However, they must be exposed to cross-functional experiences in order to make their talent bear the fruit. Only with cross-functional exposure, they will understand the business requirements correctly and can be able to offer technological solutions that will suit the business requirements of the organization.

(*c*) Technical departments should be headed by persons who are technically qualified and knowledgeable and are also exposed to the business realities, so that they can orient the technical workforce in the right direction.

(*d*) Technical personnel should be made to have contacts with the customers of the organization so that they can understand their requirements correctly; they should also be made to have contacts with the outside world, which will expose them to the happenings outside the organization and the technology strategies followed by the competitors.

(*e*) The organizational structure and the work sequence should be so designed that the technical personnel spend most of their time in their professional activities. They should not be given purely administrative works and other works that are not related to them, which will be wastage of precious resources. Such administrative and other routine works should be assigned to others who are meant for that.

(*f*) Performance appraisal system for the scientific and engineering personnel in the R&D department should be carefully designed to assess performance in terms of innovations, product/process developments, aiding the production departments with technical inputs etc., instead of merely recording their presence/compliance of certain organizational norms. In this regard, a person's efforts and progress towards innovations should also be reckoned and not necessarily the results. Results are welcome. But, failures in the path of innovation are quite normal. One who has not succeeded in bringing out innovative products, despite considerable work done in that direction, has to be assessed appropriately. Merely going by the results will not be a correct mode of assessment and it may dampen the enthusiasm of the persons concerned.

(*g*) Scientists and engineers should be offered carrier development programmes in the area of their interest/strength. They must also be continuously exposed to the latest developments in the field by deputing them to seminars, workshops, symposiums in their related areas of interest.

7.2. THE IMPORTANCE OF ORGANIZATIONAL STRUCTURE

Mintzberg defines organizational structure as under:

'It is the sum total of ways in which it divides its labour into distinct tasks and then achieves coordination among them.'

Organizational structure is a key factor that influences creativity in an organization. Size of the organization, degree of standardization, centralization and formalization have great influence on the innovating capacity of an organization.

Size

Does size has an influence upon innovation?. The answer is 'Yes'. Is a large sized firm more likely to be innovative than a smaller firm? The answer is not definite. There are arguments both for and against. Large firms have their own advantages facilitating innovation while small sized firms do have their own specific advantages that make them become more innovative. The arguments in favour of larger firms are as under:

- A bigger firm is in a better position to mobilize funds for financing its R&D activities. Since such firms will be able to spend larger amounts (in absolute terms) in R&D activities, economy of scale will also operate in the area of R&D and the firms will get benefitted more per rupee of spending in R&D activities.
- R&D expenses are shared among the products produced. Hence, in a bigger sized firm, due to higher volume of production, the R&D expenditure get loaded over a larger volume of products. A smaller firm, when it loads the R&D expenses on its production, its products may become comparatively costlier. When a smaller firm is under compulsion to keep the price lower to meet the competition from larger firms, the smaller firm will be constrained to load only a part of its R&D expenditure on the price. This is likely to erode the profitability of the organization.
- Economy of scale that a large sized firm enjoys will give it a greater advantage in terms of better maneuvering ability in all functional areas; they will be better placed to get access to vital information needed for the business which in turn will help them have greater competitive advantage. All these will go a long way in making larger firms to become more innovative in nature.
- Innovations and new product developments involve considerable extent of risk-taking. The risk-taking abilities of firms increase in proportion to their size. A bigger firm, in view of its greater financing and man-power status can take greater level of risk towards being innovative in their approach.

The arguments in favour of smaller sized firms are as under:

- Size can also be a hindrance when it comes to effectiveness of managerial control. When size becomes larger, the effectiveness of managerial control reduces (because of large number of hierarchical layers, inability to monitor progress, inability to motivate all the employees etc.,) and this may result in ineffective utilization of R&D facilities. A smaller firm can on the other hand, make better use of its available R&D facilities and resources.

- When the size becomes large, a firm may develop more rigidity, thus making it less responsive to change. A smaller firm on the other hand, will be more flexible and more adaptable to changes. The element of flexibility will help smaller firms become more responsive to the market conditions and more innovative in their approach.
- In a smaller firm, people involved in R&D activities are fewer in number and the fruits of their efforts will be visible clearly from which they can derive a lot of satisfaction and a feeling of achievement. In a larger firm, this may not be possible since many individuals might have contributed to a single achievement. Hence, the scientists and technical personnel involved in carrying out innovations will not get a sense of achievement and such an atmosphere will dampen the spirit of innovation in larger firms.
- Smaller firms have a greater degree of flexibility. They can adapt to market conditions at a much greater phase than larger firms. Larger firms, because of the many layers of hierarchy in their structure acquire greater inertia and become highly inflexible, making them difficult to adopt to changes taking place in the market.
- Smaller firms, in general, have comparatively lesser resources. Paucity of resources may, at times act as a blessing in disguise since smaller firms will become comparatively more cost cautious than larger firms in choosing new, innovative projects and employees of small sized firms remain greatly motivated in view of lesser resources and closer association between the colleagues in a firm. Hence, smaller firms register greater degree of success than larger firms in introducing new, innovative products into the market for a given amount spent towards this.

Formal/Informal Organizational Structure

In general, organizational structure can be broadly divided into the following two categories:

(*a*) Organic structure (or flexible structure)

(*b*) Mechanistic structure (or rigid structure).

Organic structure is characterized by the absence of hierarchy, thereby allowing a lot of flexibility. Mechanistic structure on the other hand, is characterized by a rigid hierarchy, thereby exercising strict controls.

In an organic structure, the channels of communication will be open, allowing free flow of information throughout the organization. As against this, in a mechanistic organization, the communication channels are highly structured and regulated. Hence, the flow of information is more prone to meet with bottle-necks in a mechanistic structure. Since an organic structure does not follow a strict hierarchy, decisions are taken based on the expertise of the individuals whereas in a mechanistic organization, decisions can be taken only by those who are given the authority to do so as per the structure of the organization. Though an organic structure does not exercise any strict control on the operations, it places greater emphasis on getting things done. The mechanistic structure follows a laid-down procedure in taking decisions/getting things done. As seen from the above, it is the more flexible and freely adaptable organic structure that can better stimulate creativity in an organization than a rigid and rule-based mechanistic structure. Even if the organic structure can not be followed for the entire organization, it would be better to follow this structure for such departments that are involved in R&D and new product development activities.

Centralization/Decentralization

Centralization refers to concentration of power/decision-making authority at the top management while decentralization refers to sharing of authority with lower levels of management. According to Fayol, 'everything which goes to increase the importance of subordinates is decentralization and everything which goes to reduce it is centralization'.

In a highly decentralized organization, there are only a few levels of hierarchy. This means that the decision-making power is spread out. Such a structure leads to more responsive and more accurate decisions since the decision points are closer to the actual places of action where decisions are needed. For an innovative organization, the organizational structure should be a decentralized one so that decisions can be taken fast and good ideas won't get struck up in the hierarchy.

Standardization

Standardization in organizational structure refers to forming rigid rules, policies and guidelines and not permitting deviations as far as possible. Bureaucratic organizational structures have a greater degree of standardization. They are more suitable for complex large sized organizations that carry out routine activities. A tall hierarchy, clear well defined roles and responsibilities, rigid policies, guidelines and rules are the features of it. Such a structure is not suitable for encouraging creativity and innovation in organizations.

7.3. THE NEED FOR IMPROVED RELATIONSHIP BETWEEN THE DIFFERENT FUNCTIONAL DISCIPLINES

In the traditional functional organization, employees are grouped by their discipline. Hence, we find the existence of different functional departments in a traditional functional organization. Every lower level employee in a particular department works under the direction of a sub-functional manager who is specialized in the functional discipline. The many sub-functional managers of a particular discipline report to a senior functional manager in the discipline. Every functional division has its role defined clearly. Every employee in a particular functional discipline is motivated to ensure better performance of his/her division. Occasionally, there can be certain issues that may overlap two or more functional divisions. When such overlaps occur, the role of each discipline is sorted out through discussions. In such a well-defined organizational structure that is divided on the basis of functions, the authority-responsibility relationship of the members is well defined and is made known to all. Every functional manager who controls the resources pertaining to his/her division also control the performance of the division.

The traditional functional organization will function smoothly provided all the tasks that are required to be performed are known in the beginning itself, so that they can be assigned to the different functional divisions according to their category. When all the tasks are apportioned between the different functional divisions and when there are no/minimum overlapping tasks, the organization will function smoothly, without much disturbance. Since each division has its task cut out, there will be no/minimum interaction between the different divisions and in spite of this, the organizational functions will be performed as planned. However, such an organizational structure is not very much suited for a research focused, development oriented organization. This is because, in most of the developmental works, all the tasks that are required to be performed will not be known in the beginning itself. New tasks will emerge during the course of the developmental works which need to be assigned to some person/ group. Another challenge is that even out of the known tasks to be performed, some of the tasks may require resources from more than one functional area. Many of the tasks may be overlapping two or more functional areas. Since all the tasks can not be known at the beginning of the execution stage and as all the tasks can not be fit into one functional division exclusively, a formal functional organization will not be a correct choice for organizations that are research/development focused, since the formal functional structure will suffer from the drawbacks of improper coordination and inadequate integration.

What is required for an innovation focused organization (or even for any production oriented organization that wants to retain long term competitive advantage), is an improved functional relationship across the different functional disciplines. This can be better achieved by Project Management approach wherein personnel from different functional departments will be deputed to the project team that will work on innovation/ new product development initiatives.

The table given below shows how the different functional departments can be of help in a new-product development process.

Department	Activities focused towards new product development
Engineering Department	Carrying out product design, finalizing the product and process parameters
Marketing Department	Providing product development teams with information on the market, during pre-development, development and post-development periods
Purchase Department	Interacting with suppliers of raw materials, components, parts and finalizing purchase deals
Production Department	Developing prototype, building up pilot plant, resolving teething problems in prototype/pilot plants, attempting at cost reduction techniques, improving process capabilities
R & D Department	Identification of new technologies, developing new product/process designs

7.4. THE STRUCTURE FOR AN INNOVATIVE ORGANIZATION

The traditional organizational configurations advocated by Taylor, Fayol and Weber were based on the principles of division of labour. Division of labour in turn leads to the formation of supervisory cadres in different divisions and a leadership hierarchy with a single centre of authority and control at the top. Such traditional organizational structure concentrates more on efficiency of the operations. Focusing on efficiency makes the organizations to stick to defined methods of operation that will improve efficiency and avoid deviations that would bring down the efficiency. However, the environments in which innovations can flourish are complex, uncertain and more turbulent. Static organizational structures with rigid division of labour cannot provide the required flexibility and agility required for an innovative organization. Innovative organizations require a structure that offers a lot of flexibility and agility and provides barrier-free communication, knowledge sharing and freedom of expression.

There is no established structure for organizations that can support innovation. The suitable structure for an organization is to be designed keeping in view the requirements of the individual organizations. Some of the requirements of the structure of an organization that will support innovation can be summarized as under:

- Lower degree of formalization.
- Decentralized decision-making.
- Reduced hierarchy.
- Absence of bureaucracy.
- Formation of adhoc project team.
- Interaction between project teams without formal coordination rules.
- Free and flexible interaction between departments.
- Coordination with customers.
- Guidance and conflict management as the role of the top management.
- Fuzzy and generalized role definition of employees.

7.5. PROJECT MANAGEMENT APPROACH

A project-based organization is one that is built around specific projects. According to Harison, a project is a non-routine, non-repetitive, one-off undertaking, normally with discrete time, financial and technical performance goals. Project Management Institute, USA defines Project as 'a temporary endeavour undertaken to create a unique product or service'. A specific characteristic of project is that it is a one-off undertaking which means that once the objectives are accomplished, the project comes to an end. Projects are undertaken by a team of workers who are specifically assigned to the project team from different functional departments.

A project starts when a project idea emerges. The project idea may be to create some product that does not currently exist in the organization. The idea may also relate to some service or process. For example, when a new idea regarding a new manufacturing process emerges or when an idea about a new marketing method emerges or when, say, a new corporate strategy is thought off, it indicates the beginning of a project. In an organization that manages technology, some of the technology management strategies like licensing, franchising, joint-venture, mergers & acquisitions etc., can all be considered as individual projects and these can be effectively executed by following Project Management methodology. These are considered as projects since they are one-time undertakings and once the objectives are reached, they come to an end. For example, when a joint-venture is considered as a technology strategy, the project begins with the thought process of going for a joint-venture and ends with the formation of a joint-venture company.

A project team will consist of people with expertise/skills in different functional disciplines. Members are drawn from different functional disciplines and assigned to a specific project. When teams are appointed by drawing people from different functional departments, an overlay organization called 'Matrix organization' emerges (Refer Fig. 7.1)

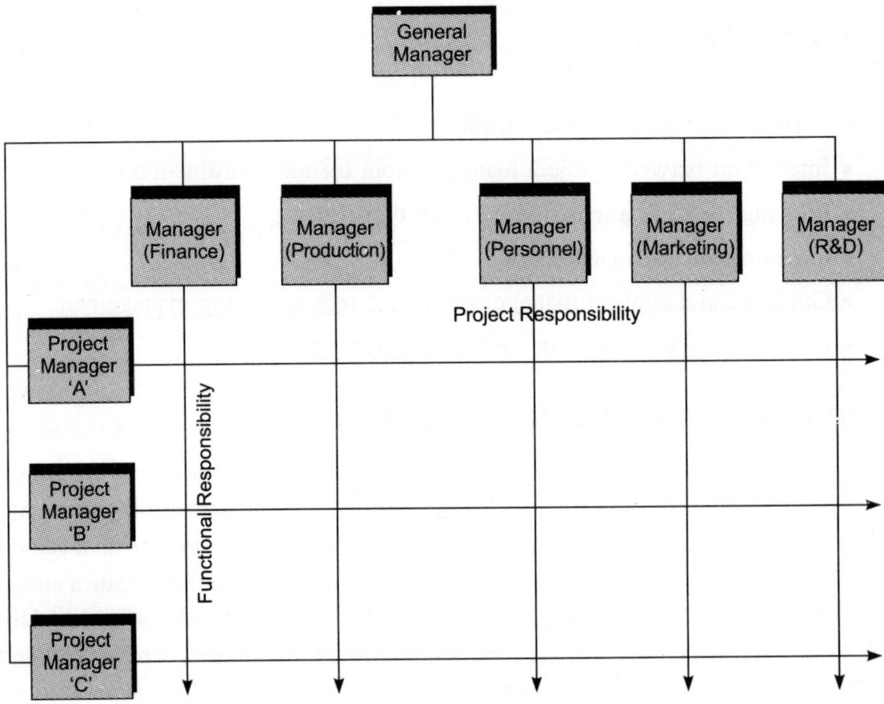

Fig. 7.1 Matrix organization

In a matrix organization, the personnel working in the project are under the control of their respective functional managers and project managers. In other words, authority over the personnel is shared between the functional managers and project managers. It is the responsibility of the project manager to coordinate the efforts of personnel in different functional departments towards reaching the project objectives. The personnel continue to maintain their departmental affiliation though they come under the control of both functional managers and project managers. Once a particular project is completed, the team is dissolved and the team members join with their respective functional departments.

Creating a project oriented organization is not simply forming teams and entrusting project works to the teams. The organizational culture should be made adaptable to project oriented functioning. The formal functional organization may be required to be redesigned so that it becomes more dynamic in accepting changes. The organization should have the ability to dismantle teams once projects assigned to them are completed and to reform the team once a new project to work with is identified. The scope for project form of management is very wide in an organization that is innovation oriented.

Project teams can be formed for developing a new product, for developing a new process, for improving an existing product/process, for effective transfer of technology, for solving some of the customers' problems, for solving some marketing problems, for carrying out a turn-around strategy etc. Project form of organization is considered as the ideal one for effectively implementing any technological/business strategies. Incremental innovations on products, new product/process development etc., can be better handled by a project management approach.

7.6. THE ROLE OF A LEADER IN AN INNOVATIVE ORGANIZATION

Most of the organizational functions, if left alone will focus only on their internal matters. The marketing department will focus on promotional activities, the sales department will focus on improving sales, the finance department will focus on budgeting, funds mobilization etc.; the production department will focus on improving productivity, the R&D department will focus on technological innovations etc. Though every department will function with a view to strengthening its domain, the common thread will be missing, and the activities of every department may not be in line with the organizational objectives. It is the responsibility of the top management to give the required direction to each department so that each department will align itself in tune with the organizational objectives. This vital role of unifying the different departments and ensuring that they focus on their individual objectives in tune with the organizational objective is the role of the leader. It is his responsibility to see to it that all the organizational members work as an unified team. The different functional departments of an organization, let to their choice, will not themselves volunteer to coordinate their activities with a focus on the organizational objectives. If the strategic plan of an organization is to achieve technological supremacy through R&D activities and technological innovations, the leader should take the initiative to coordinate the activities of the different functional departments towards the strategic objectives of the organization.

Leaders are required for two purposes, viz.

(1) to integrate and coordinate the resources, and

(2) to give the right direction for the organization to prosper.

In innovation focused organizations, leaders have a still greater role to perform. In an organization, leaders are present in any cadre and may belong to any functional discipline. These leaders are those who occupy pivotal positions (i.e., key roles) in organizations. It is not a single individual who is at the helm of affairs, who alone is the leader. An organization will have persons who occupy key positions at different levels in the different functional disciplines, whose decisions will have an influence on the organizational performance. These persons are all leaders, though they occupy different positions in the organizational hierarchy. The role of a leader in a technology driven organization in creating an innovative culture are discussed below:

- The leader should create a supportive environment that is conducive for innovation:

A leader must understand the overall business objectives of the organization and should lead his team in that direction. For infusing the culture of innovation in the organization, the leader shall frame suitable policies. The leader shall ensure that a supportive environment prevails in the organization. Decisions are vital for any business. An organization that is focused on innovation will be required to make hard decisions frequently. Managers at lower and middle levels and even some who are at the top level may not always come out with rational decisions quickly. There will be a tendency on their part to go too much into analysis before taking decisions. Employees at all levels exhibit this tendency because of lack of confidence about the outcome of decisions or due to their reluctance to experiment with the unknown. Delay in taking right decisions will cost an organization heavily. Hence, leaders shall be watchful to see that decisions do not get held up anywhere in the organization. When they find one, they should immediately attend to it and take a quick, rational decision, which according to them is the right decision under the given circumstances.

Another important factor that is responsible for the creation of a supportive environment is delegation of authority to the subordinates. In an innovation focused organization, at many points in the organizational hierarchy, many decisions will be taken. A leader must know how to delegate authority effectively. He/she should delegate adequate authority to his/her subordinates. Delegation of authority shall prevail throughout the organization and every employee at each level in the organizational hierarchy should have some powers delegated to him/her depending upon his/her position in the organizational hierarchy.

The leader should retain only critical and strategic decisions with him/her and should delegate all routine decisions to the various people in the organization. This will give enough encouragement to the employees to involve wholeheartedly in the process of innovation. The leader should also make it known to all the employees that failures in the path towards innovation will not be viewed seriously as long as the efforts taken are genuine and the decisions taken are rational and justifiable. This will infuse confidence in the minds of the employees to go ahead with testing and giving shape to their innovative ideas.

- The leader should establish necessary mechanisms in the organization that supports innovation.

An encouraging and empathic leader alone can not create an innovative culture. For this, there must be proper system in place. Framing employee supportive policies will remain only as policies and will not see the light of implementation unless there are adequate mechanisms for the implementation of the policies. For example, if cross functional communication and coordination are to be encouraged as per the policy of the organization, there must be a mechanism to bring the employees of different functional streams together and to permit sharing of information and ideas between them. For achieving this, interdepartmental meets can be made as a part of routine organizational activities, at pre-determined intervals. If the vision of the organization is to make the organization a technology leader in the chosen technology, ample rewards must be given for research and developments in the chosen field of technology. Rewarding the employees who come up with significant contribution will act as an incentive for others to follow. Establishing a reward system is an effective mechanism that will make the employees appreciate the genuine intentions of the top management.

For ensuring free flow of communication (both between and within the different functional departments in an organization), there can be a system of sharing the e-mail addresses of all the employees, including all the top management personnel and the chief executive. An interactive session between all the employees can be arranged at periodical intervals to discuss the issues of common interest and interdepartmental issues. This will create an informal atmosphere and will help diffuse ideas vertically as well as horizontally (i.e., both laterally across the different departments and linearly within each of the functional departments.)

- The leader should allocate adequate resources to the R&D activities and for innovative practices:

Resources are always scarce. Every department competes for resources. If technological developments and innovative practices are to be encouraged, these activities should be allotted their share of budget. Since the results of R&D efforts may not be immediately visible and as all the innovative ideas may or may not mature into commercially viable products, the amount spent on R&D efforts and innovations will not give immediate monetary returns. Hence, there can be a tendency on the part of the employees in other departments to look down upon the effectiveness of R&D department and hence, most of the members of the organization will not favour greater resource allocation to the R&D department. The leader should be one who realizes the long term benefits of the investments in R&D activities and convinces his team about the need to wait and watch, without coming to immediate conclusions about the usefulness of the money spent on R&D efforts.

7.7. RISKS AND UNCERTAINTIES ASSOCIATED WITH TECHNOLOGY

Whenever a new technology is introduced in an organization, whether it is an indigenously developed technology or a technology acquired from outside, whether the technology relates to product or process, the new technology will be received by the members of the organization only with skepticism and lot of apprehension. This is because the fear of the unknown affects most people. Change always creates mental chaos and disruption. Change is resisted because people are comfortable with the way in which they carryout their routine activities and are less prepared to accept any change. Hence, proper interaction and coordination between all the functional departments is a must for implementing a new technology in an organization successfully. The minds of the employees are the breeding ground for technology. If a new technology is implanted in an organization without proper preparation of the employees, it will not take off effectively. Hence, the first risk that an organization may face in technology management is resistance to change and unpreparedness to accept a new technology by the employees. This needs to be understood and handled properly.

Coming to technology per se, there can be risks associated with it in the course of putting the technology into use. For example, developing a new chemical may create unknown toxic effects. Producing a new drug may reveal unknown side effects which are detrimental to health. The effluents generated due to the introduction of a new technology may be harmful. Lack of training in operating a new plant, lack of knowledge about a new process may lead to problems and the organization may run the risk of not putting the technology into proper use. Training of personnel in the areas of new technology is a prerequisite for the successful management of technology.

Another problem that is usually encountered in high technology areas is the failure in the management of technology rather than failure of technology itself. Nuclear energy provides an apt example for this. The Chernobyl meltdown in Ukarine, the problems associated with Three Mile Island, USA and the Fukushima nuclear disaster in Japan were not failures of technology, but were only failures in the management of technology. A pertinent question here is that why such failures happen. No doubt, those who were in charge of operation of the nuclear power plants might have been well trained in operating the plants. There could have been no lack of knowledge about the technology. It is in fact due to lack of knowledge about the harmful effects of faulty operation of the nuclear power plant, lack of awareness of the extent of damage that can be caused by minor lapses in the safety measures and lack of concern for the damages that it could cause to humanity. This being so, the responsibility can not be entirely shifted to those few employees who are involved in the day-to-day operations of the plant. The management has a greater responsibility to see to it that nothing goes wrong at any place and at any point of time. The management must keep necessary check points and counter check points in place to ensure that nothing goes wrong when the procedures that are laid down are followed systematically. Nothing should be left to the judgment and discretion of individuals. An effective poka-yoke is very much desired in such situations. It is the responsibility of the top management to ensure proper management of technology. Technology disasters like the meltdown of nuclear plants, leakage of harmful chemicals from chemical plants etc., happen due to deploying technologies with total lack of system perspective and total disregard to social responsibility. The top management should realize its responsibility and introduce technology after ensuring that every precaution is taken and all the employees are trained and sensitized in the handling of technology and the aftereffects of mismanagement of technology. This will avoid risks associated with the management of technology.

7.8. ORGANIZATIONAL LEARNING

Just as individuals learn from their experiences, organizations also learn. They learn from the experiences of their members. Over a period of time, the organizational members gain both positive and negative experiences, which acts as a repertory of knowledge. The difference between individual learning and organizational learning is that, an organization is said to learn only when the individuals in the organization share among themselves their experiences. Without sharing of experiences, no organizational learning will take place, in spite of the individual organizational members having gained a lot of experience.

"*A learning organization is a group of people working together to collectively enhance their capacities to create results they really care about*."

– *Peter Senge*

"*It is team learning, not individual learning,*
that adds to organizational learning."

– *Peter Senge*

When the different teams in an organization learn, it makes the organization as a whole to learn.

Organizational learning is a process of knowledge acquisition by an organization. The importance of organizational learning can not be underestimated. It is one of the crucial components for achieving competitive advantage over competing firms. A firm achieves competitive advantage if it possesses a resource that the other competing firms do not possess. A firm can sustain its superior position as long as its competitors are not able to acquire the crucial resource/resources that distinguish the firms in terms of competitive advantage. The resources that a firm owns can be tangible or intangible. Tangible resources (or assets) can be easily acquired by all firms. The only limitation may be the financial resources required for acquisition of the asset. Contrary to this, an intangible asset that a firm owns, that has given the firm some form of competitive advantage, can not be easily acquired by other firms operating in the same domain. While tangible assets can be easily identified measured and duplicated, intangible assets are not easily amenable to identification, measurement and duplication. For example, an innovative culture prevailing in an organization is an intangible asset that will not be visible apparently. And, it will take a long time and prolonged efforts to inculcate innovative culture in a firm. Hence, a firm that enjoys competitive advantage because of the innovative culture can not be easily overcome by its competitors. Organizational learning is another intangible asset which can help a firm to achieve sustainable competitive advantage over its competitors.

The two notable contributors to the field of organizational learning are Chris Argrys and Donald Schon. According to them, organizational learning is the result of organizational inquiry. In any organization, there are always differences between planned achievements and actual achievements. Whenever this difference is noticed, the members of the organization who are involved in the process deliberate among themselves, engage in inquiry and problem solving and attempt to set things right. In the process of their interaction with the team members and in their attempt to arrive at a solution to the problem at hand, they learn many things. The learning of the individual members and the sharing of their knowledge between themselves lead to addition to the knowledge pool of the employees which is an asset for the organization. Thus, gathering and sharing of knowledge takes place in the process of organizational learning.

The focus on learning has been gradually getting shifted from individual learning to organizational learning. As individuals grow in stature and strength by acquiring knowledge, through the process of learning, organizations also grow and become more effective and competitive.

Organizational learning process has three distinct stages, viz.,

(1) knowledge acquisition,

(2) knowledge sharing and

(3) knowledge utilization.

Knowledge acquisition stage refers to the development or creation of insights and skills. For example, arranging a training programme for the employees on the emerging technology is a process aimed at knowledge acquisition. The individual who participates in the training programme might acquire knowledge. But, the organization acquires knowledge only when the knowledge acquired by the individual is shared and utilized in some form or the other. Thus, dissemination of knowledge becomes an important element for the organization to acquire knowledge. Hence, organizations should take concerted efforts for better dissemination of knowledge.

7.9. KNOWLEDGE MANAGEMENT

Collins English Dictionary defines knowledge as 'the facts, feelings or experiences known by a person or a group of people'. Information is obtained from data while knowledge is derived from information. Knowledge is more meaningful than information since knowledge, includes familiarity, awareness and understanding gained through experience apart from information. From an organization's point of view, knowledge management refers to a multi disciplinary approach for achieving the organizational objectives by making the best use of knowledge. From a business organization's point of view, knowledge refers to the knowledge regarding markets, customers, competitors, products, processes, technologies, employee details, their strengths, qualifications, capabilities, weaknesses and limitations and all other data/ information that help the organization to manage its business better and to generate profits and add value. Data and information will become knowledge only when we know how to make use of them for the purpose of value addition. In 1970's, Peter Drucker made it known that information and knowledge are organizational resources. In 1980's, knowledge was acknowledged as a very competitive asset.

Thus, knowledge management can be defined as the process of making use of data and information and converting them into knowledge through enabling the employees in an organization individually and collectively and making use of the knowledge so gained for the betterment of the organization. In short, it is about application of the collective knowledge of the entire workforce to achieve specific organizational goals. It is essentially about facilitating the process by which knowledge is acquired by the members of the organization, shared between them and utilized by all of them for the betterment of the organization. The objective of knowledge management is to ensure that people get the knowledge they need, at the time and at the place they need it. In other words it is providing with the people the right knowledge at the right time, in the right place.

Do organizations possess knowledge?

We can understand when it is said that a particular individual has knowledge on a specific domain. Organization is only a legal entity. It has no life. Can an organization acquire or possess knowledge? The answer is a firm 'Yes'. If it is taken for granted that organizations can acquire and possess knowledge, the next obvious question is: 'Is the organization knowledge, the sum total of the knowledge of the individuals in the organization?'. Before answering this question, we should distinguish between an individual's knowledge and an organization's knowledge. When the knowledge of the individuals are embedded in an organization, sharing of knowledge takes place. This sharing of knowledge between the members of the organization leads to the creation of additional knowledge. This additional knowledge is due to the interaction between the organizational members. This additional knowledge proves the point that the whole can be more than the sum of the parts. It is akin to synergy that takes place when two or more different domains interact. Thus, the knowledge base of an organization is not simply the sum total of the knowledge of the individuals who make up the organization, but it is more than that. Figure 7.2 shows a diagrammatic view of organizational knowledge.

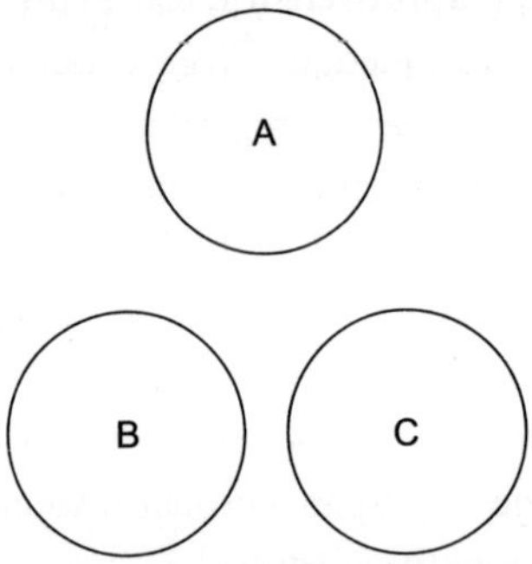

Total knowledge = A + B + C

Fig. 7.2 (a) Individual knowledge base

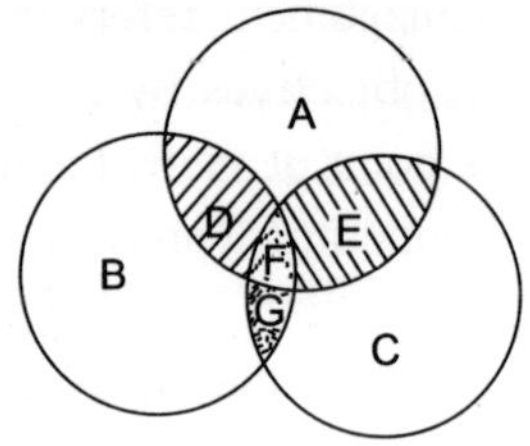

Total knowledge = A + B + C + D + E + F + G

Fig. 7.2 (b) Organizational knowledge base

It is this additional knowledge that an organization acquires due to interaction among individuals that gives strength to the organization to continue despite some of its employees leaving the organization and some others joining afresh. The pool of knowledge developed and retained by the organization through its operations is not lost when some employees leave because the remaining employees will be possessing the knowledge of those who are leaving. Such knowledge retention in an organization is made possible because of the interaction and sharing of knowledge among the employees. This gives the required strength to the organization to continue its operations unaffected. It is as if an organization, as an entity separate from its employees, possesses knowledge required for the smooth running of its operations. This organizational knowledge is unique to a firm and can not be shared with other firms.

As we know, data gathered are converted into information and this additional information forms part of knowledge addition by the organization. Knowledge acquired by an organization in its process of learning can be classified into two types:

- Explicit knowledge
- Tacit knowledge.

Explicit knowledge is that part of knowledge that can be made known to all by way of putting them in black and white in the form of codes, manuals, guidelines etc.

This is a systematic knowledge and it can be readily communicated and shared through print media, electronic media and other formal modes. Once explicit knowledge is codified and stored in some form, it can be retrieved, used and re-used any number of times to solve problems of similar nature. Thus, explicit knowledge connects people with valuable, reusable knowledge.

Tacit knowledge is the knowledge that an individual in an organization acquires that is internal to the individual and that can not be easily passed on to other members of the organization. Tacit knowledge is that component of knowledge that is understood without being openly expressed. The reason for it being not openly expressed is that words are insufficient to express. According to Polanyi, Tacit knowledge refers to knowing more than we can tell or knowing how to do something without thinking about it. Thus, tacit knowledge is a very personal and subjective form of knowledge Hence, it can not be reduced to manuals, reference guides, books, databases etc. The knowledge of a master craftsman falls under the category of tacit knowledge.

7.9.1. Features of Knowledge Management

For a technology driven organization, Knowledge Management (KM) plays an important role. Some of the features of Knowledge Management are:

(*a*) KM as a process, collects, organizes and classifies information from within and from outside the organization.

(*b*) KM deals with dissemination of the collected information throughout the organization so that every member of the organization will get the required information at the time when he/she needs it.

(*c*) KM captures explicit knowledge residing in the minds of the employees and stores them in electronic or in some other form in a central repository so that the knowledge can be made available to any employee who needs it.

(*d*) KM analyses and organizes information available in a company's computer database and shares this knowledge throughout the organization so that accessibility of inter departmental information becomes much easier and free from any barriers.

(*e*) Any organization will be in need of important data/knowhow/details like forecasts, budgets, patent details, formulae, production processes, designs, material specifications, reference works etc., KM ensures that all such data/ information are gathered and organized and made available instantaneously.

7.9.2. The Need for Knowledge Management in an Organization

- Knowledge has become an asset of top-most value. It adds value to other resources. Knowledge infuses quality into products/services offered by an organization, thereby improving the organization's worth.

- Customer needs and expectations are to be assessed correctly if an organization wants to succeed. Moreover, customers quite often change their preferences based on feedbacks obtained from others, past experiences etc. Knowledge Management helps an organization to correctly assess the customer expectations and to act accordingly.
- Knowledge Management can help in repositioning of products, in identifying the products that are to be withdrawn from the production line etc.
- When an employee leaves an organization, the knowledge, skills and experiences possessed by the employee is also likely to leave the organization. Knowledge Management can help the company retain such knowledge, by proper documentation and dissemination of knowledge among the employees. Except tacit knowledge, other forms of knowledge can be retained.
- Knowledge Management can help an organization to take leadership position in bringing about the required changes in the organization in order to reengineer the business/ business processes.
- Empowering employees with more knowledge and keeping them updated on the latest trends will help them offer better service to their clients.
- Businesses expand globally. Most businesses have competitors located throughout the world. To survive in the global competition, organizations must have knowledge of things happening worldwide, at least in their respective domains. Knowledge Management using the state-of-the-art computer technology can deliver the required knowledge in time.
- Knowledge assists an organization in decision making. Decision support systems can help take effective decisions on the basis of knowledge gained and stored about earlier projects and the reasons for their success/failure.
- The business rule of survival of the fittest has been redefined as survival of the knowledgeable. This is because the economy has become knowledge-based and organizations are competing with each other only on the basis of their knowledge base.

7.9.3. Knowledge Audit

Knowledge audit is an investigation into an organization's knowledge health. It is more of a qualitative evaluation. Knowledge audit tries to answer the following questions.

- What are the knowledge assets possessed by the organization and where are they?
- What are the knowledge needs of the organization, keeping in view the growth of knowledge outside the organization?

- What is the knowledge gap present in the organization? (which is the difference between the expected knowledge and the available knowledge)
- How does knowledge flow in an organization among the organizational members? Are there constraints for the free flow of knowledge and if so is it due to people or due to system?

(a) Preparing a knowledge inventory

This is taking a count of the knowledge assets possessed by the organization. It involves collecting and categorizing the knowledge assets.

[*As we are aware knowledge can be of two types, viz., explicit knowledge and tacit knowledge. Explicit knowledge is formal, systematic knowledge which can be easily communicated, documented and shared while tacit knowledge is purely personal in nature and can not be easily communicated. The challenge of knowledge management lies in identifying which part/element of the tacit knowledge can be captured and made explicit so that this part of knowledge can be shared. For the component of tacit knowledge that can not be captured, the way left out is to connect the possessors of tacit knowledge with the seekers of tacit knowledge. This is very crucial but invisible area which requires the attention of knowledge management professionals.*]

Drawing up a knowledge inventory for explicit knowledge includes the following:

- Identifying the knowledge locations in the various systems/sub-systems of the organization.
- Knowing the types/categories of knowledge held by the organization in the forms of various documents, databases both in hard and soft form.
- Knowing how the knowledge resources are organized and how easy it is for the employees to access the knowledge sources.
- Extent of usage of the knowledge resources by the employees.
- The quality of the knowledge base and its relevance to the organization.

In respect of tacit knowledge, the inventory will extract information as to what type of tacit knowledge is owned by whom, how they acquire such knowledge (viz., through learning and development or through on-the-job training).

(b) Assessing the knowledge needs of the organization

Knowledge audit has to identify the type of knowledge needed that will help the organization to achieve its objectives. For achieving this task, employees are contacted and details about the knowledge needs of the organization are gathered from them through interviews, questionnaire-based surveys, facilitated group discussions etc. The respondents should be given to understand clearly as to what is expected of them when they give their views/feedback on the knowledge needs of the organization. As this is a conceptual idea, they should be guided properly. As a simple tool, they may be asked to visualize the goals and objectives of the organization and to identify the types of knowledge which if made available would help reaching the goals and achieving the objectives in a much better way.

(c) Identifying the knowledge gap

A comparison of the knowledge inventory and the knowledge need will throw light on the knowledge gap that exists. In arriving at the knowledge gap, it shall be ensured that only those knowledge that will support the organization in achieving its objectives, but do not find place in the knowledge inventory are to be identified and spelled out.

(d) Analysing the knowledge flow

Knowledge flow refers to the movement of knowledge within the organization. This phase of the analysis finds out how people locate the source of knowledge in the organization that they need, how they access the knowledge and also and how they share the knowledge that they have, with others. This is also a conceptual analysis and is done by interacting with the employees of the organization and obtaining their inputs/feedback from through interviews, questionnaire and facilitated group discussions. Any block/barrier to knowledge flow will indicate either of the two things, viz.,

(*i*) The employees are not sensitized about the importance of knowledge flow so that they will participate willingly in knowledge sharing.

(*ii*) The organization may have certain rules/policies which act as barriers for the free flow of knowledge.

(e) Summary of the knowledge audit

A meticulously and diligently conducted knowledge audit will be of very great help to an organization to strengthen its knowledge base and to capitalize on its strengths in terms of knowledge. Without carrying out a knowledge audit, knowledge management will not be effective. Knowledge audit is a continuous process since the knowledge needs of the organization will keep changing in tune with the technological developments taking place over a period of time.

7.10. CHANGE MANAGEMENT

Change Management is the planned, structured process for ensuring that changes planned are implemented smoothly and completely and the benefits envisaged due to the change are achieved.

Any change does not take place in an organization in isolation. It affects the entire organization and all the members of the organization will experience the change. Hence, if we want to manage change effectively, it should be not dealt with in isolation, but the wider impacts of change throughout the organization should be handled.

Inventions, innovations, product development, process modification etc., bring about great changes in organizations in the way in which organizations operate. Hence, change management is a part of technology management, as technology always brings about changes in organizations.

7.10.1. Areas of Change Management

There are three major areas where change needs to be managed in an organization. They are:

(*a*) Change of organizational structure,

(*b*) Change of physical organizational setting, and

(*c*) Technological change.

(a) Change of organizational structure

The structure of an organization is the base upon which the operational policies of the organization are formed. Organizations may find it necessary to change their structure in order to introduce new products, to change the manufacturing process, to modify the organizational operations, to adapt to the changes that are taking place in the industry or in the market place, to remain competitive in the field, to suit the requirements of mergers/acquisitions etc. Changes in the organizational structure also become necessary when the existing structure has not been found effective over a period of time and suit the requirements of strategy being implemented etc.

In carrying out the required changes in the organizational structure, it is advisable to involve employees from all levels of the organization in the planning stage. A few frontline employees from each department may be asked to participate in planning meetings. They can offer ground level insights and can also disseminate steps being taken for effecting change in the organization with the other employees. This will ensure that the entire organization will become aware of the process of change management being undertaken in the organization.

The employees shall be explained clearly about the reasons for the changes that are being attempted, the benefits that would accrue to the individual employees and to the organization due to the changes. The possible hurdles like downsizing of workforce, repositioning of employees etc., shall also be convincingly explained.

To start with, the planned changes in the organization may be introduced in one department at a time, This will help identify unidentified, unforeseen issues if any which can be solved/ corrected before implementing the required changes in the other departments.

(b) Change of physical organizational setting

The physical setting of the work/work environment may be required to be changed due to the following reasons:

(*i*) due to technological change, demanding change of machinery & machinery layout

(*ii*) for improving productivity by rearranging the production facilities

(*iii*) for fulfilling regulatory norms stipulated by the concerned authorities (Example: Environment protection authorities may give directions that certain polluting industries should be shifted to places at a certain distance away from the city limit.)

(*iv*) due to social pressures (Example: Polluting industries may not be permitted in a thickly populated region due to the objections raised by the public.)

Of the above four causes, the first two causes relate to an organization's internal issues while the last two causes are external to the organization. An organization can have a definite plan to handle its internal issues since these are already known to the organization. However, external influences can not be predicted accurately. The uncertainty resulting due to change of physical organizational setting can be to some extent avoided if the organization takes into consideration social and environmental factors before setting up the plant. Plant location decisions are to be taken keeping the distant future in view and taking into account the social and environmental factors.

(c) Technological change

Technology refers to the scientific knowledge and activities that are involved, making use of tools, equipments, machinery, methods and information to transform inputs into an organization as outputs of value. The outputs may be products or services. Technological change is a change caused by technical advances in production methods. It refers to the overall process of invention, innovation and diffusion of technology. No organization can be immune to the impact of technology and technological changes.

Factors causing technological change may be internal or external to the organization.

Determinants of Technological Change	
Internal	**External**
A technology that has become obsolete	Emergence of a new technology.
A technology that has become less efficient, unsafe and hazardous	Emergence of a highly efficient and safe technology.
In-house inventions and innovations	Technological advances in the specific industry & Technological advances made by the country as a whole.
Controlling costs to gain competitive cost advantage	Govt.'s initiatives towards economic development of the country; Govt.'s industrial and economic policies.
Organization's plans to become quality leader, to improve efficiency of operations	Changes in customer preferences.

Technological change demands greater response from the organizational members. To keep them ready to face any technological change, the training department of the organization should be proactive in its approach and design training programmes suitably. Thus, in order to embrace technological change, the training function itself must undergo a change. The trainers must have expertise in the latest technologies. Hence, wherever necessary, expert trainers may be brought from outside. The two areas where technological change is prominent are change in product design and change in process design.

Change in Product Design

Product design refers to the complete details of the product to be manufactured. It includes the following:

(*a*) Size, shape, weight of the product.

(*b*) Materials to be used for the manufacture of the product.

(*c*) Technical specifications about the product.

(*d*) Product features.

(*e*) Components, parts that form part of the product and their complete specification.

Product design is normally found to consume about 7% to 8% of the product development budget, but it accounts for about 80% of the final cost of the product.

Designing the product right first time itself has been the cherished objective of product developers, because this will reduce costly rework and redesign which will add to the product development cost. It is pertinent to note that the machinery/ equipments required for production, the plant layout, the production process etc., depend very much on the product design. Hence, changing the product design will affect all the above aspects of production. Before attempting to change any product design, its consequences on the entire production process needs to be studied in totality and the preparedness of the organization to implement the changes shall be ascertained.

Changes in the product design may be necessitated due to one or more of the following reasons.

(*a*) Changes in customer preferences.

(*b*) Gaining competitive advantage by way of cost reduction and value addition. Cost reduction may be aimed at by changing the design parameters, product features, material specifications, process parameters etc., while value addition may be aimed at by improving the efficiency of the product, adding more functions, improving product reliability, improving product quality etc.

(*c*) Advancements in technology which aids the product as well as the production process.

(*d*) Extending the product life cycle of a product that is already in its maturity stage by adding additional features that will retain the customers for some more time.

(*e*) Government stipulations, putting restrictions on some of the product's features, production processes etc.

Change in Process Design

Process design in a manufacturing unit refers to the specific steps involved in the production process and the linkages among the different steps that will enable the inputs to be converted into outputs (called 'products'). Efficient design of production process is equally important as the product themselves. A proper process design ensures that products of the desired quality are produced at the minimum cost and within the specified dates so that delivery dates are honoured. Process design can be changed due to the following two reasons:

(*a*) A change in product design will necessitate a change in process design to suit the new product/modified version of the existing product. When an organization has decided to change the product design, change in the process design is thrust upon the organization.

(*b*) In respect of the existing products, the organization may aim at improving the quality of products, reducing the process wastes, reducing the processing time, improving productivity, improving process efficiency etc.

7.10.2. Dr. John P Kotter's Change Management Steps

Prof. Dr. John P Kotter, Konosuke Matsushita Professor of Leadership, Emeritus at Harvard Business School, after 30 years of research came to a stunning finding that 70% of all major change management efforts in organizations fail. The findings revealed the urgent need for effective change management. Kotter outlined a eight step process to avoid failure in bringing about the desired changes in organizations. These steps recommended by Kotter are discussed below.

1. *Establishing a sense of urgency*

The employees should be convinced about the need to bring about the change and the importance of acting immediately towards it. This is an important step. It had been found that close to 50% of the companies that failed to implement the required changes in them had failed to understand the importance of this important step. It is also found that leaders tend to underestimate the importance of creating a sense of urgency in the minds of the employees to accept the change. People have a tendency to resist any change as they do not want to come out of their comfort zones. The other reasons for resisting change are, fear of the unknown, need for security, force of habit and selective information processing. Hence, the first requirement is to make the employees understand the necessity of accepting the change and making them mentally prepared and making them feel the urgent need to bring about the required change in the organization.

2. *Building the guiding team*

This is forming a group and delegating the group with the required powers to lead the change. No singe individual, however knowledgeable and skillful he/she maybe, can lead change in an organization single handedly. Hence, it is advisable to entrust the task to a team. The team members should have the right mix of knowledge and skills and should be drawn from different levels. The group members should have proven leadership qualities.

3. *Developing the right vision*

A right vision is essential to have a direction. A clear vision motivates the employees to take action in the right direction. Since vision gives the direction to all the employees in an organization, the actions of different people get oriented in the same direction and hence coordination between them becomes easier.

4. *Communicating the vision for buy-in*

This refers to ensuring that as many people understand and accept the vision. The vision should be simple, clear and vivid and should convey the same meaning to all, so that communication will be effective.

5. *Empowering broad-based action*

This refers to removing obstacles/barriers and unleashing people to do their best work. Often it will be found that the internal organizational structure will be at odds with the changed vision. In such cases, the organizational structure should be refined/ realigned in such a way that it can be supportive of the vision.

6. *Generating short term wins*

This refers to setting aims that are capable of being achieved in the short run. Short term successes are essential since it gives the confidence to pursue further for achieving the long term goals. Kotter's study had shown that companies that experience significant short term wins by 14 to 26 months after the initiation of change process begins, are much more likely to complete the transformation. The short term successes should be visible. Such short term successes are proof that the efforts and sacrifices of people have started paying off. Short term successes build up the momentum of the change process and will attract reluctant and neutral people also into the streams that all the organizational members will start contributing towards the organization accepting the change.

7. *Never letting up*

This refers to consolidating the gains and producing more change without giving up the efforts. The employees must be encouraged to have determination and perseverance to complete the task of effecting the changes completely so that the organization can reap the benefits in the long run. The leader's role is very crucial in this stage since any let up in efforts will pull down the level of commitment of the members and will spoil the entire effort.

8. *Making the change stick*

This is the stage when the effects of changes will be visible. The need during this stage is to weave the change in the organizational culture and to reinforce the new norms and values in every existing and new employee.

Review Questions

1. 'People form an important asset in the process of managing technology' – Explain
2. 'Organizational structure is a key factor that supports exploration of innovative ideas' – Explain.

3. What are the requirements of an organizational structure that will encourage and support innovation?
4. Explain the structure of a Project based organization.
5. Explain the role of a Leader in creating innovative organizations.
6. Explain the risks and uncertainties associated with technology and how they can be handled.
7. Explain the organizational learning process and its importance for knowledge acquisition.
8. Define the terms 'Knowledge' and 'Knowledge Management'. Distinguish between individual knowledge and organizational knowledge.
9. What are the essential features of Knowledge Management? Justify the need for Knowledge Management in an organization.
10. Define 'Knowledge Audit'. Describe the steps involved in conducting a Knowledge Audit.
11. Define 'Change Management'. Describe in detail the three major areas where change is to be managed in an organization.
12. What are the steps advocated by John Kotter for managing change in an organization?

Intellectual Property Rights

8

CHAPTER

8.1. TYPE OF PROPERTIES

Property is any asset owned by an individual or by an entity. The owner of the property has absolute right over the property and others cannot lawfully use the property, without proper authorization/consent by the owner of the property. Properties can be broadly grouped under the following three heads:

(*a*) Immovable property,

(*b*) Movable property, and

(*c*) Intellectual property.

Out of the above, immovable and movable properties are tangible in nature, while intellectual property is intangible in nature. Factory land and building falls under the category of immovable property. Machinery, equipments, vehicles etc., fall under the category of movable property. As we know, the owner of an immovable or a movable property has exclusive right to use them. No one other than the owner has the right of use. The owner, however, can legally authorize another person to use his/her property.

8.2. INTELLECTUAL PROPERTY

Intellectual property is a class of property that is created by human intellect. Human beings possess intellectual faculty that distinguishes them from animals. By virtue of their intellectual faculty, human beings have evolved greatly and have progressed to a state of highly civilized society. Animals have not been able to do so. What distinguishes human beings from animals is the intellectual faculty possessed by the human beings.

Patents, Designs, Trademarks, Copyrights etc., are some of the intellectual properties. Just like immovable and movable properties, intellectual property is an asset that can be bought, sold, mortgaged, licensed and gifted.

According to The World Intellectual Property Organization (WIPO), Intellectual Property includes the rights relating to the following:

- Inventions in all fields of human endeavour
- Scientific discoveries
- Industrial designs
- Trade–marks, Service marks, Commercial names and Designations
- Literary, artistic and scientific works
- Performances of performing artists, phonograms
- Protection against unfair competition
- All other rights resulting from intellectual activity in the industrial, scientific, literary or artistic field.

8.3. INTELLECTUAL PROPERTY RIGHTS (IPR)

Rights over immovable and movable properties are governed by the law of the country. For example, a person can acquire an immovable property for a consideration. The proof of the transaction needs to be registered with the concerned statutory authorities by way of a sale deed/other legal document that transfer title to the property in favour of the buyer. All relevant records that are in the name of the seller are to be transferred to the name of the buyer. Then, the buyer of the property becomes the rightful owner. His/her right over the property is protected through the laws of the country and no other person can create any kind of encumbrance on the property without the consent of the owner. Similar to the legal rights generated over immovable and movable properties, legal rights created over intellectual properties are termed as Intellectual Property Rights (IPR). Intellectual Property Rights are created and protected by the relevant laws of the country.

8.4. NEED TO PROTECT INTELLECTUAL PROPERTY

Just as the ownership of immovable and movable properties is protected by appropriate laws, the intellectual properties also need to be protected in order to safeguard them from infringement. Intellectual Property is more concerned with technology which is intangible. For example, a new product/process invention done by a company is a property of the company and the company needs to be given protection against infringement of the invention by others. The laws related to IPR offer this protection. The needs for protecting IPR are discussed below:

(*a*) Intellectual properties are emerging as a form of new wealth and give power to nations. Unless protected, the intellectual property generated in a particular country may be stolen by players in other countries which will be a great loss of national wealth.

(*b*) Within a country, the intellectual properties need protection in order to help the owner of the property to gain and maintain advantage of his intellectual property.

(*c*) In the absence of statutory protection, there will be lesser interest shown in inventions due to the fear of inventions being infringed upon by others. Such a situation will create uncertainty in the minds of inventors and will discourage R&D efforts in an organization.

(*d*) The R&D costs for developing new products/processes are considerably high and at times may very much exceed the expected/estimated cost since a lot of trials and reworks may be needed to give shape to the inventive ideas. Hence, such huge costs in R&D efforts need to be reaped back by companies through increased returns. Companies invest in R&D efforts only with the hope that they would take back their investment at some point of time. Thus, there is a need to protect intellectual properties in order to encourage the culture of inventions among the companies of a country. This will give them the required statutory and moral support to proceed with their mission of creating new products/processes that will help the industry grow technologically.

(*e*) Protecting IPRs will help bring out better and affordable products to the consumers which will lead to economic growth and social benefits.

8.5. THE DISINCENTIVES OF INTELLECTUAL PROPERTY RIGHTS

Intellectual property, when protected gives the investor what is due to him/her as a creator of a new product/process. In the absence of such a protection for the intellectual property, there will be no encouragement/incentive for R&D initiatives. Thus, protecting intellectual property rights creates an environment conducive for further growth in R&D efforts. However, protecting intellectual property rights also has certain disadvantages some of which are discussed below.

- When intellectual property rights are protected, it affects the consumers directly since the consumers are in a situation to pay higher price for patented products than for non-patented products. Thus, the monopoly power enjoyed by the patent owners put the consumers at a cost disadvantage.
- The patent holder, by virtue of the exclusive right over the patent does not permit others to improve upon the original patent and bring out further innovations on the products/processes. Since derivative innovations off the original patent are not allowed to flourish, a patent once registered fails to realize its full profit potential. A single investor will have his/her own limitations in terms of men and material resources and expertise in the field of invention. Hence, the patent holder who enjoys exclusive right over the

patent may not be able to improve upon the product/process on his own. The patent holder's apprehension that others would exploit the potential benefits of his/her invention prevents him/her from disclosing the technology/know-how to others. Thus, it is the people/society at large that is affected as it would take a long time for the new technology to become available for the benefit of the masses.

- It often so happens that the original inventor does not reap the fullest financial rewards that the invention is capable of giving. On the contrary, it is the entrepreneurs who are in the second tier who adopt/adapt the inventions of others who gain greater profit as they do not have to spend heavily in R&D activities.

In spite of the above arguments that are posed against protection of intellectual property rights, the benefits that such protection gives to the society are far great and they outweigh the disadvantages. Hence, protection of intellectual property rights has come to stay and will only get further refined and strengthened in the course of time.

8.6. INTELLECTUAL PROPERTY VERSUS INDUSTRIAL PROPERTY

Industrial property is a division of intellectual property. Among intellectual properties, patents, industrial designs and trademarks fall under the category of industrial property since these are concerned with industrial products. The other forms of intellectual properties are copyrights, trade secrets, geographical indications, protection of life forms, domain names, traditional knowledge etc.

8.7. PATENTS

Patents are legal rights granted (in the form of a valid document) to an inventor for the exclusive use of his/her invention. The invention should have been made employing the scientific/technical knowledge of the investor. Patents are granted by the Government/sovereign authority of the country and are valid for a limited period (called 'term' of patent). After the expiry of the term, the owner of the patent loses his exclusive right over it and the patent becomes a public property. During the tenure of the 'term', the patent holder has to keep the validity of the patent alive by payment of periodical renewal fees. If the renewal fee is not paid, the validity will expire and the patent holder will stand to lose his exclusive right over the patent.

In India, patents are governed by The Patents Act, 1970, The Patents (Amendment) Act, 2005 and The Patents (Amendment) Rules, 2006.

If an inventor does not apply and get patent rights for his invention, but goes ahead with commercializing the invention, he loses the right to register the patent in his name since by virtue of the commercialization without registration of patent rights, the invention becomes a public property.

8.8. PATENTABLE AND NON-PATENTABLE INVENTIONS

(*a*) Patentable Inventions

All inventions can not be patented. The Patents Act requires that for an invention to be patentable, the following criteria are to be satisfied.

(*i*) Novelty

(*ii*) Inventiveness (non-obviousness)

(*iii*) Usefulness.

Novelty

The invention must be new and should not be known anywhere in the world as on the date of filing of patent application. If the inventor discloses his/her invention in the public (through any mode) before filing a patent application, it ceases to be novel and it cannot be patented. Novelty of an invention is determined through extensive search of patents already granted world wide, and by search of knowledge available in the relevant field any where in the world.

Inventiveness

The patentable product/process must involve some inventive step. It should not be obvious to a person who is reasonably skilled in the field of the invention.

Usefulness

The invention must possess utility value. It must be capable of being used for the benefit of the society. An invention that can not be made use of for any activity that is useful for the society can not be patented. The utility of an invention is assessed based on the industrial applications for which the invention will be useful as well as based on the utility of the invention to the society as a whole.

It may be noted that improvement of an invention (that has already patented or not) can also be patented provided it satisfies the above three criteria of patentability on its own.

(*b*) Non-patentable Inventions

The following can not be patented:

1. An invention that claims anything that is contrary to the well established natural laws.
2. An invention whose use or commercial exploitation could be contrary to morality/public health and could create hazards to human, animal or plant life or to the environment.

3. Discovery of a scientific principle.
4. Discovery of any living thing or any non-living substance occurring in nature.
5. Substances intended for use or capable of being used as food or as medicine or drug.
6. A method of agriculture.
7. A method of horticulture.
8. Any medicinal/surgical process that is diagnostic, therapeutic, curative or prophylactic or for any other treatment of human beings.
9. Any medicinal/surgical process for treatment of animals.
10. Plants and animals other than micro organisms in whole or any part thereof, including seeds, varieties, species and essentially biological processes for the production or propagation of animals or plants. (This means that micro organisms are patentable provided they satisfy the three essential requirements of patentability.)
11. A literary, dramatic, musical or artistic work or any other aesthetic creation whatsoever, including cinematographic works and television productions.
12. A mere scheme or rule or method of performing mental act or method of playing game.
13. A presentation of information.
14. Topography of integrated circuits.
15. An invention which in effect is traditional knowledge or which is an aggregation or duplication of known component or components.
16. Inventions related to atomic energy.
17. A mathematical or business method or a computer program or algorithm.

8.9. TYPES OF PATENT APPLICATIONS IN INDIA

According to The Patents Act, the following four types of patents can be secured.

(1) Ordinary patent

(2) A patent of addition

(3) A patent granted under convention agreement

(4) A patent application under PCT (Patent Cooperation Treaty).

Ordinary patent

An ordinary patent is a patent granted for an invention based on an ordinary application made by the inventor with the patent office. The ordinary patent application does not claim any priority over applications made in a convention country*/countries and without any reference to other patent applications under process in the patent office.(*Convention country is one which is one of the signatories to the Paris Convention for the protection of Industrial property. India is a signatory to the Paris Convention. There are 174 member countries, as of 2013.)

Patent of addition

It is a patent granted for an improvement or modification made on an already existing invention (which has been already patented or whose patent application has already been filed and is in process). The term of the patent of addition will subsist till the term of the patent of the main invention. Once the term of the patent of the main invention expires, the patent of addition will no longer remain valid.

Patent granted under convention agreement

The Patents Act defines convention country as a country who is a member of a group of countries or unions of countries or an inter-governmental organization as notified under section 133, sub-section -1 of the Act. India is a member country in Paris Convention. When a patent application has already been filed in one of the convention countries and the applicant files a patent application in India claiming priority date based on the application filed in the convention country, the application is called Convention application. The applicant should file the application in Indian Patent Office within 12 months from the date of filing of a similar application in the convention country.

Patent under PCT

The Patent Cooperation Treaty is an agreement of international cooperation in the field of patents. An applicant who files an 'international' patent application under PCT can get protection for the invention simultaneously in all the member countries. India is one of the contracting states to PCT. Such an application can be filed with the patent office of the contracting state of which the applicant is a resident or national or with the international bureau of WIPO (World Intellectual Property Organization) located in Geneva. The effect of the international application in each designated State is the same as if a national patent application had been filed with the national patent office of that State. It simplifies the process of filing patent applications since an applicant can file a single international patent application with one receiving patent office and can simultaneously get protection for the invention in up to 138 countries (contracting states of PCT) throughout the world.

The PCT — international phase must be followed by PCT — national phase. This means that the applicant, after having filed an international application, has to necessarily file another application in each country (among the countries that are the contracted states of PCT) he/she wishes to enter within 30 – 31 months (depending on the law of the designated countries) from the international filing date or the priority date, whichever is earlier. (Note: The terms filing date and priority date are often used interchangeably, but they are not the same. The filing date is the date when a patent application is first filed at a patent office. The priority date is the earliest date to which a patent application can claim priority. For example, a continuation patent application will enjoy the filing date of the application of which it is a continuation. Another example is the patent application which claims priority from a provisional application already filed.)

8.10. PATENT SPECIFICATION

The application for patent should be submitted to the patent office along with a provisional or a complete patent specification. Without a patent specification, the patent application will be incomplete and will not be accepted by the patent office. If the patent application is a convention application, it should be accompanied only by a complete patent specification and not by a provisional specification.

Provisional patent specification

It is a document that discloses the nature of the invention and it is important to establish the earliest ownership of the invention. It is a permanent and independent scientific-cum-legal document and it can not be amended subsequently. The patent law does not prescribe any format for the patent specification, whether provisional or complete. A patent application accompanied with a provisional specification does not confer any legal right to the applicant. Patent right is not granted on the basis of the provisional specification. Complete specification must be submitted to the patent office within 12 months from the date of filing provisional specification. It is also not necessary that a patent application should be first filed along with a provisional specification, to be followed by a complete specification. A patent application can be filed along with a complete patent specification in the first instance itself.

Complete patent specification

It is the document that contains all the details of the invention for which patent protection is desired. In general, a complete specification shall contain the following:

- The title of the invention.
- The field/area of the invention.
- Description of the prior act.
- Drawbacks of the prior act and the need to remove the drawbacks.
- Objectives of the invention.

- Advantages of the invention.
- Basic principles of the invention.
- Essential features and optional features of the invention.
- Description about the working of the invention, supported by drawings, working examples etc.
- Claim statements based on which legal proprietorship is being sought,

Complete patent specification is an important document. The disclosures in the complete specification are to be made carefully and correctly. The legal rights on the invention that are covered in a patent are arrived at on the basis of the disclosure in the complete specification.

8.11. PATENT SPECIFICATION VERSUS KNOWHOW

The patent law does not require that the information disclosed in the patent specification (provisional/complete) be sufficient for commercial exploitation of the invention. Though the specification will give an outline of the nature and field of the invention, finer details that are vital for converting the invention into a product/process need not be spelt out. Thus, any one who goes through a patent specification will not be able to commercialize the invention only on the basis of the details/information available in the specification.

On the other hand, knowhow covers all information that are necessary to commercialize the invention. It will include details of production methods, process techniques, designs, drawings etc. When technology transfer takes place between two companies, it is the knowhow that is traded. Since knowhow is vital for commercialization of an invention, it is kept as a trade secret and it is not shared with the public. It may be noted that a knowhow developed around an existing patent and commercialized will be considered as an infringement of the patent, unless the terms of commercialization are mutually agreed upon between the patent owner and the knowhow developer who opts for commercialization.

8.12. 'PATENT PENDING' TERMINOLOGY

When the term 'patent pending' is referred anywhere, it indicates that the inventor has already filed the patent application disclosing a new invention, the acceptance of which is pending at the patent office. No inventor should use the term 'patent pending' before filing the patent application with the patent office. Merely by filing an application with the patent office, the applicant does not get any legal rights on the invention disclosed in the application. The patent rights emanate only after the grant of patent by the patent office. However, the patent rights granted will have retrospective effect from the date of the application or the priority date* whichever is earlier. The purpose of informing 'patent pending' is to make to known to the public that a patent for the invention has already been applied for and it will act as a warning notice to others.

8.13. 'TRUE AND FIRST' INVENTOR

Every patent application should indicate the name(s) of the 'true and first' inventor(s). The true and first inventor(s) means the person(s) who has/have developed the invention for which patent is applied for, by applying his/her/their intellectual ability. The inventor need not be restricted to one person. In the present day, R&D programs are done by people from across different disciplines and each will have his/her contribution. In view of the multidisciplinary nature of research activities, there will be more than one person who can be termed inventor. The patent law does not limit the number of persons to be included as true and first inventor. It may be noted that the true and first inventor has to be a natural person. A company, firm or organization can not name itself as the inventor in the patent application. Though a company/firm/organization can be an applicant for patent, there should be one or more natural person(s) named in the application as true and first inventor who would have assigned the invention in favour of the company/firm/organization.

8.14. PUBLICATION OF PATENT APPLICATIONS

All patent applications (except those applications that are considered prejudicial to the Defence of the country and those that are incomplete) are published in the journal of the patent office after 18 months from the date of filing of the application or the date of priority whichever is earlier. Once published, the complete specification, designs/ drawings etc., can be inspected by any one at the appropriate patent office, by making a written request to the Controller and on payment of the prescribed fee.

8.15. PATENT SEARCH

Before resources are committed towards invention in a particular field/area, it is advisable to conduct a patent search so that it will avoid the possibility of reinventing the wheel. Venturing upon an invention without proper patent search will only bring

* The Paris Convention for the Protection of Intellectual Property provides that once a person files a patent application in any one country that is a party to the convention, the applicant is entitled to claim priority for a period of 12 months and the filing date of the first application is considered as the priority date. Thus, the applicant need not file the patent applicant simultaneously in several countries that are signatories to the Paris Convention. However, to claim priority, the applicant has to file an application with the country (where he/she wants protection) within 12 months from the date of filing the first application.)

embracement at a latter stage. It happens many times that companies carry out patent search after developing an invention and before filing the patent application. A conscious decision has to be taken not to entertain such a course of action as this may end up in wastage of time and resources if the same invention has already been done and registered by some other party. Also, patent search is not a one time affair. Even after an invention is ventured upon and during the course of developing the invention, the patent search is to be done at frequent intervals to ensure that the invention being attempted is not a duplication of work already done by somebody else. Patents are getting registered in every country in many spheres of activities. The National Patent System of each country classifies patents already granted into different categories and sub-categories. In India, the patents granted are available under 'Indian Patent Classification System.' Also, at international level, International Patent Classification System is available. The web sites of WIPO (World Intellectual Property Organization) and USPTO (United States Patent and Trademark Office) can be referred, apart from the websites of the Patent Office of the respective countries, for knowing the patents already granted.

8.16. IMPORTANT POINTS ON PATENTS

It must be clearly understood that there is no international or global patent. An inventor who wants protection for his/her invention in the form of patent right has to file a patent application with each country where he/she wants to have protection. An inventor who wants to seek protection in more countries than in his/her home country can make use of PCT to register his/her patent in the designated countries. In this connection it may be noted that each country is free to grant or refuse patent based on scrutiny by its own patent office. The fact that patent has been granted by one country does not mean that every other country in which patent for the same invention is applied will grant the patent. Also refusal of granting patent by one country does not bar another country to consider the patent application for the same invention and grant patent.

In India, the patent application is required to be filed in any one of the four patent offices (located at Delhi, Mumbai, Kolkata and Chennai), according to the territorial jurisdiction of the applicant or the first mentioned applicant (in the case of joint applicants). The territorial limits are decided on the basis of the place where the applicant normally resides or has a place of business or the place from where the invention actually originated.

In India, the term of every patent is 20 years from the date of filing of patent application irrespective of whether the patent application is filed with provisional or complete specification. In respect of patent applications filed under PCT the term of 20 years begins from International filing date.

It is the sole responsibility of the patentee (the party who possesses/has been granted patent) to ensure that his/her patent is not infringed upon by somebody. If the patentee comes to know about any such infringement it is the patentee who has to file a suit against the infringer for the infringement.

A mere idea or concept can not be protected by a patent. For obtaining a patent, the idea/concept has to be crystallized in the form of a product/process at least at the laboratory level. However, if the inventor feels that the idea is a potential one capable of being commercialized, he/she can protect the idea by an indirect means by filing a provisional specification along with the patent application. The inventor can, after submission of the provisional specification, work upon the idea and give shape to the idea and develop a product/process and then file a complete specification with the patent office. Thus, the inventor can get an indirect protection for the original idea.

Statement of claim is an important requirement of the complete specification. It is the legal operative part of the patent that defines the legal rights of the patent. When a patent applicant fails to make a specific claim, he/she can not get any legal right over the invention, despite he/she describing the invention in the body of the complete specification. According to the Patent Act, anything that is not claimed is deemed to be disclaimed and it becomes the public property. Hence, the statement of claims should be carefully prepared, taking into account the legal implications. It may be noted that the claim statement need not relate to a single claim. There can be more than one claim, provided the claims are based on a common invention.

8.17. INDUSTRIAL DESIGNS

In India, Industrial Designs are covered under The Designs Act, 2000. The act defines the term 'Design' as under:

"Design" means only the features of shape, configuration, pattern, ornament or composition of lines or colours applied to any article whether in two dimensional or three dimensional or in both forms, by any industrial process or means, whether manual, mechanical or chemical, separate or combined, which in the finished article appeal to and are judged solely by the eye; but does not include any mode or principle of construction or anything which is in substance a mere mechanical device.

Design does not include any trademark as defined in Clause (v) of Sub-section (1) of Section 2 of the Trade and Merchandise Marks Act, 1958 or property mark as defined in Section 479 of the Indian Penal Code or any artistic work as defined in Clause (c) of Section 2 of the Copyright Act, 1957.

The Designs Act defines the term 'Article' as under:

'Article' means any article of manufacture and any substance, artificial, or partly artificial and partly natural and includes any part of an article capable of being made and sold separately."

Since the definition of 'Design' excludes any mode or principle of construction, the act recognizes that protection is given only for the aesthetic appearance of the products rather than any technical aspects since technical aspects of products are more suitable for protection through patents. Industrial designs make a product attractive and appealing to the eye, thereby improving the commercial value of the product. Furniture, toys, cases, household utensils, electronic gadgets and appliances etc., are some of the examples of industrial designs.

An important requirement of 'Design' is that the design should be applied on any article by an industrial process. Designs that are of artistic nature and that do not require an industrial process like paintings, sculptures etc., do not come under the purview of The Designs Act, 2000 and hence such designs can not be registered.

'Appealing to the eye' is another attribute of a design. The features of a design are judged solely by the eye. It is the visual appeal that defines a design. Hence, the design on any article should be visible apparently. Any design that is concealed inside an article that is not visible when looked from outside can not be registered. For example, a design inside a cupboard that can be seen only when the cupboard is opened, can not be registered.

The Design should not include any trademark and it should be distinguishable from known designs or a combination of known designs.

An applicant who wants to get his/her design registered has to apply to the Patent office. Just as in the case of patent application where the applicant files a patent specification, (either provisional or complete), the applicant who wants to register his/her design has to file a representation sheet. The representation sheet describes the article on which the design has been applied and the requirements of a representation sheet are available in Design Rules 11, 12 and 14. (Please refer 'Manual of Designs Practice and Procedure' published by the Office of the Controller General of Patents, Designs and Trademarks.)

The proprietor of the registered design has the exclusive right to apply the design to any article in the class in which the design is registered. For the purpose of registering the designs systematically, designs are categorized into different classes and sub-classes, based on the classification of goods/articles on which the design is applied.

Any product will have some functional utility and the buyer of the product buys the product mainly for its functional utility. However, consumers are attracted by the appearance of the products, apart from their functional utility. Since designs add value to products, it is an intellectual property and needs to be protected. The term of a registered design is 10 years from the date of registration, which can be extended by a period of 5 years on application.

Designs that are primarily literary in nature or artistic in character cannot be registered under the Designs Act and these works can not get protection under the act. The following items fall outside the scope of the Designs Act and can not get protection under the Designs Act, 2000.

- Calendar, certificates, forms, greeting cards, leaflets, medals
- Maps, Building plans
- Labels, tokens, stamps, cartoons
- Religious symbols
- Mere mechanical contrivance
- Buildings and structures
- Flags, emblems or signs of any country
- Parts of articles not manufactured and sold separately
- Layout designs of integrated circuits
- Mere workshop alteration of components of an assembly
- Mere change in size of article
- Any principle or mode of construction of article.

The Controller of Patents, Designs and Trademarks shall grant a certificate to the proprietor of the Design once the Design is registered. The registration of Design gives the proprietor of the design 'Copyright' in the design for the period of registration. Copyright gives the exclusive right to the proprietor to apply the design to the article belonging to the class in which it is registered.

After registration of a Design, the Controller causes publication of the prescribed particulars of the Design to be published in such manner as may be prescribed and thereafter the Design shall be open to the public for inspection on payment of the prescribed fee.

8.18. TRADEMARKS

There are four types of marks that are considered as Intellectual Property. They are: Trademarks, Service Marks, Certification Marks and Collective Marks.

Trademark is a word, phrase, name, symbol, logo, image, a group of letters or numbers, a device (or a label), color, a combination of colors, smell, sound, movement, shape of goods, packaging or a combination thereof used by the company to identify its products/services and to distinguish them from the products/services of others. A few examples of Trademarks are given below:

The purpose of Trademarks is to make consumers know the source or origin of the product. It is to help them identify the manufacturer. Manufacturers who infuse quality and reliability into their products gain customer goodwill and their Trademarks enjoy customer confidence and loyalty. Trademark can be owned by an individual, a business organization or by any legal entity. Since Trademarks get embedded in the minds of the customers, they stand for the quality of the products that they represent. For example, let a company with well-established and popular Trademark comes out with a totally different new product. The new product will have customer acceptance by virtue of the company's Trademark even before the new product gets tested by the market for its quality and features. Thus, trademarks carry the goodwill earned by companies.

When a Trademark is registered, the symbol ® is used along with the Trademark while the symbol™ is used when the Trademark rights are claimed by the user but the mark has not yet been registered.

The following are considered as infringement of Trademark:

- Retaining the essential features a Trademark and making a few additions and alterations to it.
- Taking another Trademark as a whole and making a few additions and alterations.
- Counterfeiting, i.e., using a Trademark that is basically undistinguishable from another Trademark.
- When a Trademark appears not to be different from another Trademark, thus creating confusion in the minds of the consumers.

In India, a registered trademark is valid for a period of 10 years which can be renewed for another 10 years at a time.

The following are not registerable Trademarks as per the Trademarks Act, 1999:

1. Marks devoid of any distinctive character or not capable of distinguishing the goods or services of one person from those of others.
2. Marks which indicate quality or other descriptive character of the goods.
3. Marks which have become customary in the current language or in the bona fide or established practice of the trade.
4. Marks that are likely deceive public or cause confusion.
5. Marks comprising scandalous or obscene matter or likely to hurt religious susceptibilities of any class or section of the citizens in India.
6. Marks prohibited under Emblems and Names (Prevention of Improper Use) Act, 1950.
7. Marks shape of which results from the nature of the goods themselves.
8. Marks that would be disentitled to protection in the court of law.
9. Marks which are identical or similar to an earlier Trademark and the respective goods are identical or similar.
10. Marks which are identical or similar to an earlier Trademark, but the goods are not similar.

Trademark Search

A trademark search is a comprehensive way of researching a name, logo or slogan for use. It is highly advisable to conduct a trademark search before submitting an application for a trademark registration. This is to be done in order to check if similar Trademark has already been filed in India. If so, the owner of such Trademark may raise opposition for the registration and this may delay the process of Trademark registration. A basic trademark search includes pending applications for trademarks in India and trademarks already registered.

Filing of Trademark application

Trademark application is filed with Trademark office. The Trademark application can be filed for more than one class of goods in one application.

Examination of application

After an application is submitted, the Trademark Office will examine the registerability of the application. The office checks the distinctiveness of the Trademark, similarity with Trademarks already registered, submission of required supporting documents etc., and decides on the registerability of the application. If the application is accepted, the Trademark Office issues an acceptance order.

Publication

Trademark applications that are accepted by the Registrar are published in the Trademark Journal. Any interested party may file a notice of opposition to the registration of the mark within 3 months from the date of publication.

Opposition

When the Trademark is advertised in the Trademark Journal, any interested third party can oppose the registration of the Trademark within the 3 months from the date of publication of Trademark journal. Normally opposition comes from the owner of an earlier Trademark that looks similar, the person/business entity that has applied for registration of a similar Trademark, whose registration is pending and the person/business entity that has been using a similar Trademark, but has not yet applied for registration.

The procedure for resolving opposition is as under:

- The Opposition Notice is filed by the opposing party in Form No: TM-5 within three months from the date of publication of the Trademark.
- The Trademark Registry office sends one copy of the Notice of Opposition in form No: TM-5 to the applicant/applicants.
- The Applicant sends his Counter- Statement in triplicate in Form No. TM-6 to the Trademark Registry within two months period.
- The Trademark Registry then sends one copy of the Counter Statements to the Opponent.
- On receipt of the Counter Statement, the opponent files his evidence by the use of an affidavit supported by documentary evidence of the use and advertisement of the mark to the Trademark Registry. The opponent also sends one set of his evidences to the Applicant simultaneously.
- On receipt of the documents from the opponent, the Applicant files his evidence by way of an affidavit and documentary evidence of the use and advertisement of the mark to the Trademark Registry. The applicant also sends one complete set to the opponent.
- On receipt of the documents from the Applicant, the opponent files his rebuttal evidence within one month.
- After completion of these formalities, the Trademark Tribunal fixes a date and time for addressing arguments by both the parties through their attorneys and the case is decided by the Trademark Tribunal.

When no opposition is received, or when the time period given for raising any opposition has expired, the registrar will go ahead with registering the Trademark applied for.

8.19. TRADE NAMES

Trade Names are different from Trademarks. While Trademark identifies the goods manufactured (or products), Trade Name identifies the company itself. The Company name is the legal name of the business entity and it is the name registered with the statutory authorities. In India, the company name is registered with the Registrar of Companies (ROC). The Trade name mostly resembles the Company name and can have minor modifications. For example, Kentucky Fried Chicken Pvt. Ltd., is the company name (which is the legal name of the business entity), while the Trade name used by the company is Kentucky Fried Chicken. It's Trademark is shown below:

Although a company may use its Trade name for commercial purposes, it can use only its legal name for contracts and other formal situations. Trade names are mostly used by companies to market their products or to promote their brands.

8.20. SERVICE MARKS

A Service Mark is a Trademark used by some countries to identify a service rather than a product. For example, United States uses Trademarks for products and Service Marks for services. Some examples of Service Marks are given below:

Indian Trademarks Act treats products and services equally and offers only Trademarks both for products and services.

8.21. CERTIFICATION MARKS

A Certification mark certifies the nature of goods and services to which it has been applied. Certification mark on a product shows that there exists a certification agreement between the manufacturer of the product and an organization with national accreditation for both testing and certification. (For example, Bureau of Indian Standards (BIS) is the organization that tests and certifies industrial products in India and a certification by the BIS confirms that the products meets the requirements in terms of specifications, quality etc., as prescribed by the BIS.) The certifying organization, apart from testing the products prior to the issue of the certificate, also carries out periodical audits to check that the quality standards are met. Some examples of certification marks are given below.

	Wool Mark — identifies goods that contain 100% wool.
ISI	ISI Mark for industrial products — Certifies that the product conforms to a set of standards laid down by the Bureau of Indian Standards.
CE	European Commission Mark — Certifies that the product complies with safety, health or environmental requirements set by the European Commission.
FPO	Fruit Products Order Mark — A mandatory mark for all processed fruit products in India; Certifies that the product was manufactured in a hygienic, 'food-safe' environment.
भारत सरकार GOVERNMENT OF INDIA AGMARK एगमार्क	AGMark — Certifies agricultural products in India, assuring that they conform to a set of standards approved by the Directorate of Marketing and Inspection.
	BIS — Hall Mark — Certifies purity of Gold jewellery.

8.22. COLLECTIVE TRADEMARKS

A collective trademark is a Trademark owned by an organization, such as an association. The members of the association use the Trademark to identify themselves with a level of quality or accuracy, geographical origin, or other characteristics set by the organization.

Collective trademarks differ from Certification Marks in the sense that Collective trademarks will be used by particular members of the organization/association which owns them, while Certification marks can be used by anybody who complies with the standards defined by the owner of the particular certification mark (i.e., the Certifying institution/organization)

	A Mark of the Institute of Chartered Accountants of India. (a collective Trademark)
	A Mark for Darjeeling Tea – Certifies that the tea contains 100% tea originating in the Darjeeling region of India and that the blend meets other specifications established by the certifier. (a certification Mark)

8.23. COPYRIGHTS

Copyright literally means the right to make a copy of an original literary or artistic work. Copyright is an intellectual property and it protects the literary, musical, dramatic, graphic or other artistic works in which the creator of the work expresses his/her intellectual concepts. The creator of copyrightable expression is called the author. Copyright protection in India is governed by The Copyright Act, 1957 (Amended in 1983, 1984, 1992, 1994, 1999 and 2012). The requirement of an artistic work for getting copyright protection is that it should be in a tangible or material form, i.e., it should be capable of being touched, seen or heard. The Copyright Act defines the term 'Copyright' as under:

"Copyright" means the exclusive right subject to the provisions of this Act, to do or authorize the doing of any of the following acts in respect of a work or any substantial part thereof, namely:

(*a*) In the case of a literary, dramatic or musical work, not being a computer programme —

(*i*) to reproduce the work in any material form including the storing of it in any medium by electronic means;

(*ii*) to issue copies of the work to the public not being copies already in circulation;

(*iii*) to perform the work in public, or communicate it to the public;

(*iv*) to make any cinematograph film or sound recording in respect of the work;

(*v*) to make any translation of the work;

(*vi*) to make any adaptation of the work;

(*vii*) to do, in relation to a translation or an adaptation of the work, any of the acts specified in relation to the work in Sub-clauses (i) to (vi).

(*b*) In the case of a computer programme —

(*i*) to do any of the acts specified in (*a*) above;

(*ii*) to sell or give on commercial rental or offer for sale or for commercial rental any copy of the computer programme:

Provided that such commercial rental does not apply in respect of computer programmes where the programme itself is not the essential object of the rental.

(*c*) In the case of an artistic work —

(*i*) to reproduce the work in any material form including depiction in three dimensions of a two dimensional work or in two dimensions of a three dimensional work;

(*ii*) to communicate the work to the public;

(*iii*) to issue copies of the work to the public not being copies already in circulation;

(*iv*) to include the work in any cinematograph film;

(*v*) to make any adaptation of the work;

(*vi*) to do in relation to an adaptation of the work any of the acts specified in relation to the work in Sub-clauses (i) to (iv).

(*d*) In the case of cinematograph film —

(*i*) to make a copy of the film, including a photograph of any image forming part thereof;

(*ii*) to sell or give on hire, or offer for sale or hire, any copy of the film, regardless of whether such copy has been sold or given on hire on earlier occasions;

(*iii*) to communicate the film to the public.

(*e*) In the case of sound recording —

(*i*) to make any other sound recording embodying it;

(*ii*) to sell or give on hire, or offer for sale or hire, any copy of the sound recording regardless of whether such copy has been sold or given on hire on earlier occasions;

(*iii*) to communicate the sound recording to the public.

The copyright is a statutory right and the Copyright Act does not stipulate that registration is mandatory to claim protection under the act. However, the act provides for maintaining a register for recording the names and titles of the works that are registered along with the names and addresses of authors, publishers and owners of copyrights and such other particulars as may be prescribed. The registration can be done at the office of the Registrar of copyrights in New Delhi.

India is a member country to Berne Convention for the Protection of Literary and Artistic Works. Under this convention, registration of copyright is not an essential requirement for protecting the right. Copyright on a work created in India would be automatically and simultaneously protected through copyright in all the member countries of Berne Convention. Though registration is not mandatory, the creator/author shall maintain an undisputable record of the date on which the work was created.

The terms of the copyright are as under:

Nature of the work	Term
Any literary, dramatic and artistic work	Until 60 years from the beginning of the calendar year next following the year in which the author dies.
Photograph	Until 60 years from the beginning of the calendar year next following the year in which the photograph is published.
Cinematograph	Until 60 years from the beginning of the calendar year next following the year in which the film is published.
Sound Recording	Until 60 years from the beginning of the calendar year next following the year in which the work is first produced.
Broadcast reproduction	Until 25 years from the beginning of the calendar year next following the year in which the broadcast is made.

8. 23.1. Software Copyright

With the rapid developments in the fields of Information and Technology, protection of computer software gains more importance and companies are expected to be aware of the software copyright laws. A computer software or programme can be registered as a literary work. As per Section 2(0) of the Copyright Act, 1957, 'literary work' includes computer programmes, tables and compilations including computer databases. In the case of computer programmes, the law does not require the disclosure of source code and copyright for software can be registered without revealing the source code.

Commercial Software

Commercial Software (sometimes called 'payware') is a computer software that is produced for sale. It is developed by a business entity and is licensed to customers for a fee and subject to certain conditions. The business entity that supplies the software often provides the required support, training, updates and other similar services needed by the customers to use the software efficiently. Normally, the source code is not given along with the software. However, the source code may be made available to certain users if required by them, through special license agreements.

When a person buys a commercial software, he/she acquires a license to use the software, but does not acquire its ownership. The terms of license may vary from one company to another and from one software to another. In general, commercial software licenses come with the following conditions:

- The software is protected by copyright.
- One archival copy of the software can be made which shall not be used except when the original software has failed or is damaged/destroyed.
- No modifications in the software are allowed.
- Decompiling the programming code (which is equivalent to reverse engineering of a manufactured product) is allowed only with the permission of the copyright owner.
- Derivative works (i.e., development of new works upon the original software package is not allowed without the permission of the copyright owner.

Freeware

Software that can be downloaded, used and copied without any restrictions is called freeware. The user, however, does not have access to the source code. Thus, the freeware can not be improved upon by the user, as is possible in open source software. Unlike in commercial software, the user of a freeware can not get any support from the owner of the software.

[Examples: Adobe PDF, Yahoo Messenger]

Open Source Software

This software is free to users as well as developers. Most open source software have committees that support each other and collaborate on developments/modifications. The source code is made available freely to all. Users are free to use, modify and redistribute the source code. Open source vendors generate revenue from support services and hardware that are packaged around the open source software, for which the vendor charges a fee. For any problem encountered with commercial software, the customer can avail the services of the vendor for sorting out the problems or the customer can hold the vendor accountable for rectifying the problems. For an open source software, there is no owner and hence the user can not make any person accountable for any deficiencies

[Examples: Moodle (virtual learning system), Firefox (web browser based on Mozilla), TeX (type setting language), Linux (operating system)]

Shareware

Shareware is software that a customer can use on a trial basis before paying for it. Shareware often has limited functionality in its trial version or can be used only for a limited time before requiring payment. Once the customer pays for the software, it becomes fully functional, the user is registered and there will be no time restrictions for the usage of the software. In effect, after payment by the user, the software will acquire the status of commercial software and the copyright conditions applicable for commercial software will be applicable for the shareware also. Shareware acts a popular mode for small developers to capture the market.

[Examples: Norton Anti virus, Anyvideo converter, Kalkulator]

8.24. GEOGRAPHICAL INDICATIONS

Geographical Indication (G.I.) is a name or sign used with certain products that correspond to a specific geographical location (a town, region or country). The products may be agricultural products, natural products or manufactured goods. G.I. informs the consumers that the product is produced in a particular place and that it has certain characteristics that are specific to that place of production. Protection of G.I. in India is governed by the Geographical Indications of Goods (registration & Protection) Act, 1999. The act provides for registration of G.I. relating to goods in India. The Controller General of Patents, Designs and Trademarks acts as the registering authority.

Most commonly, a Geographical Indication consists of the name of the place of origin of the goods. Some of the examples are as below:

G.I.	Category	State of origin
Coorg Orange	Agricultural product	Karnataka
Kuthampully Saree	Handicraft	Orissa
Mysore Silk	Handicraft	Karnataka
Mysore Agarbathi	Manufactured product	Karnataka
Kachipuram Silk	Handicraft	Tamilnadu
Coimbatore Wet Grinder	Manufactured product	Tamilnadu
Malabar pepper	Agricultural product	Kerala
Kovai Cora Cotton	Handicraft	Tamilnadu
Thanjavur Paintings	Handicraft	Tamilnadu

Application for registering Geographical Indications can be filed by an association of persons, or any organization / authority, who represent the interests of the producers of the concerned good. The applicant shall file an Affidavit, clarifying how the applicant claims to represent the interest of the group. After a G.I. is registered, any person claiming to be the producer of the good designated by the registered G.I. can file an application for registration as an authorized user of that G.I. The authorized user gets the right to use the G.I. in relation to the goods in respect of which it is registered.

By registering a Geographical Indication in India, the rights holder can prevent unauthorized use of the registered Geographical Indication by others and promote economic prosperity of producers of goods produced in a particular region.

G.I. is an important intellectual property for a country like India that is richly endowed with natural and agricultural products. G.I. registration in India will help improve the economic prosperity of the produces of agricultural products, handicrafts and other manufactured goods. It will support the economic growth of the country as a whole, by obtaining better value abroad for products with Geographical Indications and by boosting exports of Indian Geographical Indications and by offering protection in WTO countries.

Unlike other Intellectual Properties, Geographical Indications can not be assigned, transmitted, licensed, mortgaged, pledged etc., since G.I. is a public property belonging to the producers of the concerned goods.

8.25. TRIPS

The **Agreement on Trade Related Aspects of Intellectual Property Rights (TRIPS)** is an international agreement administered by the World Trade Organization (WTO) that sets down minimum standards for many forms of intellectual properties (IP) to be followed by WTO Member countries. It was negotiated at the end of the Uruguay Round of the General Agreement on Tariffs and Trade (GATT) in 1994. TRIPS covers Patents, Industrial designs, Copyrights, Trademarks and Geographical Indications.

TRIPS is an international agreement between the member nations of World Trade Organization (WTO). It is aimed at harmonizing the Intellectual Property (IP) related laws and regulations worldwide. The TRIPS Agreement accomplishes this motive by setting minimum standards for protection of various forms of IP to be provided by the member countries, by laying down the principles applicable for the enforcement of IPR that are to be followed by the member countries and bringing about a dispute settlement mechanism for solving IPR related disputes among the member countries.

Thus, the three essential ingredients of TRIPS are:

- Establishment of standards
- Enforcement
- Dispute settlement

The objective of the TRIPS Agreement is to ensure the protection and enforcement of Intellectual Property Rights (IPR) to contribute to the promotion of technological innovation, transfer and dissemination of technology, mutual advantage of producers and users of technological knowledge in a manner that is conducive to social and economic welfare, and balance of rights and obligations, worldwide. The coverage of the TRIPS Agreement encompasses the various areas of IP including patents, trademarks, copyrights, geographical indications, industrial designs etc.

It may be noted that TRIPS Agreement is only a minimum standards agreement. The nations that are signatory to the TRIPS Agreement have to abide by these minimum standards in their national laws related to IP. The member countries can however, provide more extensive protection of intellectual property if they so wish. The member countries are free to determine the appropriate method of implementing the provisions of the Agreement within their own legal framework. India is a member country of TRIPS agreement.

Under the TRIPS Agreement, countries are under no obligation to extend protection to a particular geographical indication unless that geographical indication is protected in the country of its origin.

Prior to 2003, India did not protect geographical indications of Indian origin. In order to comply with the obligations in the TRIPS Agreement, India enacted the Geographical Indications of Goods (Registration & Protection) Act, 1999, which came into force with effect from 15th September 2003. The present geographical indications regime in India is governed by the Geographical Indications of Goods (Registration & Protection) Act, 1999 and the Geographical Indication of Goods (Regulation and Protection) Rules, 2002.

8.26. TRADE SECRETS

Trade secret is confidential information used by a business to achieve competitive advantage. Trade secret may be in the form of a secret formula, designs, drawings, manufacturing processes, techniques, instruments, instructional methods, know-how, ingredients of products, compilation of data/information used by the business etc.

A company that wants to take advantage of the special knowledge acquired by it can either opt for patenting or hold the knowledge as a trade secret. When it opts to retain it as a trade secret, it is not made known to the public and it is guarded against as confidential information. It requires considerable effort to maintain secrecy. A company normally enters into non-compete, non-disclosure contracts with its employees to protect the trade secrets.

Unlike the patents, trade secrets are not protected by law. Hence, there is the risk of a third party duplicating and using the secret information once the information gets leaked out. Under such situations, the company that originally developed the idea/ concept can not have any legal protection. Unlike patents, industrial designs and copyrights that have an expiry period, trade secrets never expire since they are not registered with any authority.

A company can sell/license a trade secret for a consideration to a third party. When a patent is registered, the patent specification filed by the inventor does not reveal everything about the invention. Certain finer aspects about the invention, especially those that are required in connection with replication and commercialization of the technology are retained by the inventor and are not revealed in the patent specifications filed by the inventor. These undisclosed information falls under the category of trade secrets. When a company transfers/sells know-how about some technology to a third party, it is the trade secret that is transferred/sold in the form of 'know how'.

8.27. LICENSING INTELLECTUAL PROPERTY AS A BUSINESS STRATEGY

For an inventor who has patented his/her invention, there are two options available to exploit the potential financial benefits of the patent. Either the patent holder can produce a product/devise a process based on the invention and commercialize the same or can license the patent right to other interested parties for some consideration. When the patent holder attempts to commercialize the invention on his/her own, it will require deployment of huge men and material resources. Though the invention made may be a very promissing one, exploiting the potential benefits of the invention commercially will require greater expertise and allocation of greater resources.

Quite often it so happens that the inventor is not resourceful enough in terms of men and material resources to commercialize the invention on his/her own. Under such situations, the inventors opt for the second option, viz., licensing. It is often found that licensing the invention works out to be a more profitable option than attempting to develop and market all possible applications of the invention. In a licensing agreement, the party who buys the technology (or any other thing that is the subject matter of the agreement) is called the licensee and the one who offers it to the licensee is called the licensor.

Advantages of Licensing

- Licensing may work out to be a more profitable and relatively less risky option for the licensor.
- For the licensee who has the expertise and capacity to commercialize the invention, licensing will be a better option since the licensee can make better use of his expertise and resources.

- When the licensor does not have the required resources to commercialize an invention, licensing acts as a route to take the benefits of the invention to the society.
- Since licensing enables faster adoption/adaptation of new technology, it is more beneficial to the society as the benefits of a new technology will reach the masses at a faster rate through licensing agreement.

The Licensing Agreement

The licensing agreement is a very important document that defines the terms and conditions between the licensor and the licensee. Since the terms of the licensing agreement are to be drafted with utmost care in order to avoid ambiguity and misinterpretation between the parties concerned, it is advisable to engage the services of an experienced attorney in the field for drafting the licensing agreement.

Some of the important clauses that form part of a licensing agreement are discussed below:

(a) Term of the licensing agreement

Every licensing agreement shall specify the term, which is the period up to which the agreement will be valid. Beyond the term of the agreement, it can not bind the parties to the agreement. The licensing agreement shall spell out the term of the license in clearer terms. There can be a provision in the agreement for extension of the term of the agreement beyond the term specified in the agreement, by mutual consent of the parties to the agreement.

(b) Grant clause

A licensor can transfer in favour of the licensee any one or more of the following rights:

1. A product
2. A process
3. Know-how
4. Right to manufacture
5. Right to market/distribute
6. Right to use the product in the production of another product

The term 'Grant' refers to that which is being delivered to the licensee through the agreement. The first thing to be done by the licensor is to decide upon the rights to be licensed. The licensor should decide upon the right/combination of rights that gives the licensor the highest value possible. Suppose a company has invented a technology that has great potential for commercialization. If the company does not have the required resources and capability to expand their activities in the diverse markets that the newly invented technology can cater to, the company may opt for licensing its technology. On the other hand, when the inventor company is financially sound enough and has the required expertise to commercialize the innovative idea, it can go ahead with production of the new product using the new technology. Suppose the company feels that it is not strong enough in marketing the new product, it can rely upon companies that have expertise in marketing and enter into licensing agreement only for marketing of the products.

The license can be exclusive or non-exclusive. The exclusive license gives the specified rights only to one licensee. The license is called non-exclusive when there are two or more licensees for the same subject matter of the license.

The grant clause in the agreement shall also specify if the licensee has the right to further grant his/her rights in favour of sub-licensees.

(c) Confidentiality clause

This is an important clause and needs to be drafted carefully. This clause is meant for restricting the disclosure by the licensee of vital information being transferred by the licensor to the licensee. The clause shall specify as to whom the information can be shared and for what period of time. It can also include a penalty/damage clause that will become operational in the event of non-compliance.

(d) Payment clause

The licensor offers a technology/know-how etc., to the licensee for a consideration. The consideration can be in the form of upfront fee, pre-determined periodical payments, periodical royalty based on a percentage of net sales etc., or a combination of these. The quantum of consideration depends on the value of the entity (a product, process, know-how, right to is manufacture, right to market etc.,) that is the subject matter of the license agreement. The value is arrived at through negotiation between the licensor and the licensee. While the licensor will be interested in recovering his investment on the invention/development of the new technology over a period of time, the licensee will be interested in getting some return for the risk undertaken by him, after meeting the consideration of the license agreement. Hence, the value of the license depends more on the expected return to the licensee than on the return expected by the licensor on the basis of the investment made by him in the invention/development of the new technology. The cost of development of a technology has got nothing to do with the value of the license, though it is a measure normally relied upon by the licensor to fix the value.

(e) Performance clause

Suppose a licensee ties up a technology with a licensor in an exclusive agreement.

If the licensee is not keen in commercializing the technology or does not succeed in commercializing the technology or does not achieve the expected levels of sale after commercializing the technology, the licensor will be at a loss. The licensor may not be earning the expected return out of the license agreement due to the incompetency of the licensee especially when the license agreement contains clauses that link consideration to performance. To avoid such situations, license agreements provide for a performance clause which stipulate achievement of certain agreed-upon goals by the licensee such as time-bound commercialization of the technology, achievement of periodical sales targets etc.

8.28. PATENT STRATEGY

Patents offer the owner very strong proprietary rights and hence extend greater scope in formulating business strategies. Most companies are better placed in managing their tangible resources and in framing business strategies on the strength of their tangible resources. Intellectual property has grown as a property of significant value and influence, in spite of the fact that it is intangible in nature. Of late, companies are differentiated on the basis of the technology that they possess and on the basis of intellectual property that they own. This being so, a company can not afford to ignore intellectual properties in its strategic decisions. While capitalizing on the intellectual properties that a company can produce/own will help the company grow, ignorance about the intellectual properties may land a company in trouble if the company unknowingly or inadvertently infringes the intellectual property of another company. Hence, it is high time companies gave due importance to intellectual properties in formulating their business strategies. A well-formulated patent strategy will help a company succeed by offering the following advantages:

1. Giving the company a temporary monopoly
2. Improving financial performance
3. Giving competitive edge

1. Temporary monopoly

Once a company has successfully invented a technology and patented a product that is based on the newly invented technology, the company enjoys exclusive right for the production of the product till the expiry of the term of the patent. Till such time the legal protection available to the company offers the company a kind of monopoly status. If the product is received well by the market, the company stands to gain a lot till the expiry of the patent's term. Hence, as a strategic decision, companies can reorient their R&D efforts towards those areas where they are strong enough and are confident of getting strongest patent protection.

2. Improved financial performance

Obviously, the temporary monopoly available to a company till the expiry of the term of the patent helps improve the revenues and profits to the company, due to the absence of competitors in the chosen field. Companies who have successfully patented their invention can also use their patent right to generate revenue through licensing arrangements whereby they will get income in the form of licensee fee, royalty etc. Thus, intellectual properties act as revenue generators,

3. Competitive edge

Patents give competitive edge to the patent owners as they are better placed in the market to face the competitors. An effective patent strategy does not restrict itself to the R&D efforts, inventions, development of new products/processes, patenting the newly developed products/processes etc. If buying a patent right (either through outright purchase or through lease agreement) from the patent holder proves to be cost effective, time saving and strategically advantageous, a company can explore the possibility of acquiring the patent right through out right purchase/leasing arrangement. Pros and cons of in-house development versus acquiring the patent right from an outside source are to be thoroughly analyzed and acted upon. A correct strategy in this direction will stand the company in good stead for a long time.

Intellectual Property Audit

Any patent strategy (or for that matter, any I.P. strategy) is incomplete without the intellectual property audit. Intellectual property audit is a systematic review of the intellectual properties owned, used or acquired by a company. Its objectives are:

- Preparing an inventory of intellectual properties that are used by the company.
- Preparing an inventory of the intellectual properties that are not put into any use by the company.
- Identifying the ownership of the intellectual properties of the company. (i.e., identifying whether the I.P. is one that is developed, patented and owned by the company or one that is acquired through some arrangement from the owners of the I.P.)
- Checking if the I.P. assets of the company are infringing the rights of others or others are infringing on the I.P. assets of the company.
- Arriving at the actions required to be taken in respect of each of the I.P. asset of the company.
- Arriving at strategic decisions for managing the Intellectual properties and maximizing the return from the intellectual properties owned/used by the company.

- Gathering information as to what happens in the underlying business and market in terms of intellectual properties.

I.P. audit helps a company to capitalize on the potential benefits of the intellectual properties owned by the company and to derive maximum benefit out of them. The advantages of conducting I.P. audit for a company are as under:

- Determining exactly the intellectual property rights owned/controlled by the company.
- Ensuring that the intellectual properties of the company are properly registered and secured.
- Suggesting a course of action for licensing and other ways of exploiting intellectual properties owned by the company.
- Revealing instances of infringements which need to be addressed.
- Revealing gaps, if any, in the I.P. right ownership and suggesting remedial steps to plug the gaps. [For example, a company might have patented a new product for its innovative functional features. Certain non-functional features might have been overlooked and might not have been patented. When such features that are part of the product and that were not patented are found to hold a greater influence in the buying behaviour of customers, it indicates a gap in the patenting of the product and the company needs to immediately fill up the gap by additionally patenting the non-functional feature also. This will help the company enjoy full fledged patent right over the product. For example, the design of the handle of a product, the colour of the product etc., might not have any bearing on the performance of the product, but may have an influence on the buying behaviour of the customers. Under such situations, protecting these aspects (of design of the handle, colour of the product etc.) also by patenting them will enable the company to obtain comprehensive intellectual property rights over all essential features of the product.]
- An I.P. audit will act as a due-diligence study in the following transactions:
  - — Licensing
  - — Merger & acquisition
  - — Joint venture
  - — Strategic Alliance
  - — I.P. acquisition

8.28.1. Patent Wall

Patent wall is a barrier of multiple interlocking patents created around a product. This is normally done for consumer products that are easy to design. Patent wall will prevent competitors from duplicating the product. In all, Gillette obtained 22 utility and design interlocking patents for the Sensor Razor (in razor blades, packaging, handle, moisturizing strip etc.,) thus creating a patent wall, so that the product can not be duplicated. This strategy is also called patent clustering.

8.28.2. Patent Bracketing

This is a patent strategy through which subsequent inventions effectively lock a competitor out of the market. For example, let a company (Company-A) that produces a particular product has invented a new technology for the production of a particular component in the product. Let the product in which this new component will be used, has say, five components in all. This means, there are four more components that make up the product. Company-A has invented new technology only one of the four components. To support the newly invented component, the other four components are also required to be modified. Suppose a company (say, Company-B) seizes this opportunity and develops a new technology for one more component of the product and patents it. Now, Company-A has two choices before it. It can invent a suitable technology for the second component on its own or it can enter into some agreement with Company-B for obtaining the technology for the second component. The second option will in all probability, will be the first choice for Company-A, since the new technology is already available. Hence, Company-A, might approach Company-B for the required technology. Company-B, which enjoys an advantageous position, can now negotiate the deal to its advantage. Company-B can either license the technology to Company-A, or might ask for a slice of share in the profit, or even acquire some shares of Company-A in return for the technology parted with etc., In effect, Company -B is said to have bracketed Company-A. It may be noted that the product that Company-A manufactures may be some thing that is totally different from the product range of Company-B. Still, Company-B could strike an advantageous deal with Company-A, purely through the patent strategy.

Review Questions

1. Define the term 'Intellectual Property'. Explain the need to protect Intellectual Property Rights.
2. What are Patents? Explain the three requirements of a patentable invention.
3. Give the list of inventions that are not patentable.
4. Explain the four types of Patent Applications as per the Patents Act.
5. What are Patent Specifications? Distinguish between Provisional Patent Specification and Complete Patent Specification.
6. Give a brief account of the Designs Act, 2000.

7. Explain the procedure for obtaining Trademarks.
8. Distinguish between Trademarks and Trade Names.
9. Define the term 'Copyright'.
10. Explain the following terms:
    (*a*) Commercial Software
    (*b*) Freeware
    (*c*) Open Source Software
    (*d*) Shareware
11. Write a short note on the following:
    (*a*) Geological Indications
    (*b*) TRIPS
    (*c*) Trade Secrets
12. Explain Licensing as a business strategy for the owner of an Intellectual Property. What are its advantages?
13. Discuss the types of Patent strategies and bring out the use of patent strategies in gaining competitive advantage.

Bibliography

Bergen, S.A.: *R&D Management*, Basil Blackwell Inc., Massachusetts, USA, 1990.

Chitale, A.K. and Gupta, R.C.: *Product Design and Manufacturing*, Prentice Hall of India Private Limited, New Delhi, 2007.

Dale, Brethauer: *New Product Development and Delivery*, American Management Association, New York, 2002.

Deborah, E. Bouchoux: *Intellectual Property Rights*, Cengage Learning India Private Limited, New Delhi, 2005.

Elaine, Dundon: *The Seeds of Innovation*, Prentice Hall of India, Private Limited, New Delhi, 2007.

John, E. Ettlie: *Managing Innovation*, Elsevier, New Delhi, 2006.

Kenneth, B. Kahn: *New Product Planning*, Response Books, New Delhi, 2001.

Kevin, Otto and Kristin Wood: *Product Design – Techniques in Reverse Engineering and New Product Development*, Dorling Kindersley (India) Pvt. Ltd., New Delhi, 2009.

Melissa, A. Schilling: *Strategic Management of Technological Innovation*, Tata McGraw-Hill Publishing Company Limited, New Delhi, 2008.

Michael, Z. Brooke and William Ronald Mills: *New Product Development*, Jaico Publishing House, Mumbai, 2008.

Paul Trott: *Innovation Management and New Product Development*, Dorling Kindersley (India) Pvt. Ltd., New Delhi, 2011.

Radhakrishnan R. and Balasubramanian, S.: *Intellectual Property Rights – Text and Cases*, Excel Books, New Delhi, 2009.

Richard Stim: *Intellectual Property – Copyrights, Trademarks and Patents*, Cengage Learning India Private Limited, New Delhi, 2012.

Robert, E. Johnson, Jr. and J. Gouglas Bate, *The Power of Strategy Innovation,* Prentice Hall of India Private Limited, New Delhi, 2007.

Shlomo, Maital and D.V.R. Seshadri: *Innovation Management*, Sage Response, New Delhi, 2012.

Suliman, Al-Hawamdeh: *Knowledge Management*, Chandos Publishing (Oxford) Limited, Oxford, UK, 2005.

Tarek Khalil: *Management of Technology*, Tata McGraw-Hill Education Private Limited, New Delhi, 2009.

Index

V